Additional Praise for *Decentralizing Finance*

Kenneth Bok's book *Decentralizing Finance* helps to demystify DeFi and goes further by explaining how traditional financial services are being unbundled by new technologies. We need more literature to explain why self-managed finance needs to be an integral component of the future digital economy.

—**Linda Jeng**, Head of Global Web3 Strategy at the Crypto Council for Innovation, Visiting Scholar on Financial Technology and Adjunct Professor at the Georgetown University Law Center's Institute for International Economic Law

Kenneth has displayed his vast experience, deep insights and thoughtful views on the fast-moving, often-misunderstood world of blockchain and distributed ledger technology, as well as digital/crypto assets with his notable knowledge and experience gained from traditional finance. His book, *Decentralizing Finance* is indeed valuable for not only the uninitiated who are seeking to learn more about this space, but also for the veteran who would gain much from Kenneth's opinions, reflections and forward-looking views, in this realm. Kenneth has managed to pack all that into less than 250 pages of clear and concise, systematic reading, which makes it so much more pleasurable to read. I would highly recommend this to anyone interested in this industry.

—**Hsu Li Chuan**, Senior Partner, Dentons Rodyk & Davidson LLP

In this book *Decentralizing Finance*, Kenneth Bok comprehensively and systematically covers the many areas that are evolving in this new world. What is clear is that the institutions and instruments in the world of finance are changing. How will it look going forward? How will it be different from the world we already know? These are the pertinent questions addressed in this book. The author gives the reader a timely and authoritative overview of how, as finance decentralizes, digital assets and distributed ledgers are bringing about fundamental change. An essential read for anyone who wants to have a competent grasp of the tools needed to analyze the new status quo.

—**Joo Seng Wong**, Founder and CEO at Spark Systems

In his book on decentralized finance, Kenneth unveils profound insights into this dynamic landscape. Kenneth's perspective on the evolving DeFi realm is truly enlightening, providing valuable understanding of trends, challenges, and opportunities. With his expertise and clarity, he demystifies DeFi's complexities, making it accessible to readers of all levels. A must-read for both novices and experts, Kenneth's book enriches our comprehension of this transformative space.

—**Yi Ming Ng**, CEO at Tribe

Decentralizing Finance

Decentralizing Finance

How DeFi, Digital Assets, and Distributed Ledger Technology are Transforming Finance

Kenneth Bok

Registered Office(s)
John Wiley & Sons, Inc., 111 River Street, Hoboken, NJ 07030, USA
John Wiley & Sons Ltd, The Atrium, Southern Gate, Chichester, West Sussex, PO19 8SQ, UK

Editorial Office
The Atrium, Southern Gate, Chichester, West Sussex, PO19 8SQ, UK

For details of our global editorial offices, customer services, and more information about Wiley products visit us at www.wiley.com.

Wiley also publishes its books in a variety of electronic formats and by print-on- demand. Some content that appears in standard print versions of this book may not be available in other formats. Designations used by companies to distinguish their products are often claimed as trademarks. All brand names and product names used in this book are trade names, service marks, trademarks or registered trademarks of their respective owners. The publisher is not associated with any product or vendor mentioned in this book.

Library of Congress Cataloging-in-Publication Data is Available:

ISBN 9781394154975 (Cloth)
ISBN 9781394154982 (ePDF)
ISBN 9781394154999 (ePub)

Cover Design: Wiley
Cover Image: © amasterphotographer/Shutterstock
Author Photo: Courtesy of Kenneth Bok

SKY10059806_111323

Everyone who works towards the greater good

"*Finance, at its best, does not merely manage risk, but also acts as the steward of society's assets and an advocate of its deepest goals. Beyond compensation, the next generation of finance professionals will be paid its truest rewards in the satisfaction that comes with the gains made in democratizing finance extending its benefits into corners of society where they are most needed. This is a new challenge for a new generation, and will require all of the imagination and skill that you can bring to bear. Good luck in reinventing finance. The world needs you to succeed.*"

—Professor Robert J. Shiller, Speech to Finance Graduates,
Finance and the Good Society

This book is dedicated to everyone working towards a more inclusive and efficient financial system.

Contents

Acknowledgments

The creation of this book was a collaborative effort, enriched by the knowledge, support, and insights of many individuals and organizations. I extend my deepest gratitude to those who played a crucial role.

Thank you to the numerous researchers and authors whose reports have been integral to this book. Their detailed insights have shaped many of the ideas and concepts presented here, and I have strived to reference their work appropriately.

Daniel Liebau: Thank you Dan for your support of this project. Your contribution to my journey in this DeFi path has been invaluable. I appreciate all the reports, introductions, and feedback you've sent my way.

A heartfelt thank you to my editors – Vithusha Rameshan, Syd Ganaden, Susan Cerra, and Purvi Patel – as well as the entire Wiley team responsible for bringing this book to life. Special appreciation goes to Carol Thomas for her meticulous copyediting. Your dedication and patience throughout the publishing process have been invaluable.

To my family, especially my mother, thank you for your love, encouragement, and understanding. Your belief in me has been a guiding force.

Timothy Draper, for being so generous with his time to speak at De/Centralize 2018 and writing the foreword for this book. The first time I had heard that Singapore was becoming a crypto hub was during an event at Draper University in San Mateo, California, back in 2014.

Special thanks to various professionals who have provided invaluable feedback and detailed commentary on the material, including Jeremy Kim, staff at the Monetary Authority of Singapore, and Lasse Clausen along with his team at 1kx.

Finally, thanks to all my colleagues, past and present, who supported me throughout this endeavor: Brandon Possin for editing and feedback on early chapters, Tim Han for previous support with De/Centralize, David Tan and Jennifer Lewis for constant encouragement and advice.

Glossary

There will be many terms that might be new to you if you are just starting out in DeFi. Crypto has a habit of reinventing itself semantically, and new terms like "web3" have emerged only recently. This can become even more confusing when we aim to cover both the crypto-native side and the regulated side of DeFi. To provide clarity, let me offer some definitions for the main terminology used in DeFi concerning assets and technology.

Blockchain: The underlying technology behind digital assets and crypto-assets. Examples: Bitcoin and Ethereum.

CeFi: Centralized Finance. These are crypto-native centralized exchanges and centralized yield platforms. They are predominantly custodial in nature. Sometimes also pointing to centralized TradFi.

Crypto: A general and informal term that commonly refers to cryptocurrency or crypto-assets. It traces its origins back to cryptography, the underlying technology that secures and encrypts these digital assets. Can also refer to the industry as a whole.

Crypto-asset: The most inclusive and general term used to describe various types of cryptographic assets. This encompasses both cryptocurrencies and utility tokens, representing a wide range of digital assets operating within the crypto ecosystem.

Cryptocurrency: A crypto-asset with specific functions as a currency within a smart contract network to pay for fees, or a crypto-asset such as Bitcoin whose dedicated function is to act as a money substitute. More commonly used than "crypto-asset," especially in the media.

DeFi: Decentralized Finance. From the Bank of International Settlements (BIS): "Decentralized Finance (DeFi) is a new financial paradigm that leverages distributed ledger technologies to offer services such as lending, investing, or exchanging cryptoassets without relying on a traditional centralized intermediary" (https://www.bis.org/publ/work1066.htm).

I define DeFi broadly as *DLT-based finance that replaces centralized databases and / or disintermediates centralized entities*. More relation to *crypto-native DeFi* but recently having relation with *DLT-enabled TradFi*, who has interest in *institutional DeFi*. A narrower definition of crypto-native DeFi would include elements of self-custody, uncensorability, and community-driven governance.

Digital Asset: A general term for any kind of asset represented on a distributed ledger. May or may not be regulated. Now often being used by the regulated world to differentiate from the speculative crypto side. Nonetheless encapsulates crypto-assets also.

Distributed Ledger Technology (DLT):   The more general class of blockchains, some of whom may not have blocks or chains, and have different consensus mechanisms. Also a preferred term on the regulated side. Examples include: Corda.

"Distributed ledger technology (DLT) refers to the protocols and supporting infrastructure that allow computers in different locations to propose and validate transactions and update records in a synchronised way across a network." (BIS, https://www.bis.org/publ/qtrpdf/r_qt1709y.htm)

Token: Crypto-assets created on a specific blockchain (L1 / L2) such as Ethereum. For example, the ERC-20 token.

TradFi: Traditional Finance. The larger world of finance whose main nodes are central banks, commercial banks, and investment banks.

Web3:   Another generalized collective term for the overarching vision of a decentralized, blockchain, and token-based internet. Where the Web2 is platform-based and centralized, Web3 is decentralized and uncensorable.

Foreword

Bitcoin holds promise. It is the promise of a wealthier world. The kind of wealth that changes everything for the people of the world. The kind of wealth that transforms the global economy to one that is faster, better, cheaper, and more frictionless than the one we have today. The kind of wealth that brings the people of the world together and allows them the freedom to operate with minimal hindrance from government regulation.

At the same time, Bitcoin holds the promise for better government. A government that can account for every profit, every transaction, and every asset without the need for more IRS agents. A government that keeps perfect records on the blockchain, so that everyone is treated fairly, and no one can cheat the system. A government that people can all be proud of: one that allows the trust and freedom of action to build a business without unnecessary restrictions or regulations, since the entire Bitcoin blockchain is perfectly transparent.

Bitcoin also holds great promise for the retailer and the shopper. A shopper that pays in Bitcoin can get a discount on the purchase, and the retailer can save on bank and credit card fees. Bitcoin and the blockchain will keep perfect records so the shopper and retailer will never have a dispute on what was purchased, when, and by whom.

Bitcoin holds great promise for the unbanked in society. The unbanked are also often the homeless, the weakest, the poorest, and the least hopeful. A Bitcoin economy can help the unbanked become a part of the global economy. The unbanked are those who have so little money that a bank cannot afford to open an account for them. Without an account, they cannot easily buy and sell anything, so they are hamstrung to operate with more friction and less technology. Bitcoin can change all that for them. A Bitcoin wallet can be opened for free. They can jump into the world economy with zero friction, and begin to get their life on a good wealthier path.

And Bitcoin holds great promise for a venture capitalist like me. I look forward to a time when I can raise money from LPs in Bitcoin, invest money in a startup in Bitcoin, have the startup pay their employees and suppliers all in Bitcoin, and have all the taxes computed and paid in Bitcoin. This walled garden of business can allow perfect records without the need for an accountant, a bookkeeper, an auditor, a tax lawyer, a transfer agent, even a tax collector. Payments of return of capital and profits to LP investors and to the VC (GP) could all be done in a smart contract waterfall without the need of anyone in house checking the math. The entirety of that business could be frictionless, honest, and automated. The government would be paid, the investors would get exactly what is coming to them, and the cost of the operation could be decreased nearly entirely.

Bitcoin was and remains the origin of digital assets, DeFi, and distributed ledger technology. It combined cryptography, proof-of-work consensus mechanisms, and ingenious economic incentives to create the world's first decentralized digital asset independent of any government. It is no understatement to say that Bitcoin was the seed, and continues to be a vital part of the current ongoing revolution of the decentralization of finance.

A Bitcoin world is a world I want to live in. A wealthy world, a prosperous world, a trusting world, a free world, a fair world.

Enjoy Kenneth Bok's book. It will take you on a journey and teach you about the path to this great world we can envision together.

Timothy Draper
Founder, Draper Associates, DFJ,
and Draper University

Introduction

The genesis block of Bitcoin bears the inscription, "Chancellor on Brink of Second Bailout for Banks." This encoded message, imparted by Satoshi Nakamoto, signaled the advent of a paradigm shift in finance: distributed ledger technology. The distributed ledger transformation is not limited to crypto speculators; it is finally reaching the echelons of central banks and commercial banks.

Cryptocurrencies bear significant risk. The collapse of entities like FTX and Terra, coupled with extreme volatility and the largely unregulated nature of the crypto realm, suggest that it might not be an ideal investment avenue for the average consumer.

Despite these risks, the innovative technology behind cryptocurrency is undeniably powerful. It empowers anyone with internet access to transact and store their own crypto-assets, opening up promising possibilities for financial inclusion. It represents the precursor of an open, global financial system without intermediaries, operating 24/7 and challenging traditional financial structures, thus paving the way for a more accessible and inclusive financial landscape.

As we will explore, blockchain technology – more broadly referred to as *distributed ledger technology (DLT)* – is spearheading dramatic changes and advancements in finance. DLT enables for an efficient, secure, and interoperable financial ecosystem, enabling faster and more inexpensive experiences for consumers and businesses. Its potential to transform payments and capital markets is enormous, extending even to implications for geopolitical dynamics.

Decentralizing Finance: How DeFi, Digital Assets, and Distributed Ledger Technology Are Transforming Finance, First Edition. Kenneth Bok.
© 2024 John Wiley & Sons Ltd. Published 2024 by John Wiley & Sons Ltd.

Decentralized Finance (DeFi) is finance operating on DLT. More accurately, I would define DeFi as DLT-based finance that replaces centralized databases and / or disintermediates centralized entities. In crypto-native DeFi, this definition may include self-custody, uncensorability, and community-based governance. In the regulated world of central banks and commercial banks, DLT is also playing a role in Central Bank Digital Currencies (CBDCs), tokenized assets, tokenized bank deposits, and institutional DeFi.

This book aims to unravel the complex world of DeFi and explore its transformative impact on finance, preparing finance and investment professionals for the future ahead.

I.1   Who Am I?

Allow me to introduce myself and how I came about writing this book.

My career began at Goldman Sachs in London, where I worked as an exchange-traded fund (ETF) trader on the Program Trading desk. My role involved using algorithms to hedge the firm's exposure to Eurozone ETFs in futures and equities markets, as well as executing orders for clients. Coincidentally, I bore witness to the unfolding of the global financial crisis in 2008 right from the trading floor. This first-hand experience with the global financial system's flaws sparked in me a conviction that substantial improvements can be made in the realm of finance.

My journey into the world of digital assets commenced in 2014, when I began researching Bitcoin and bought it for the first time. This exploration fortunately led me to invest in the Ethereum crowdsale, and also into investing my Ether into other Layer 1 platforms such as Cosmos and Tezos. Additionally, I organized a conference called De/Centralize in Singapore in 2018, bringing many world-class innovators in the industry to my home country.

Subsequently, I served as Head of Growth and Strategy at Zilliqa, a Singapore-based Layer 1 blockchain platform. During my time there, I led ecosystem and business development, supporting developers and startups looking to build on Zilliqa. I also spearheaded FinTech and DeFi strategy, fostering collaborations with FinTechs such as Xfers, which launched Singapore's first stablecoin, and HG Exchange, a regulated security token exchange.

I currently run my own boutique DeFi / FinTech advisory company Blocks.sg. I'm also an active trader and angel investor in the crypto and DeFi space. Since 2014, I've executed various strategies such as arbitrage, yield farming, and relative value in the DeFi space. On the long-only side, I've participated in numerous crowdsales, angel investments, and other kinds of advisory engagements. I'm also a pro bono mentor with R3, a leading financial DLT. Please reach out if you're building something interesting in the DeFi / FinTech space via my website: kennethbok.com

I.2   How This Book Is Organized

This book is organized into two main parts: *Crypto-native DeFi* and *DLT in Traditional Finance.*

Part I, *Crypto-native DeFi*, explores DeFi in its native setting: public blockchains on the internet. It operates in an unregulated environment, characterized by high risk, yet fosters remarkable innovation, global accessibility, and operates at a rapid pace.

Chapter 1, *What Is DeFi?*, provides an introduction to what DeFi is, offering a broad, top-down perspective and its unique characteristics, together with an examination of its size, key participants, and an exercise for you to try it yourself.

Chapter 2, *Infrastructure and Instruments*, examines the infrastructure of DeFi, with a focus on Ethereum. Basics of blockchains, cryptography, the difference between Bitcoin and Ethereum, L1s and L2s, how transactions work in DeFi, smart contracts, and types of crypto-assets.

Chapter 3, *Activities and Applications*, explores actual DeFi applications that run on L1s and L2s. Understanding how payments, trading, investing, lending, and borrowing work in DeFi. Delving into aggregation, governance/DAOs, real-world assets, and examining relevant case studies.

Chapter 4, *Risks and Mitigation*, discusses cybersecurity, software, operational and financial risks associated with DeFi and how they can be mitigated. It includes case studies. It considers the risks endemic to DeFi and the risks that DeFi poses to the broader financial system, from a global regulatory perspective.

Chapter 5, *Regulation*, considers the vital role that regulation plays in shaping DeFi's evolution. Considering DeFi's global nature, our focus lies on key standard-setting bodies like the BIS, FSB, IOSCO, and significant jurisdictions such as the US and EU. Additionally, we delve into DeFi-specific regulations related to stablecoins and decentralized exchanges.

Part II, *DLT in Traditional Finance*, delves into how DLT is being implemented by commercial banks, central banks, and other financial institutions in the highly regulated and supervised financial world, which transacts in volumes significantly larger than that of crypto-native DeFi. While innovation may move at a slower pace, this environment offers much greater integrity, stability, and consumer and business protection.

Chapter 6, *Central Bank Digital Currencies (CBDCs)*, views how CBDCs represent a highly significant development that holds the potential to transform the base layer of digital money, consequently reshaping the landscape of finance as we currently know it. The chapter includes historical context, central bank motivations for CBDCs, comparisons between retail and wholesale CBDCs, analysis of their benefits and risks, central bank preferences for permissioned DLT, and highlights developments in Nigeria, the United States, and China regarding CBDC adoption.

Chapter 7, *Asset Tokenization*, notes how nearly any kind of financial asset can be tokenized on a DLT. We explore the what, why, and how of asset tokenization, understanding its significance and implications. We also look at the impact of DLT on capital markets, across five different segments: primary markets, secondary trading, clearing and settlement, custody, and asset servicing.

Chapter 8 considers *Deposit Tokens*, which refer to commercial bank deposits represented on a DLT. In this discussion, we distinguish between CBDCs, stablecoins, e-money, and deposit tokens, understanding their unique characteristics and roles. Additionally, we explore the advantages of deposit tokens and explore case studies on deposit token projects, including the Regulated Liability Network (RLN) and initiatives from Onyx by JP Morgan.

Chapter 9, *Institutional DeFi*, investigates the ongoing efforts of central banks and commercial banks in piloting DeFi innovations within a regulated environment. We delve into how they are integrating automated market makers (AMMs), smart contracts, CBDCs, tokenized deposits, and tokenized assets. Our exploration includes considerations for institutions seeking to participate in DeFi, along with examples of pilots. Additionally, we explore FX as a key asset class for AMMs and examine the BIS's concept of a Unified Ledger.

Chapter 10, Conclusion, provides an overview of the current DeFi situation and looks ahead to what the future of DeFi might be.

I.3   Scope of This Book

A brief note on the scope of this book, taking into account the wide-ranging topics of finance, technology, law, and regulation we are going to cover.

I.3.1   In Scope

1. *All types of DLT*: This includes both public blockchains and permissioned DLT.
2. *All types of finance*: This encompasses traditional finance and crypto finance, both regulated and unregulated.
3. *Infrastructure, applications and technology*: While it is impossible to encompass every aspect within this domain, I have endeavored to address the most significant themes and core technologies of DeFi.
4. *Law and Regulation*: The legal and regulatory landscape plays a central role in shaping the future prospects of DeFi. Recognizing the complexity of individual country specifics, I have taken a high-level approach to address the overarching themes in this domain.

1.3.2 Out of Scope

1. *Non-financial applications of DLT*: While DLT holds potential across various domains, such as supply chain management, healthcare, and transport, this book focuses solely on DLT applications within the finance-related context. Non-financial applications of DLT are considered out of scope for this work.
2. *Non-financial Web3 applications*: The emerging Web3 certainly has many overlaps with crypto-native DeFi, such as social media and gaming. In order to focus on our finance theme, this is also out of scope for this book.

1.4 Disclaimers

1. *No endorsement of specific DeFi apps*: The mention of any specific DeFi apps or crypto-assets are for educational purposes and do not constitute endorsements.
2. *Rapidly changing information*: The information in this book is subject to change quickly. The volatile, highly innovative and dynamic nature of crypto may mean that things mentioned in the book could be different by the time you read them.
3. *Author's positions*: At the time of writing, I may have positions in crypto-assets and some of the startups mentioned in the book. I hold a position in Credix, and I may also have some holdings in Bitcoin and Ether.
4. *Not financial advice*: This book is not financial advice. Please do your own research. The author takes no responsibility for any investment decisions or outcomes made based on the information provided.
5. *Views of the author only*: The views expressed in this book are solely those of the author and do not represent the views of any other organization, including any organizations mentioned.

1.5 Corrections

Please contact me at ken@blocks.sg for any corrections to the material.

Part I

Crypto-native DeFi

1

What Is DeFi?

I've developed a new open source P2P e-cash system called Bitcoin. It's completely decentralized, with no central server or trusted parties, because everything is based on crypto proof instead of trust.

—Satoshi Nakamoto

Decentralized Finance (DeFi) is an alternative financial infrastructure that is open, permissionless, and interoperable, built on public blockchains such as Ethereum. DeFi consists of a wide variety of internet-native applications and protocols that enable existing financial activities such as trading, investing, and payments, and also for entirely new financial capabilities. DeFi applications, being permissionless by design, are available for retail and institutional investors to utilize globally, with only an internet connection and sufficient knowhow being the prerequisites required to participate in DeFi. Like many emergent movements and technological trends, DeFi outpaces regulation and many aspects of DeFi are unregulated and suffer from a lack of standards necessary in financial applications. Nonetheless, DeFi represents an entirely new way to deliver financial services and could interface with traditional finance as well as financial technology (FinTech) in many ways.

Interfaces for DeFi take place through software tools and infrastructure already built for the existing cryptocurrency system, such as blockchains, managed infrastructure, web-based browser wallets, centralized and decentralized exchanges, and the plethora of tools available for creating and maintaining decentralized applications (dApps). A more detailed explanation of the infrastructure, instruments, and applications will be covered in the following chapters.

Historically, core DeFi applications such as Uniswap and Aave occurred earlier in about 2018, but DeFi only came into prominence in Q2 2020, "DeFi Summer," when the *total value locked-up* by smart contracts skyrocketed above

Decentralizing Finance: How DeFi, Digital Assets, and Distributed Ledger Technology Are Transforming Finance, First Edition. Kenneth Bok.
© 2024 John Wiley & Sons Ltd. Published 2024 by John Wiley & Sons Ltd.

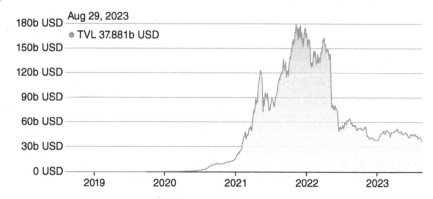

Figure 1.1 Total value locked-up in DeFi (2019–2023).
Source: https://defillama.com/

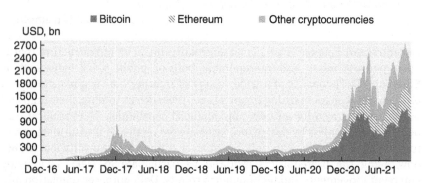

Figure 1.2 Market capitalization of all cryptocurrencies (2016–2022).
Source: Thompson Reuters Eikon, OECD. https://www.oecd.org/daf/fin/financial-markets/Why-Decentralised-Finance-DeFi-Matters-and-the-Policy-Implications.pdf

US\$100 billion, coinciding with a bull market in cryptocurrencies which peaked in late 2021. See Figures 1.1 and 1.2.

Within the cryptocurrency industry, DeFi is an established vertical, with well-defined business models and product offerings. Other key verticals in crypto include general-purpose blockchains (L1 / L2s), Games, Non-Fungible Tokens (NFTs) and stablecoins. dApps are built on a specific blockchain, which results in distinct ecosystems for each blockchain. Each blockchain thus tends to have a DeFi ecosystem which consists of key dApps which serve a specific niche or function, such as decentralized exchanges, aggregators, and lending / borrowing platforms. dApps are also able to be multi-chain or cross-chain, allowing for bridging and aggregation of liquidity and functionality across multiple blockchains. The majority of DeFi apps are on Ethereum, although there now exist DeFi applications and ecosystems on other L1s such as Solana, Binance Smart Chain, Polkadot, and Avalanche.

On a broader level, DeFi is being analyzed and monitored by many TradFi industry participants, and also supranational organizations such as the Bank of International Settlements (BIS), the Organisation for Economic Co-operation and Development (OECD), and the International Organization of Securities Commissions (IOSCO), with all three having produced reports and analysis on DeFi. The reports assess risks to global financial stability and implications to regulation and policy, but strike a cautiously optimistic tone to the technological innovations which DeFi and smart contracts might bring to finance as a whole.

> DeFi applications have the potential to provide benefits to financial market participants in terms of speed of execution and transaction costs, driven by the efficiencies produced by DLT-technological innovation and disintermediation of third parties replaced by software code of smart contracts. DeFi could possibly allow for a more equitable participation of users in markets depending on the design of governance arrangements. Given the open source nature of protocols, DeFi may promote innovation in financial services and could have some potential to promote financial inclusion depending on the design and transaction arrangements (e.g. fees charged).
> —Why Decentralised Finance (DeFi) Matters and the Policy Implications, p. 10, OECD

DeFi has tremendous potential to lower transaction costs, improve financial inclusion and facilitate financial innovation through its global, open nature. It could prove as significant as FinTech in enabling a more democratic access to financial services by way of projects such as MPesa. It could reduce fees associated with financial services for lower-income groups and small businesses. Given its nascent nature, DeFi faces significant structural and cultural challenges towards these aspirational goals.

DeFi is not without its risks, a topic we will explore in detail in Chapter 4. Some of the highest-profile collapses in crypto, although primarily related to centralized crypto, have had ripple effects on DeFi as well. Two such examples are Terra and FTX.

The implosion of the Terra ecosystem and UST, an algorithmic "stablecoin," was one of the biggest cryptocurrency collapses in history, affecting thousands of retail users and institutions involved in crypto asset trading and investing. At its peak, the market capitalization of LUNA, the token of the Terra ecosystem, was US$36 billion and UST was the third largest stablecoin (behind USDT and USDC) with a market capitalization of US$18 billion.[1] Many people flocked to the promise of 19.5% per year rate that Anchor (a yield platform operated by Terra) paid out until it all collapsed very suddenly. The collapse of Terra was the beginning of a cryptocurrency financial contagion which led to the collapse of several other cryptocurrency firms including Celsius, Three Arrows Capital, BlockFi, FTX, and others.

1.1 The Role of Intermediaries in TradFi

A core tenet of DeFi is the disintermediation of financial intermediaries with the blockchain. Intermediaries are middlemen. If DeFi seeks to replace intermediaries through software, then it is only appropriate to ask what those existing functions are. How will blockchain-based software enable them?

Most financial entities such as banks, exchanges, and insurance companies are intermediaries. Intermediaries perform the important functions of connecting those who have capital (investors and lenders) with those who seek capital (entrepreneurs and borrowers) in accountable, rigorous, auditable, and risk-prudent processes. Intermediaries are core to the healthy functioning of the global financial system, and enable monetary and fiscal policy to be transmitted from central banks and governments down to businesses and consumers.

Global financial centers such as New York City, London, Shanghai, and Singapore are also frequently associated with good rule-of-law, infrastructure, and governance that enable financial market participants to operate stable businesses. This is critical in fast-changing financial environments that demand a tremendous amount of interconnectivity.

Intermediaries perform a large number of roles, including investor protection, market integrity, and other systemically important functions. Regulators ensure intermediaries meet these goals through licensing requirements and legal enforcement.

Two examples of financial intermediaries are stock exchanges and banks. The New York Stock Exchange (NYSE) is the world's largest stock exchange, with an average daily trading volume in the hundreds of billions of dollars. By facilitating order books for different stocks and supporting the millions of orders that change price and size constantly on a millisecond basis, the NYSE allows for buyers and sellers of stocks to trade with one another securely and with low transaction costs. Stock exchanges enable traders to find the other side of the transaction, at the right price.

Banks that you and I have accounts with are also financial intermediaries. Banks accept deposits from savers and lend money to businesses and borrowers, who have to pass screening from the banks in light of their credit scores and other estimates on their ability to pay. This screening is a key role in making sure that loans are financially viable and that borrowers ultimately are being economically productive.

Banks are also fundamentally in the business of matching their assets and liabilities and ensuring that the interest they earn from their borrowers is higher than the interest paid to their lenders. Banks hedge and control their financial risk through the money markets (short term debt markets).

One of the key issues of DeFi is that most of the lending takes place pseudo-anonymously (anonymous but having a distinct blockchain address) and is based on overcollateralization. This is in large contrast to the way loans are disbursed in TradFi as discussed briefly earlier. We will examine some initiatives such as decentralized identity and credit scoring that seek to bridge this gap.

1.2 Definitions

For the scope of this book, I will define DeFi in two ways: narrow and broad. A narrow definition of DeFi:

> DLT-based finance that is self-custodial, uncensorable, and community-driven.

A broader definition of DeFi:

> DLT-based finance that disintermediates centralized entities.

There do not exist many formal definitions of DeFi, and distinctions vary between industry practitioners and academics. Nonetheless, here is a summary of the key features of DeFi, with both narrow and broad definitions.

The one feature that most industry practitioners and academics agree on is the non-custodial or *self-custodial* aspect of DeFi. That is, users are able to own their crypto assets directly through the use of private keys and not rely on a third-party custodian to custody their assets. For clarity, I will henceforth refer to non-custodial as self-custodial, since that tends to be less confusing.

The other feature around DeFi custody which stems from public blockchains is that *smart contracts* (computer code executed on the blockchain, to be covered in Chapter 2) can custodize crypto. Smart contracts can hold funds and enable for a wide range of functionality owing to the programmable nature of the blockchain. Many of the DeFi protocols, such as automated market makers and borrow / lending platforms, utilize this feature of smart contract custody.

The second feature of DeFi is that it should be *uncensorable*, both on the transaction layer and the protocol layer. For example, if you are using Uniswap on Ethereum, both Uniswap (the application) and Ethereum (the protocol) must not have the ability to censor your transaction – that is – have no way of stopping your transaction. In direct contrast, a relationship where your assets are held or custodized by a central entity is referred to as centralized finance or CeFi.[2] Figure 1.3 shows a decision tree to differentiate between DeFi and CeFi.

The third feature of DeFi, especially within crypto, is about incentives for specific groups of actors for doing particular tasks and distributed governance. In other words, DeFi is *community-driven*. Some might call these DAOs, or distributed autonomous organizations. The majority of DeFi projects have a circulating governance token that is designed for token holders to be able to

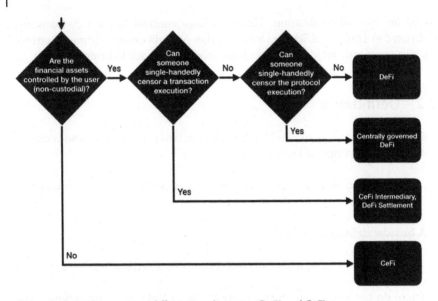

Figure 1.3 Decision tree to differentiate between DeFi and CeFi.
Source: Qin, K., Zhou, L., Afonin, Y. et al. (2021). CeFi vs. DeFi – Comparing Centralized to Decentralized Finance. arXiv:2106.08157

propose and vote for issues that are material to the ongoing functioning of the project. For example, in Curve (a decentralized exchange), the CRV token is used for the control of the emission gauge of the rewards in the staking pools. The extent to which decentralized governance actually is decentralized is another topic of discussion that has been discussed by BIS[3] and other research into governance.

More broadly speaking, the core mission and tenet of DeFi is *disintermediation*. This is also in line with a similar sounding "decentralization." A broader definition of DeFi is financial disintermediation with smart contracts and blockchains. To be more precise, smart contracts that run on *public* blockchains, since private blockchains are limited by design. In regards to this broader definition of DeFi, *DeFi* and *crypto* are almost interchangeable by meaning.

The adoption of DeFi from TradFi institutions is also promising. One example is the tokenization of regulated securities and putting them on-chain to be used in DeFi-style trading pools as collateral. Thus, I would argue that the definition of DeFi is broadening from the crypto-native perspective. Just as with Central Bank Digital Currencies (CBDCs) and permissioned blockchains, innovations in crypto have readily transposed to the centralized world, albeit in piecemeal ways that fit within existing mandates, requirements, and processes.

1.3   Other Characteristics of DeFi

Here are a few more key characteristics of DeFi that set it apart from TradFi. Some of them are advantages, some of them are disadvantages and there are some that are both. Here are the key ones that will help you to understand DeFi from a high-level perspective.

1.3.1   Interoperability / Composability

DeFi applications and protocols are designed to be "money legos" – being able to interoperate with one another with application programming interfaces (APIs). Complex transactions may involve multiple calls to multiple applications in one transaction. Interoperability of applications and protocols allow for easy aggregation and other kinds of abstraction, such as dashboards.

1.3.2   Transparency

DeFi takes place on smart contracts, which are by nature transparent and auditable. Like open-source software, this makes it easy to audit the code. Verification of transactions is also easier in a transparent system: for example, for a simple token transfer from Alice to Bob, Alice would not even need to ask Bob if he has received the token to verify the transaction has completed – all she needs to do is to look at his address on the block explorer.

1.3.3   Openness

DeFi is designed to be permissionless and open. One does not need to provide any kind of identification to the blockchain in order to open a wallet or account. In theory, this has great potential for DeFi to serve the billions of the unbanked and underbanked who do not have formal identification or have challenges opening a bank account.

The other dimension of openness is open-source. Many DeFi applications have their source code posted on software development platforms such as GitHub where developers can collaborate, audit, and re-use software code. This is arguably positive for innovation as a much larger set of developers, beyond those who work in TradFi, have the ability to work on financial software.

1.3.4   Decentralized / Peer-to-peer

Decentralization can occur on different levels and layers. Miles Jennings of *a16z* has offered a categorization of decentralization in web3 into three categories: technical, economic, and legal.[4]

In most countries, the banking sector is concentrated in a few players. This hurts the consumer as there is less competition and other kinds of behavior such as price setting. Decentralization enables for a more open-playing field and for open-access to financial infrastructure. On the flip-side, there is also no one to call when things go wrong, and promotes a greater level of risk-taking due to the unregulated nature of DeFi.

DeFi takes peer-to-peer business models in FinTech to the next level. DeFi enables individuals to lend and borrow from one another, using DeFi platforms as the intermediaries. We'll examine some of these businesses in Chapter 3.

1.3.5 Unregulated

It is not just the novelty of DeFi that makes it a "wild west." The entire basis of financial regulation (currently) is around licensing and centralized control over known corporate entities, and individuals who can be subject to enforcement actions if rules are not complied with. The fundamental architecture of DeFi and its global nature makes it difficult to regulate, as there are no centralized entities to censure, and DeFi companies can move or choose one regulatory regime over another (regulatory arbitrage). In DeFi, pseudo-anonymity (i.e., I know you by your on-chain address, but not your real name) is an accepted norm. There are teams that operate on this basis that have received funding from venture capital (VC) firms,[5] and there have also been cases where founders have abused this norm of anonymous developers to create an illusion of success.[6]

1.4 The DeFi Stack

The following framework is from Fabian Schär, Professor at the University of Basel, describing the five layered DeFi stack:

1. **Settlement Layer**
   This is the core layer of the blockchain and consists of the node operators, consensus mechanisms, and the hardware that powers it such as PoW (Proof-of-Work) mining rigs, GPUs (Graphics Processing Units) and CPUs. Different blockchains may have vastly different architectures and there is an entirely separate line of analysis that looks to compare them. (You can see my presentation on L1 comparisons on my website.)[7] This is the foundational layer of DeFi.

2. **Asset Layer**
   This layer consists of the assets that are issued on the blockchain, and may differ by token type. In Figure 1.4, ETH is the native crypto-asset of the Ethereum blockchain, and is directly linked with the core blockchain as it is

The Decentralized Finance Stack

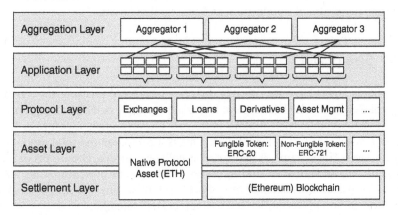

Figure 1.4 The DeFi stack.
Source: https://research.stlouisfed.org/publications/review/2021/02/05/
decentralized-finance-on-blockchain-and-smart-contract-based-financial-markets

utilized in staking, miner rewards, and other incentives that power the blockchain. The ERC-20 standard specifies fungible token contracts, and the ERC-721 standard specifies non-fungible token contracts.

3. **Protocol Layer**
   This layer consists of the smart contracts that power specific applications such as decentralized exchanges, borrowing and lending platforms, and derivatives platforms. These are written in the native programming language of the blockchain, in the case of Ethereum: Solidity and Vyper. Other tools such as IDEs (Integrated Development Environments), libraries and debugging tools assist developers with writing and deploying smart contracts on-chain.

4. **Application Layer**
   This is the front-end of the protocol layer. This is what the typical user sees via a Graphical User Interface (GUI) and where interactions and transactions occur between the protocols and the user's wallets. Components of the application layer such as graphics and other middleware are often hosted off-chain on centralized servers, cloud providers, or newer decentralized equivalents such as InterPlanetary File System (IPFS).

5. **Aggregation layer**
   The aggregation layer is yet another layer of abstraction above the application layer, and aggregates across different protocols and applications to provide the user with the best possible price and execution (for trading applications), visualize the user's positions across all the DeFi applications they are using, or perform other complex operations across multiple DeFi applications.

Chapter 2 will examine the settlement layer and asset layer. Chapter 3 will examine the protocol, application, and aggregation layers.

1.5   Size of DeFi

How big is DeFi? Here we can rely on a few metrics to measure the size and scale of DeFi, and whether or not it is actually "eating TradFi," as its supporters would say colloquially. (Nibbling perhaps?) One common measure is *Total Value Locked-up* (TVL) (Figure 1.5). This is a proxy for the total amount of crypto assets "locked up," or deposited as collateral in smart contracts of trading platforms and borrow / lending platforms. As of time of writing (Aug. 2023) TVLs (across all blockchains) are ~US\$37.5 billion, down from the peak of ~US\$250 billion in December 2021. (Source: DefiLlama.)

It should also be noted that there are many critiques of the TVL metric. The primary criticism being that it is an inflated number due to multiple counting of the same asset. For example, if a user deposits 100 ETH into Aave (a borrow / lending platform) and borrows 40 ETH (assuming a 40% collateralization ratio), the same user could subsequently deposit the same 40 ETH and borrow 15 ETH. The TVL metric counts 140 ETH even though there was only 100 ETH to begin with. The same is also true for "liquid staking" platforms such as Lido Finance where ETH can be staked for stETH, which in turn can be used in other DeFi applications.

The other measure, which pertains to the wider adoption of crypto, would be the number of *global crypto owners* Figure 1.6). Crypto.com's "Crypto Market Sizing" report in January 2023 estimates 425 million global crypto owners in December 2022.

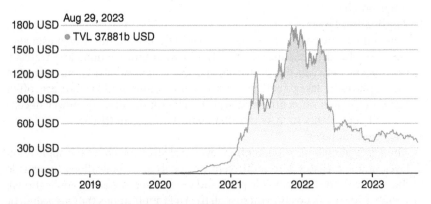

Figure 1.5 Total value locked-up in DeFi (2019–2023).
Source: https://defillama.com/

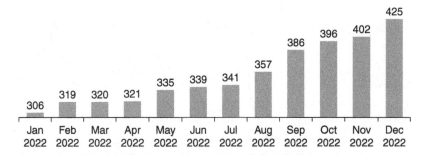

Figure 1.6 Total number of global crypto owners (in millions).
Source: Crypto.com, Crypto Market Sizing. https://content-hub-static.crypto.com/wp-content/uploads/2023/01/Cryptodotcom_Crypto_Market_Sizing_Jan2023-1.pdf

The third category would be *volume of transactions* (Figures 1.7 and 1.8). Coingecko estimates that the volume for all decentralized exchanges is US$84.17 billion, and represents 13.88% of CEX (centralized exchange) spot trade volume.

From these measures we can surmise that DeFi is quite cyclical and dependent on the broader bull / bear markets in cryptocurrencies, but on the whole has demonstrated significant growth in the last 3 years and continues to cannibalize market share from centralized crypto exchanges.

1.6 Key Participants in DeFi

DeFi is (at present) predominantly a subset of crypto. Thus the key actors in DeFi are similar to those in crypto. Nonetheless, this could change as DeFi evolves (especially with putting real world assets on-chain) and has more integrations with FinTech and TradFi.

1.6.1 Developers and Entrepreneurs

Developers typically focus on certain projects or a blockchain ecosystem as it takes time to build up expertise in the native programming language of the blockchain. Electric Capital has some great analysis of the number of developers in the crypto / DeFi / web3 space.

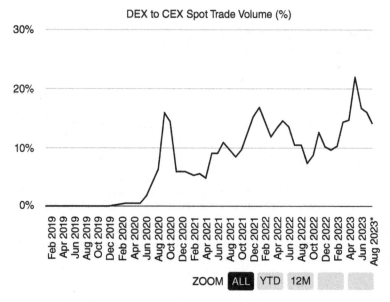

Figure 1.7 DEX to CEX volumes.
Source: The Block, Coingecko

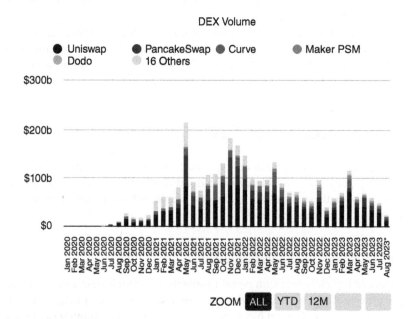

Figure 1.8 DEX volumes.
Source: The Block, Coingecko

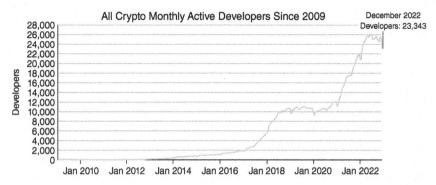

Figure 1.9 Web3 active developers since 2009.

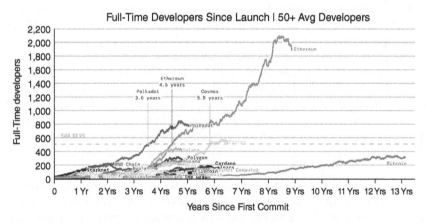

Figure 1.10 Web3 active developers since launch.
Source: Electric Capital Developer Report https://medium.com/electric-capital/
electric-capital-developer-report-2021-f37874efea6d

From Figure 1.9 we can see that the number of software developers in the Web3 space in total has been steadily increasing to an all-time high of 23,343 in December 2022. Figure 1.10 (an interesting one for anyone looking to compare ecosystems) shows the growth of monthly active developers (on GitHub) since the launch of the blockchain. We see that Ethereum leads the pack, followed by Polkadot, Cosmos and Solana.

There exist a wide variety of ways for entrepreneurs to collaborate and find co-founders offline and online – through local networking events, hackathons, accelerator programs, grant programs, discord channels, and online forums.

In December 2021, *The New York Times* ran an article about tech executives and engineers quitting big tech companies such as Google, Meta, and Amazon to join crypto.[8] While this should be taken with a pinch of salt (given it was near the height of the last bull market), it highlights the vote of confidence that some of the best and brightest in tech have in crypto.

1.6.2 Institutions

1.6.2.1 Venture Capital Funds

Web3 and Crypto-specific venture capital (VC) funds account for a substantial portion of growth of the industry, and predominantly pursue a long-only strategy. Unlike web2 VCs, who have a longer holding period, web3 VCs can exit and reap the rewards of their investments as soon as tokens become liquid in the market. The lifecycle of web3 investments when tokens are involved tend to be much shorter than the typical 6–10 years in a traditional VC.

Nonetheless, this has been getting longer due to longer vesting periods and a general shift towards higher levels of commitment to the startups (i.e., not selling the token when it suits, but being invested for the longer term, and also participating in governance).

Figure 1.11 presents a detailed breakdown of fundraising across various cryptocurrency categories from 2017 to 2022. It's evident that 2021 and 2022 were notably robust years for investment. This was particularly true for sectors like infrastructure, NFTs/Gaming, and DeFi.[9] Many software and tech VCs have had a strong focus on web3 and DeFi in the last few years, for example a16z, which had closed their fourth crypto fund totaling US$4.5 billion in May 2022, and has raised a total of US$7.6 billion across all crypto funds.

> We are excited about developments in web3 games, DeFi, decentralized social media, self-sovereign identity, layer 1 and layer 2 infrastructure, bridges, DAOs & governance, NFT communities, privacy, creator monetization, regenerative finance, new applications of ZK proofs, decentralized content & story creation, and many other areas.
>
> *—Chris Dixon, a16z*[10]

Traditional VC firms such as Sequoia Capital[11] and Lightspeed Venture Partners[12] have also raised funds focused on liquid tokens and digital assets. Crypto-native VCs (i.e., their first fund was a crypto-specific fund) of note include Paradigm Capital, Multicoin Capital, Pantera Capital, and Polychain Capital. Many crypto exchanges also have their own VC arms, for example, Coinbase Ventures, and Binance Labs.

1.6.2.2 Hedge Funds

Hedge funds are not constrained by long-only strategies or buy and hold mandates. Like their TradFi hedge fund brethren, they employ a wide variety of strategies that may be market-neutral, relative value, arbitrage, discretionary,

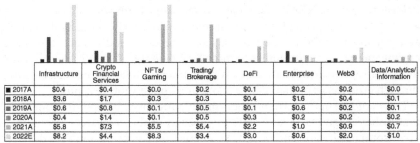

Annual Amount Raised by Category

■ 2017A ■ 2018A ■ 2019A ■ 2020A ■ 2021A ▦ 2022E

	Infrastructure	Crypto Financial Services	NFTs/ Gaming	Trading/ Brokerage	DeFi	Enterprise	Web3	Data/Analytics/ Information
■ 2017A	$0.4	$0.4	$0.0	$0.2	$0.1	$0.2	$0.2	$0.0
■ 2018A	$3.6	$1.7	$0.3	$0.3	$0.4	$1.6	$0.4	$0.1
■ 2019A	$0.6	$0.8	$0.1	$0.5	$0.1	$0.6	$0.2	$0.1
▦ 2020A	$0.4	$1.4	$0.1	$0.5	$0.3	$0.2	$0.2	$0.2
▦ 2021A	$5.8	$7.3	$5.5	$5.4	$2.2	$1.0	$0.9	$0.7
▦ 2022E	$8.2	$4.4	$8.3	$3.4	$3.0	$0.6	$2.0	$1.0

⊗ THE BLOCK | Research

Figure 1.11 Crypto / blockchain deals in 2017–2022 by category.
Source: The Block Research
Note: Amount in billion US Dollars.

event-driven, or quantitative in nature. DeFi hedge funds may look for discrepancies in cryptocurrency prices across DEXs, CEXs, and across different blockchains and look to lock-in short term, market-neutral profits. Hedge funds may also engage in yield-farming, staking, and borrowing / lending with DeFi applications and protocols.

The (now) infamous Three Arrows Capital (that has been in the news due to its meteoric rise[13] and fall[14]) had their origin in FX trading and at their peak their NAV was rumored to be in the multiple billions.

1.6.2.3 Market Makers

Jump Trading, GSR, Cumberland DRW, Wintermute, and QCP Capital are some of the largest market makers in crypto, and are engaged in making markets in the thousands of cryptocurrencies trading both on centralized and decentralized exchanges. Many have their origin from making markets in TradFi equities, commodities, FX, and other derivatives, and employ sophisticated HFT technology and techniques to capture spreads with the use of algorithms. When you are trading on an exchange, you might well be trading with one of these institutions.

1.6.2.4 Exchanges

Some of the largest decentralized exchanges are Uniswap, SushiSwap, PancakeSwap, Curve Finance, Serum, Raydium, and dYdX. A hallmark characteristic of DEXs is that they are permissionless: they do not need KYC (Know-your-customer) information to trade. These can be automated market makers or limit order book-based. We will examine how these work in greater detail in Chapter 3.

1.6.2.5 Foundations and L1s / L2s

Blockchains such as Ethereum, Avalanche, Solana, Binance Smart Chain, Polkadot, Polygon, NEAR, Algorand, Cosmos, and Tezos will all have a corporate structure that promotes the multi-fold mission of encouraging developers and startups to build on their blockchain, validators and miners to dedicate capital and hardware resources to mine / validate their blockchain, and investors (retail and institutional) to invest in their native token. Funds can be raised through crowdsales of their native token or through venture capital.

This could be in the form of a non-profit entity (e.g., Ethereum Foundation) that disburses grants to accelerate the growth of the ecosystem, promote its open-source software, and organize conferences. For-profit software development companies such as ConsenSys (specializing in the Ethereum blockchain) develop decentralized software services and applications for the blockchain. These software development companies work for corporations and governments looking to build projects on the specific blockchain ("Layer Ones – L1s") as well as derivative networks ("Layer Twos – L2s").

1.6.2.6 Retail Investors and Users

DeFi has become a mainstay for many crypto users as it is very convenient to perform transactions on DEXs. DEXs have enabled for a long-tail effect (i.e., being able to enable liquidity for many more tokens that would otherwise not be available on CEXs) and the best price for a less liquid token is often found on a DEX.

Automated market makers such as Uniswap pioneered the ability for retail investors to participate in the upside of market making, which traditionally was only available to large and sophisticated trading houses (as mentioned earlier). Retail investors can deposit crypto-assets to liquidity pools and receive LP (liquidity provider) tokens as representations of pro-rata shares of the total pool. Liquidity providers earn prorated trading fees charged by the pool, and sometimes the native token of the platform by participating in these activities. Such innovations are also beginning to translate to more complex products such as options with decentralized options vaults (DOVs).

Other methods of earning yields on DeFi platforms include lending, borrowing, and staking. Investors who believe in the growth potential of DeFi platforms may also hold tokens in DeFi applications. The value of these tokens may be derived from the potential and utility of the application or other kinds of business models. The DeFi Pulse Index, maintained by DeFi Pulse, is one example of an index of liquid DeFi tokens[15] on Ethereum, which includes Uniswap, Aave, Maker, Synthetix, Compound, Yearn, SushiSwap, and Kyber.

1.6.2.7 Traditional Institutional Investors

An increasing number of institutional investors are becoming more interested in DeFi in large part due to the yields that are much higher than in TradFi, especially in a low / near zero interest rate environment. (This is now changing with the Fed Funds rate at 2.25–2.5% at time of writing.) Many of these yields come from staking, lending, liquidity mining, AMM pools, and yield farming.

Nonetheless, significant compliance issues around AML, CFT, KYC, and the numerous risks of DeFi continue to limit institutional investors participation in DeFi. Many other innovations are enabling institutions to onboard onto DeFi, including compliance, RegTech, custody, trading, aggregation, anti-frontrunning systems, identity, and other institutional grade solutions.

Lending / borrowing platforms such as Aave and Compound have launched permissioned DeFi liquidity pools (Aave Arc and Compound Prime respectively) to cater specifically for these requirements. Financial institutions are also looking into putting regulated securities on-chain as collateral for DeFi activities. One such example is French financial services company Societe Generale (SocGen), which issued €100m of covered bonds to itself on the Ethereum blockchain in 2019.[16] SocGen is at time of writing, looking to borrow 30m DAI from the MakerDAO platform, using the tokenized bonds as collateral.[17]

Many of these innovations are promising (or interesting at the least) and we'll talk about institutional adoption of DeFi more in Chapter 5.

1.7 DeFi and FinTech

Throughout the book, I'll be using quite a lot of jargon terms. I'll also be attempting to make some higher-level observations about the industry, so for clarity, let me define some key terms here:

DeFi
Crypto-native, self-custodial, uncensorable, and community-driven platforms such as decentralized exchanges, borrow / lending platforms, and aggregators.
Examples include: Uniswap, Aave, Compound, Synthetix, MakerDAO
CeFi
These are crypto-native centralized exchanges and centralized yield platforms. They are predominantly custodial in nature.
Examples include: Binance, Gemini, Coinbase, Crypto.com, BlockFi
TradFi
The "normal," much larger financial world that lives in skyscrapers in Wall Street and Canary Wharf. These are banks, financial institutions, pension funds, stock exchanges, and insurance companies, who deal in equities, FX, commodities, and fixed income instruments in the trillions every day.
Examples include: JP Morgan, Goldman Sachs, BNP Paribas, Bank of America

	Regulated	Smart Contract Based/ "Decentralized"	Startup/Innovation Orientation
DeFi	✗	✓	✓
FinTech	✓	✗	✓
Banking/TradFi	✓	✗	✗

Figure 1.12 Comparisons of DeFi, FinTech and TradFi.

FinTech

Software and technology oriented, regulated platforms that look to disrupt traditional financial services. These are payment services gateways, robo-advisers, neo-banks / digital banks, Buy Now Pay Later (BNPL) platforms, personal finance management platforms, and P2P platforms.

Examples include: PayPal, Stripe, Ant Financial, Adyen, LendingClub

DeFi and FinTech may sound similar, as both are fundamentally software-driven technological revolutions in finance, but DeFi fundamentally uses smart contracts and blockchain technology. FinTech might not utilize blockchains at all. For comparisons see Figure 1.12.

The key characteristics of DeFi are the use of smart contracts and tokens. The global, internet-native nature of token flows and smart contract interaction make DeFi fundamentally different from FinTech. One of the most promising use cases for crypto and DeFi is to enable more efficient cross-border value transfers, and could reduce costs for remittances and enable a greater degree of financial inclusion, since these costs tend to impact the poor more. Money movements within DeFi take place on blockchains which are global by default. FinTechs for the most part are regulated by a local financial authority or regulator, and will nearly always build in processes to satisfy know your customer / client (KYC), anti-money laundering (AML), and combatting the financing of terrorism (CFT) requirements.

The usage of digital assets / crypto is thus part of this disintermediation. We can also say that DeFi is a subset of FinTech, given that FinTech is much about the use of software in disintermediating human labor. Nonetheless, it is my own perception that they are still currently used in fairly distinct terms, owing to the narrow definitions of self-custodial, uncensorability, and distributed governance.

1.8   How Can I Try DeFi?

I'm a big believer in learning by doing, and combining theory with practice. I'm assuming you picked up this book with an intent to learn more about this new world. I'm going to stick my neck out and say this: if you haven't bought any crypto before, owning and transacting in a small amount of stablecoin might be one good way to get your feet wet. But let me say this first: *you can participate in DeFi without speculating.* You will need a small amount of crypto to pay for transaction fees, but you can absolutely use DeFi just with stablecoins. I can't guarantee that you won't get hacked or run into technical problems, but there's at least less chance of the value fluctuating wildly than other types of crypto like Bitcoin or Ethereum. It will give you a visceral sense of what DeFi is, beyond the theory.

If you're completely new, here's how I recommend you do it:

1. You'll need to open an account with a reputable crypto exchange.
2. You'll need to transfer some fiat into the exchange and buy USDC and a small amount of the native cryptocurrency of the blockchain you intend to use for "gas" (transaction fees).
3. Download and install the crypto wallet on your phone, mobile browser, or computer.
4. Create your wallet. You'll need to store your private key / seed phrase in a safe place, like a password manager. *Never show anyone else this.*
5. Transfer the USDC from the exchange to your crypto wallet.
6. Voilà! You're now a self-sovereign individual. Try paying your friends and family with USDC next time you split the check.
7. When you're done with the experiment, convert the USDC back into fiat via the exchange and back into your bank account.

Here are some recommendations:

Stablecoin: USDC
Blockchain: Solana or Polygon. Both have low gas fees and should not require more than a few dollars of SOL or MATIC for a few transactions
Wallets: Metamask (Polygon, Browser-based), TrustWallet (Polygon, Mobile-based) or Phantom (Solana, Mobile-based)

Cybersecurity and cyber hygiene are key skills while swimming in the shark infested waters of crypto. Store your private keys / seed phrases carefully and don't interact with applications you don't trust. Be careful of phishing attacks, and other kinds of scams that proliferate on Telegram, Discord, and the general crypto sphere. You've been warned!

If you're going deeper, you might want to buy a hardware wallet such as a Ledger Nano S. Hardware wallets can be used with browser wallets such as Metamask and Phantom and are a safer way of transacting in DeFi.

1.9 Where Does DeFi Meet TradFi?

At present, DeFi–TradFi links are still experimental due to the numerous challenges of compliance and risk as mentioned earlier. This could change as technology, operations, standards, and risk management improves in DeFi. Let's discuss some of the major crossovers that currently exist with DeFi and TradFi.

1.9.1 Stablecoins

Stablecoins are an important topic in DeFi and are arguably the biggest crossover point between DeFi and TradFi. We'll cover stablecoins in more detail in Chapter 2, but here is a brief overview.

Stablecoins are digital assets that circulate on public blockchains such as Ethereum, and are 1:1 representations of fiat currency. Some of them may be actually stable and some may not be. I say this beforehand because the label itself may mislead people into thinking that they are actually stable, when very often it is an aspiration. (See the UST / Terra collapse) They are issued by private companies who may or may not hold an equivalent amount of fiat (or short-term debt) in reserve to back the quantity of stablecoins they create.

The two largest in circulation are USDT and USDC (issued by Tether and Circle respectively) and have market capitalizations of US$66.5 billion and US$54.2 billion respectively at time of writing (Aug. 2022). Stablecoins are increasingly being used for cross-border transfers and a stable store of value that is crypto-native. They are used extensively in DeFi in liquidity pools, borrowing / lending platforms, and other staking and trading operations.

Stablecoins are a major bridge between crypto and fiat as they are representations of real-world value, but exist in a crypto-native infrastructure.

1.9.2 Central Bank Digital Currencies (CBDCs)

The parallel innovation that Bitcoin and crypto have spurred at the central banking level of finance (i.e., above the commercial banking layer) is with Central Bank Digital Currencies (CBDCs). The major difference here between stablecoins and CBDCs is that stablecoins are issued by private companies, whereas CBDCs are issued by central banks and governments. Which would you trust? Which would you hold? For the vast majority of people and businesses, the answer is fairly clear. The counterparty risk with CBDCs is much lower than that of stablecoins.

Strictly and technically speaking, CBDCs are not a part of DeFi yet. Most CBDCs pilots have been on permissioned networks and not public blockchains. It may seem odd to some, especially the libertarians, to be even discussing CBDCs in a book about DeFi. Nonetheless, I think this is a topic well worthy of coverage, given some of the latest developments with central banks. If governments eventually decide to utilize CBDCs on public blockchains, it would represent a quantum leap in DeFi adoption and utilization.

CBDCs and stablecoins may also combine in ways that harness the best in each system, in what Tobias Adrian, Financial Counselor and Director of the Monetary and Capital Markets Department at the IMF, has called a "synthetic CBDC" (sCBDC). In an sCBDC system, stablecoins may be used by the private sector and harnessing the innovative potentials of the private sector in distribution, interoperability, and utilization of money, whereas CBDCs are used as collateral for the stablecoins.

> A synthetic CBDC is essentially a public–private partnership that encourages competition between eMoney providers and preserves comparative advantages. The private sector concentrates on innovation, interface design, and client management. And the public sector remains focused on underpinning trust.
>
> —Tobias Adrian, Stablecoins, Central Bank Digital
> Currencies, and Cross-Border Payments:
> A New Look at the International
> Monetary System, May 2019.

In March 2022, the central bank of Brazil – the Banco Central do Brasil (BCB) – selected a number of crypto, DeFi, and FinTech companies such as Aave, Visa, ConsenSys, and Microsoft as part of the Lift Challenge Real Digital to develop pilot projects to evaluate CBDC use cases.[18]

1.9.3 Real World Assets (RWA) and Tokenized Assets

There are a number of startups and companies looking to bring real world assets on-chain, or otherwise connect real world assets with crypto. Most of them involve tokenizing the asset and could involve asset pools, which aggregate and segment the risk. Some of them that have a public-facing website are: Credix, Goldfinch, Maple, TrueFi, and Centrifuge. (Disclosure: I am an investor and advisor to Credix.)

Credix is a credit marketplace that currently enables FinTechs in Latin America to source for debt investors using USDC on Solana,[19] and currently has a loan book of US$17.5 million. Institutions that are already participating in DeFi can access yields up to 14% APY that are diversified from the more cyclical DeFi yield market. The onus of credit scoring and screening is left to the FinTechs and Credix facilitates the on-chain to off-chain value transfers and credit pool structuring.

Centrifuge takes an "asset-agnostic, wide-ranging approach that allows users to bridge limitless forms of RWA over to the DeFi space."[20] Centrifuge currently has a wide range of assets listed on its platform, ranging from real estate loans, revenue-based financing, and cash advances from a variety of issuers.

Unlike other DeFi platforms, the majority of RWA platforms require KYC identification, which may be issued in the form of a non-transferable token, and may be available for accredited investors only.

On the institutional side, two examples of bond issuance on public blockchains include the SocGen issuance of €100m of covered bonds in 2019, and another €100m, 2-year bond by the European Investment Bank (EIB), in collaboration with Goldman Sachs, Santander, and SocGen in 2021.[21] The EIB digital bond project was also selected for Banque de France's CBDC program. Both were issued on the Ethereum public blockchain. Some have taken to calling this method of bond issuance on blockchains as "smart bonds."[22]

1.9.4 Permissioned DeFi

Permissioned DeFi pools such as Aave Arc and Compound Prime are promising innovations that allow institutional investors to be able to participate in DeFi. These are institutional versions of the publicly available Aave and Compound platforms, but satisfy institutional requirements for KYC, AML, and CFT compliance, as well as enterprise-grade security. These networks consist of known institutional participants that are whitelisted by RegTech providers such as Fireblocks.[23]

We'll also examine the innovations of some TradFi institutions, such as central banks and commercial banks, that are exploring what is being referred to as institutional DeFi in Chapter 9. For these institutions, controlling access is critical for compliance and regulatory reasons, and there are several techniques to achieve this.

1.10 What are the Risks of DeFi?

DeFi is definitely a nascent and experimental field where there are many risks. One should be aware of these risks before investing significant amounts into DeFi. For anyone monitoring the news about crypto – it should be clear – not a week goes by without a hack or bug in crypto causing multimillion dollar losses. These losses occur as a result of cybersecurity issues, operational risks, technological risks, and other systemic risks in DeFi. Frontrunning (MEV) occurs frequently and retail users may not even realize they are front (and back) run when they are interfacing with DEXs. Only time will tell if these issues can be addressed with standards, regulation and technology.

We will take a closer look at some of the risks in Chapter 4.

1.11 Chapter Summary

DeFi is a new financial architecture that is built on the internet. It is built with goals of openness, accessibility, and interoperability. Even though it is still experimental, substantial amounts of capital have already been invested in DeFi and crypto is clearly a global phenomenon. DeFi seeks to disintermediate centralized financial intermediaries with public blockchains. A narrower definition of DeFi is blockchain-based finance that is self-custodial, uncensorable, and community-driven. There are many initiatives that are crossover points with DeFi, FinTech, and TradFi, and we definitely could see more integration going forward.

On a structural level, DeFi is built with a very different architecture from TradFi – the blockchain – and the technology is constantly evolving and upgrading. In the next chapter, we answer, how does it work? Let's take a look at Infrastructure and Instruments.

Notes

1. UST's peak circulation was in May 2022 before its dramatic collapse https://messari.io/asset/terrausd/historical
2. There are some that conflate the terms CeFi and TradFi, but in this book I will use CeFi to designate centralized crypto-specific finance, and TradFi for traditional finance.
3. https://www.bis.org/publ/qtrpdf/r_qt2112b.htm
4. https://a16z.com/wp-content/uploads/2022/04/principles-and-models-of-decentralization_miles-jennings_a16zcrypto.pdf
5. https://www.nytimes.com/2022/03/02/technology/cryptocurrency-anonymity-alarm.html
6. https://www.coindesk.com/layer2/2022/08/04/master-of-anons-how-a-crypto-developer-faked-a-defi-ecosystem/
7. https://kennethbok.com/resources
8. https://www.nytimes.com/2021/12/20/technology/silicon-valley-cryptocurrency-start-ups.html
9. https://www.tbstat.com/wp/uploads/2022/12/Digital-Asset-2023-Outlook.pdf
10. https://a16zcrypto.com/crypto-fund-four/

11. https://www.sequoiacap.com/article/a-block-step-forward/
12. https://www.businesswire.com/news/home/20220712005073/en/Lightspeed-Raises-Over-7-Billion-to-Fund-Early-and-Growth-Stage-Entrepreneurs-Around-the-Globe
13. https://www.bloomberg.com/news/articles/2021-05-25/ex-credit-suisse-traders-amass-billions-of-dollars-of-crypto?sref=Fet8J5HC#xj4y7vzkg
14. https://www.bloomberg.com/news/articles/2022-07-22/three-arrows-founders-en-route-to-dubai-describe-ltcm-moment?sref=Fet8J5HC
15. https://www.tokensets.com
16. https://www.coindesk.com/markets/2019/04/23/french-lender-societe-generale-issues-112-million-bond-on-ethereum/
17. https://forum.makerdao.com/t/sg-forge-socgen-risk-assessment/15638
18. https://liftchallenge.bcb.gov.br/site/liftchallenge/en
19. https://labsnews.com/en/news/business/a55-defi-loan-modality/
20. https://www.gemini.com/cryptopedia/centrifuge-crypto-tinlake-tokenization-real-world-assets
21. https://www.eib.org/en/press/all/2021-141-european-investment-bank-eib-issues-its-first-ever-digital-bond-on-a-public-blockchain#
22. https://en.wikipedia.org/wiki/Smart_bond_(finance)
23. https://www.fireblocks.com/blog/permissioned-defi-goes-live-with-aave-arc-fireblocks/

2

Infrastructure and Instruments

2.1   The Infrastructure of DeFi

What is a blockchain? What are smart contracts? In this chapter we'll unpack some of the core technologies that drive DeFi. For many of us (read: not software engineers), the deep inner workings of computer science will be less relevant and we will only need to know the basics or a high-level understanding, in the same way most people don't really know how their car works. What's more important is to know how to drive, and what the risks are with driving. I'll be doing this in the same vein, and providing you with a high-level understanding so at least you'll be able to appreciate how DeFi works.

Nonetheless, if you are technical, and want a full understanding of how Bitcoin and Ethereum works – I recommend you check out *Mastering Bitcoin* (Antonopoulos 2017) and *Mastering Ethereum* (Antonopoulos and Wood 2018). Both will go into the details of the computing, mathematics, and protocol architecture, using Bitcoin and Ethereum as the key examples. Those details may not be relevant to all blockchain systems, but they are a great starting point.

There have been many building blocks before DeFi, and this chapter will describe some of the background, mostly surrounding Bitcoin and Ethereum. Ethereum was the first L1 and the first smart contract platform, and many of the first DeFi applications such as Uniswap and Compound were built on them. Currently, there is an intense competition between many of the newer L1s such as Solana, Polkadot, NEAR, and Avalanche for flows. In the same way that MacOS and Windows can result in totally different types of applications – DeFi ecosystems can differ as well, depending on the L1.

Decentralizing Finance: How DeFi, Digital Assets, and Distributed Ledger Technology Are Transforming Finance, First Edition. Kenneth Bok.
© 2024 John Wiley & Sons Ltd. Published 2024 by John Wiley & Sons Ltd.

2.2 Basics of Blockchains

Blockchains are a shared and immutable list of records (blocks) that are sequentially linked to each other with cryptographic methods (Figure 2.1). Sometimes also referred to as *distributed ledger technology* (DLT), blockchains combine several technologies and methods in their implementation, including distributed computing, cryptography, and economic incentives. Blockchains enable trust through the security of the network. They maintain a common and constantly updating source of truth, among a large set of parties that may not trust each other.

Public blockchains enable participants to interact, transact, and contribute to the network in a permissionless fashion: no authorization from any centralized party is required. Validators (miners) maintain the network in exchange for economic rewards: usually the native crypto-asset of the blockchain. Blockchains are also usually transparent. Transactions can be viewed publicly with the use of block explorers or through running one's own node.

The first blockchain, Bitcoin, was created by the pseudo-anonymous Satoshi Nakamoto in 2008. It was the first cryptocurrency to solve the *double-spending problem* in a decentralized system. The design of Bitcoin has inspired other blockchains such as Ethereum, which was the first of many subsequent *general-purpose blockchains,* representing a dramatic upgrade in capability, namely, allowing for blockchains to run code, execute smart contracts, and act as a global computer. These properties enabled DeFi to emerge.

General-purpose blockchains, also referred to as "Layer 1s" or "Layer 2s" (L1s / L2s), are the fundamental operating layers of DeFi. In particular, since Ethereum was the earliest L1 and has the most active DeFi ecosystem, we will use Ethereum as the prime teaching example in this book, for describing how general-purpose blockchains work, and for the DeFi applications built on top of these L1s. This is not to say that another L1 could not overtake Ethereum in

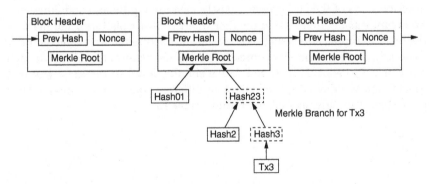

Figure 2.1 Blockchain structure.
Source: Bitcoin White Paper, Satoshi Nakamoto[1]

the future: innovation in this space is rapid and the possibilities are open-ended. We'll also take a brief look at how L1s compare to one another and what characteristics they are compared against.

2.2.1 Components of Blockchains

Blockchains usually consist of the following:

- A peer-to-peer (P2P) network that connects users and nodes;
- A set of rules that determine how consensus in the network is achieved (consensus algorithm);
- A chain of records (blocks) that are cryptographically linked together, that acts as the verified and valid record of the system;
- An incentivization and payment scheme that rewards and charges various actors in the network for providing and using resources;
- A set of rules for the emission of the native cryptocurrency; and
- Open source software implementation of the above (clients).

2.2.2 Cryptography

Cryptocurrencies got their colloquial name, "crypto," from cryptography. The Ancient Greek root of crypto, *kryptós,* means "hidden or secret." Cryptography has a large role to play in keeping the internet safe: this is the same technology that ensures your messages on instant messaging platforms are safe from prying eyes, and that your credit card numbers, passwords, and other sensitive information are kept secure when you enter them on e-commerce sites and other software platforms. Cryptography is also a key technology in blockchain. Three main methods of cryptography that are used in blockchains are *hash functions, public key cryptography,* and *digital signatures.*

2.2.3 Hash Functions

> *One-way hash functions are a cryptographic construct used in many applications. They are used with public-key algorithms for both encryption and digital signatures. They are used in integrity checking. They are used in authentication. They have all sorts of applications in a great many different protocols. Much more than encryption algorithms, one-way hash functions are the workhorses of modern cryptography.*
>
> —Bruce Schneier[2]

Hash functions transform data of arbitrary size to a fixed size. Hash functions are one-way, meaning that they are used to transform the input to the fixed size output, it is impossible to generate the original input just with the hash. Why is this useful?

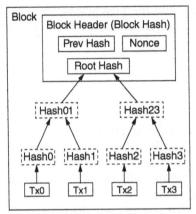

Transactions Hashed in a Merkle Tree

Figure 2.2 Merkle Tree in a blockchain.
Source: Bitcoin White Paper, Satoshi Nakamoto[3]

Hash functions are what link (or chain) the blocks together. They're an easy way to determine if the original data have changed, and serve as a method of data fingerprinting. A fingerprint is a small, verifiable imprint of your uniqueness: the same is true for a hash. Merkle trees (Figure 2.2) are a way to combine hash functions and allow for "efficient and secure verification of the contents of a large data structure."[4]

Hash functions are also used in proof-of-work-based blockchains such as Bitcoin. This is why Bitcoin miners are measured in "hash rate" or "hash power" – this is their ability to perform a number of hashes a second.

Cryptographic hash functions are specific types of hash functions that have special properties that are useful for blockchains. Ethereum utilizes the Keccak-256 cryptographic hash function and a special type of Merkle tree called Patricia Merkle trees.

2.2.4 Public-key Cryptography and Digital Signatures

Public-key cryptography (PKC) is a system that uses pairs of keys: a public key (viewable and shareable by others) and a private key (to be kept secret by the owner). Public keys are derived mathematically from the private key. In Ethereum, public addresses are similar to bank account numbers, and private keys are similar to the PIN code used to access the account. PKC allows for the authentication and verification of transactions.

Let's look at two examples to illustrate the basic workings of PKC. In the first case (Figure 2.3), Bob wants to send a message to Alice. He knows her public key but not her private key. He encrypts the message with Alice's public key

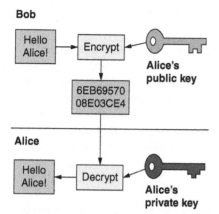

Figure 2.3 Encryption and decryption using public-private key pair.
Source: Wikipedia

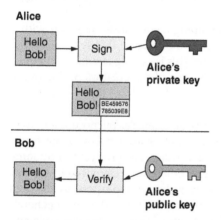

Figure 2.4 Digital signing and verification with a public-private key pair.
Source: Wikipedia

and sends the message to her. Only Alice can decrypt and view the message with her private key, ensuring confidentiality.

In the second case (Figure 2.4), Alice wants to send Bob a message. She signs the message with her private key. Since Bob has access to her public key, he is able to verify that the message in fact was from her. This is an example of a *digital signature*. Just as real-world signatures, digital signatures prove that the rightful owner of the address has approved of a message or transaction. When you are approving transactions in DeFi, digital signatures ensure that no-one else but you has the authority to do so.

2.3   Bitcoin and Ethereum

Think of the difference between something like a pocket calculator and a smartphone, where a pocket calculator does one thing, and it does one thing well. But really, people want to do all these other things. And if you have a smartphone, then you have a pocket calculator as an app, you have a music player as an app, you have a web browser as an app, and pretty much everything else. So basically, [Ethereum is] taking that same kind of idea of increasing the power of the system by making it more general purpose and applying it to blockchains.

—Vitalik Buterin

This quote was a good analogy that Vitalik Buterin, the inventor of Ethereum, gave to describe the difference between Bitcoin and Ethereum. Bitcoin does one thing well: tracking where each Bitcoin is, and who owns how much Bitcoin at any given time. The *consensus state* of Bitcoin is relatively simple: the ledger of the units of Bitcoin and the addresses.

Ethereum does the same task of maintaining a consensus state, but with a *data store*. Whereas Bitcoin is money on a blockchain, this is what makes Ethereum a computer on a blockchain. Since this is getting technical and deep into computer science land, let's hear from one of the creators of Ethereum, Gavin Wood:

Ethereum tracks the state transitions of a general-purpose data store, i.e., a store that can hold any data expressible as a key–value tuple. A key–value data store holds arbitrary values, each referenced by some key; for example, the value "Mastering Ethereum" referenced by the key "Book Title." In some ways, this serves the same purpose as the data storage model of Random Access Memory (RAM) used by most general-purpose computers. Ethereum has memory that stores both code and data, and it uses the Ethereum blockchain to track how this memory changes over time. Like a general-purpose stored-program computer, Ethereum can load code into its state machine and run that code, storing the resulting state changes in its blockchain. Two of the critical differences from most general-purpose computers are that Ethereum state changes are governed by the rules of consensus and the state is distributed globally. Ethereum answers the question: "What if we could track any arbitrary state and program the state machine to create a worldwide computer operating under consensus?"
—Mastering Ethereum, *Andreas Antonopoulos and Gavin Wood*

This is quite a paragraph, so let's unpack this.

First off – what's a general-purpose computer? There's a computer in your microwave. That's *not* a general-purpose computer. It serves a specific purpose – helping you to heat up your food in the myriad of ways possible – different timings, heat settings, and so on. A general-purpose computer is like a desktop computer, laptop, or a mobile phone: allowing for new software programs to be installed. The architecture of a general-purpose computer allows for all sorts of new functions we haven't even thought of yet. General-purpose computers are open-ended and multipurpose. Another technical term that you might come across when reading about Ethereum's general-purpose nature is "Turing complete."

Second, why would you need a computer that's global? Isn't the internet already a global computer? Aren't platforms like Facebook or Google massive computer networks already?

The answer is that Ethereum allows for anyone with an internet connection to access and interface with it, and that it allows for one shared truth of what the network state is. That is – we can't disagree as to what your token balance is on Ethereum, and we also can't disagree as to whether, say, a program has been run or not. We can't disagree on the effects of that program either. Ethereum ensures agreement, amongst any party that decides to use Ethereum. Isn't that amazing?

This also means that transactions in Ethereum are quite unlike those on FinTech platforms or banks, where it is possible to contact them and reverse the transaction if it was made in error. There is no-one to call and transactions are irreversible on public blockchains.

In short, Ethereum is a world computer that tracks and maintains a consensus state. Computers run programs. Nodes in Ethereum thus maintain consensus of state changes that are caused by users or programs.

If you're still confused about this, don't worry. It will become clearer as we move along with the decentralized applications.

There are many aspects to cover as to how Ethereum works: accounts, smart contracts, transactions, and tokens to begin with. But first, a brief overview of permissioned and public blockchains.

2.4 Permissioned vs Public Blockchains

One of the big dividing lines between blockchains that you will find is between the permissioned and public blockchains. The line is sometimes not so obvious in the way different companies and individuals market the term "blockchain." The result is that newcomers to blockchain will find it confusing as they read different books, listen to different speakers on the internet, and so forth. So let me shine some light on this, based on my experience, so you are at least aware of what this dividing line is and why it exists.

Permissioned blockchains limit nodes on the network to *known* participants. This implies two key points that cause many dramatic differences with public blockchains. As the name suggests, permissioned blockchains require permission to join the network. This implies that someone, or some entity has the authority to admit or prohibit new participants into the network. This implies centralization. That is the first point.

The second difference is around network resources. Why would someone want to contribute resources – hardware, software, capital, and labor – to a network? For public (permissionless) blockchains, the incentive is the native crypto-asset of the network. Validators and miners contribute resources to the network in order to earn these rewards. Crypto-assets also are used to pay for utilization of network resources, "gas," and prevent users from spamming the network.

Permissioned blockchains are usually privately funded by the enterprises (or consortium) that decide to use them. The motivation for participants in permissioned blockchains tend to come from specific mandates of these enterprises or consortia. This allows for permissioned blockchains not to have a native crypto-asset at all.

Some permissioned blockchain platforms include Hyperledger (from the Linux Foundation, with multiple variants), Corda (from R3), and Quorum (a permissioned version of Ethereum). They are often used in enterprise settings where specific requirements such as KYC / KYB (know your client / business) and other compliance requirements favor more control and knowledge about the network. Scalability of these networks may also be higher.

Nonetheless, due to the centralization of permissioned blockchains, some argue that permissioned blockchains do not provide the key feature of trustlessness through the network.

Metcalfe's law estimates that the value of a network is proportional to the square of the number of the users of the network. It's hard to argue against the success of public blockchains in this regard. Public blockchains enable anyone with an internet connection to access crypto, join, and build on the network if they so wish. The network effects achievable with open and interoperable systems is very significant.

Nonetheless, permissioned blockchains definitely have a place in solving problems in highly regulated industries such as finance where there are strict compliance requirements on banks. The sheer volume that financial institutions transact is a major factor in favor of permissioned DLT. The difference between the two could well be a "B2C vs B2B" type of distinction. We will discuss permissioned blockchains in more detail in Chapter 6.

2.5   L1s and L2s

Remember how I said that general-purpose blockchains, or L1s, are the funda-mental operating layers of DeFi? Well, this begs the question, which other L1s are there? How do they compare? How do they interact? How do they create different DeFi capabilities? While a full analysis and explanation of different L1s is simply too much detail to go into for the purposes of this book, let me highlight some of the key characteristics of L1s. Let's take a look at two tables from Galaxy Digital Research (Tables 2.1 and 2.2).

The *consensus algorithm* (Table 2.1) is the method in which blockchains reach agreement about the present state of the ledger. It must take into account how some nodes might fail, or behave in ways that are harmful or irresponsible. Two that you will commonly find are proof-of-work (PoW) and proof-of-stake (PoS). Most blockchains are moving towards PoS as it is more energy efficient, allows for greater decentralization, and it allows for sharding (resulting in greater throughput). In PoW systems, the longest chain of blocks is the valid version of the blockchain. In PoS systems, nodes may lose some of their stake in a mecha-nism known as "slashing" – penalties that are imposed due to downtime or double-signing. Both are behaviors that the network seeks to minimize. Consensus algorithms detail these rules for nodes, in computer code. Consensus algorithms also have important consequences on the security of blockchains.

The *transactions per second (TPS)* metric seeks to measure the throughput of the L1. This is a key metric as it looks to measure how fast a blockchain can process transactions. This is also where a great deal of innovation is happening to deliver high throughputs with newer L1s. By comparison, Visa can handle over 24,000 TPS[5] and PoW Ethereum can handle 15 TPS (PoS Ethereum looks to upgrade this significantly to 100,000 TPS). The speed of a blockchain tends to be higher in more centralized and less secure blockchains, as Vitalik Buterin's trilemma (Figure 2.5) suggests:

The trilemma posits that only two out of the three key attributes of scalabil-ity, decentralization, and security can be achieved in a blockchain.

Decentralization of a blockchain can be measured in a few ways. The first: the concentration of the validator or miners according to percentage of total stake or hash power. The Herfindahl score, a measure used in competition law and antitrust policy, can be computed using the squares of the stake (or hash power) of the validator set.

The other way to estimate decentralization is by the barrier to entry for validators. This is represented in Table 2.2, which lists the requirements of a validator node, for proof-of-stake systems. The higher the requirements, the less decentralized the blockchain will be.

EVM dApp support refers to the ability of the L1 to interface with Ethereum-based systems. This could be in the form of browser plug-ins, block explorers,

Table 2.1 Layer 1 comparisons.

Network	Consensus	Launch	Market Cap	DeFi TVL	% of Supply Staked	Annual Inflation Rate	Block Time (sec)	Transactions Per Second	EVM dapp Support
Ethereum	PoW	2015	$536bn	$163bn	6.80%	4.20$	13.35	15*	Yes
Binance Smart Chain	PoS/PoA	2020	$89bn	$32.2bn	76%	-2.35%	3	55-220	Yes
Solana	PoS/PoH	2020	$68bn	$12.4bn	78%	7.50%	0.53	50,000	Upcoming
Cardano	PoS	2017	$66bn	0	70%	5.70%	20	250	Upcoming
Polkadot	PoS	2020	$55bn	$321m	56%	10%	3	100,000**	Upcoming
Terra	dPoS	2019	$17bn	$9.8bn	35%	1.34%	6.6	10,000	No
Avalanche	PoS	2020	$15bn	$8.7bn	57%	5.57%	1.9	4,500	Yes
Algorand	pPoS	2019	$11bn	$83m	48%	29%	4.4	1,200	No
Internet Computer	PoS	2020	$8bn	Unknown	49%	Uncertain	0.12	Uncertain	No
Near	PoS	2018	$5bn	$45m	39%	5%	1	100,000	Yes
Tezos	PoS	2018	$280m	$147m	75%	4%	31	40	No

Source: Galaxy Digital Research
Data: Protocol Blogs, CoinGecko, Coin Metrics, Defi Llama, Various Other Sources
* ETH2 is estimated at 100k TPS:
** Polkadot is an estimate

Table 2.2 Validator node specifications.

Network	Processor	Memory	Storage	Req. Min. Stake*	Req. Min. Stake (USD)**
Ethereum 2.0	CPU > 2.80 GHz	16gb	>100gb	32 ETH	$140,000
Binance Smart Chain	12 Core CPU	48gb	2tb	10,000 BNB	$5,480,000
Solana	CPU > 2.5 GHz	128gb	500gb	No min.	N/A
Cardano	2 Core CPU > 2GHz	12gb	50gb	340 ADA	$680
Polkadot	CPU > 4.20 GHz	64gb	80-160gb	120 DOT	$6,000
Terra	4 Core CPU > 2.80 GHz	32gb	2tb	No min.	N/A
Avalanche	CPU > 2 GHz	>6gb	>200gb	2.000 AVAX	$148,000
Algorand	4 Core CPU > 2.50 GHz	4-8gb	100gb	0.1 ALGO	$0.32
Near	CPU > 2.80 GHz	16gb	200gb	3.59m NEAR	$39,490,000
Tezos	CPU > 2.0 GHz	4-8gb	60gb	1 XTZ	$6.27
Internet Computer	CPU > 3 GHz	36gb	3.2tb	1 ICP	$45.68

Source: Galaxy Digital Research

Data: Protocol Blogs, CoinGecko, Staking-Rewards.com. Various Other Sources

*Minimum to run a validator node, not to delegate to another validator:

** as of Nov. 4, 2021

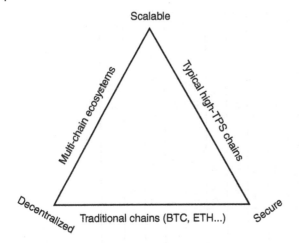

Figure 2.5 The blockchain trilemma.
Source: Vitalik Buterin's blog[6]

infrastructure, and tools that are already available for the Ethereum ecosystem. There is still a large advantage for L1s to be Ethereum virtual machine (EVM) compatible, as there will be a pre-existing base of users, developers, and infrastructure providers. The Metamask plug-in developed by ConsenSys, for example, has over 10 million monthly active users.[7]

Another dimension (not in Table 2.1) is *monolithic vs modular* blockchains. Some have also labeled modular blockchains as heterogeneous blockchains.[8] Some examples of modular / heterogeneous blockchains include Polkadot, Cosmos, Celestia, Polygon, and Avalanche. Modular blockchains allow for developers to create sub-blockchains, usually linked to the main blockchain, which can be built in a modular fashion. Modular blockchains may be composed depending on specific requirements that may utilize different execution, settlement, consensus, and data availability characteristics. Again, these may have implications on security, decentralization, and scalability of these blockchains. Monolithic blockchains like Solana may benefit from the centralization of liquidity within one ecosystem that does not require bridging.

Lastly, *L2s* are scalability solutions built on top of L1s. The Lightning Network for Bitcoin is one such example of an L2. In Ethereum, some of the leading L2s include Arbitrum, Optimism, zkSync, and Starkware. They may use technologies such as optimistic rollups and zero-knowledge rollups.

2.6 Accounts, Keys, Wallets, and Addresses

Let's come back to the micro and look at how accounts, keys, wallets, and addresses work in DeFi.

2.6.1   Accounts

There are two types of accounts in Ethereum: *externally owned accounts (EOAs)* and *contract accounts*. EOAs have private keys. Contract accounts do not. Essentially, EOAs are controlled by human beings, whereas contract accounts are controlled by smart contracts. When you use MetaMask or a Ledger, you are using an EOA. An example of a contract account would be a Uniswap smart contract for a token swap – liquidity pool. Both EOAs and contract accounts have unique addresses and it is impossible to tell them apart just by looking at the public address.

It is free to create an EOA, whereas it will cost gas to create a contract address (usage of network storage).

Multi-signature wallets are used in settings where the account needs to be owned / controlled by a group of individuals. Just like joint bank accounts, various rules can be set over the authorization of transactions (m-of-n). In Ethereum, a multi-signature wallet must be set-up using a contract account, since multi-signatures are not natively supported by EOAs.

2.6.2   Keys

Public-key cryptography is used to create public and private key pairs for EOAs. Private keys are made of 64 hexadecimal characters. Public keys can be derived from private keys, but not the other way around. Private keys are not used in the Ethereum system directly, and should not be stored or transmitted on Ethereum. Authorization is by means of digital signatures, which are created by the private keys.

In practice, private keys are rarely seen by end-users. They are usually encrypted and stored in special files, and managed by wallet clients. What end-users usually see and use as a proxy for their private keys are mnemonic seed phrases of up to 24 words. This seed phrase can be used to recreate the master private key in a *hierarchical deterministic* wallet.

2.6.3   Wallets

Wallets are systems used to store and manage keys. *Hierarchical deterministic (HD)* wallets (Figure 2.6), secured by a mnemonic seed phrase are common due to a few features:

- Privacy: Different keys can be generated for each transaction, allowing for one's transaction balance and history to be hidden
- Multi-chain: Unlimited number of keys can be generated for multiple cryptocurrencies
- Usability: There is a lower chance of error when writing down the seed phrase (as opposed to a hexadecimal sequence)
- Convenience: In an organizational setting, child keys can be assigned to specific departments

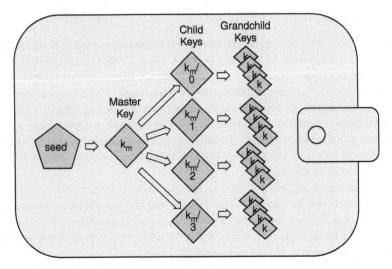

Figure 2.6 Hierarchical deterministic wallets.
Source: *Mastering Ethereum*

A few common standards enable wallet best practices, which are a contribution from the Bitcoin community, including BIP-32, BIP-39, BIP-43, and BIP-44.

2.6.4 Addresses

Public addresses in Ethereum are hexadecimal (base 16) numbers derived from the last 20 bytes of the Keccak-256 hash of the public key. The 0x prefix denotes hexadecimal format.

As an example, here's Vitalik's address: 0xAb5801a7D398351b8bE11C439 e05C5B3259aeC9B (if you're on a digital version of this book, you can click on the address and see what Vitalik holds and his trade history, on Etherscan – the block explorer for Ethereum).

The ability for individuals to choose not to link their real-world identities with their on-chain addresses is what pseudonymity means. In the above example, Vitalik willingly doxed himself, to prove a point.[9]

2.7 Transactions

Transactions are initiated by EOAs. They are signed messages originating from an EOA, transmitted by the network, and recorded on the blockchain. Smart contracts don't run autonomously – they must be called by transactions initiated from EOAs.

Transactions in DeFi have some unique characteristics that set it apart from TradFi.

2.7.1 Block-by-block Settlement

Settlement takes place on a block-by-block level. The more *block confirmations* there are, the more certain that the transaction has actually settled. It denotes the number of blocks that have been mined since the block that included your transaction. The higher the number of block confirmations, the lower the probability of disagreement amongst miners of the version of the blockchain that included your transaction. For example, FTX and Coinbase require 10 and 35 confirmations respectively, for Ethereum transactions to be considered final.

2.7.2 Irrevocable

As mentioned earlier, transactions in DeFi are irrevocable and irreversible by design. There is no central administrator or intermediary to reverse transactions. Mistakes can and do occur.[10] If errors do occur, the only course of remedy is to have the recipients send back the funds.

2.7.3 Composable

This is one of the key novel features of DeFi. Transactions may call multiple smart contracts and EOAs and change the state of the blockchain across multiple addresses, on a block-by-block level. Transactions may involve complex smart contracts that are effectively infinitely customizable. We will look at what these programs and applications are in Chapter 3.

2.7.4 Atomic

Transactions in DeFi are atomic: either the entire transaction executes, or none at all. If any individual step of the contract fails, the entire contract is reverted and does not execute. Gas is still charged by miners up to the point of failure. This allows for novel applications such as Flash Loans: uncollateralized loans which can be borrowed and paid back in one block.

2.7.5 Gas

In order to allocate the scarce resource of compute and memory on the blockchain, a fee called gas is charged for transactions. Without charging a fee for transactions, certain smart contract programs may run indefinitely, and users may spam the network.

The transaction fee in Ethereum currently (EIP-1559) is as follows: Gas limit * (Base fee + Tip).

The gas limit is the maximum amount of gas the user is willing to pay for the transaction. The base fee is set by the Ethereum network according to network usage. The tip is an optional fee that can be included to incentivize miners to include your transaction in the current block. An additional limit "Max fee per gas" can also be specified. If (Base fee + Tip) is more than "Max fee per gas," the transaction does not execute.

2.7.6   Mempool / MEV

The mempool (memory pool) is a waiting area for transactions that have not been included in a block and are unconfirmed. Nodes run a series of checks to determine if the transaction is valid, if the signature is valid, if funds are available, and other checks.

Due to the public visibility of the mempool, a phenomenon known as MEV (Maximal Extractable Value) has many consequences on execution of transactions and market dynamics. Just like HFT (High frequency trading) firms in TradFi, professional crypto trading teams scan and exploit short-term trading opportunities due to the mempool. Here are some examples.

Generalized frontrunning is possible with bots that scan the mempool for profitable transactions. The bot will copy and submit the transaction with a higher gas fee, frontrunning the transaction. Backrunning the transaction is also possible: when the victim's transaction moves the price on the local exchange, the trader can execute another arbitrage transaction to close the gap with the broader market.

The BIS has raised the various issues involved with MEV,[11] citing that MEV might form an "invisible tax" on regular market participants, and resemble front-running and insider trading activities that would be considered illegal in traditional financial markets.

2.8   Smart Contracts

The term *smart contracts* were originally coined by the computer scientist Nicholas Szabo in the 1990s. He writes:

> A smart contract is a computerized transaction protocol that executes the terms of a contract. The general objectives of smart contract design are to satisfy common contractual conditions (such as payment terms, liens, confidentiality, and even enforcement), minimize exceptions both malicious and accidental, and minimize the need for trusted intermediaries. Related economic goals include lowering fraud loss, arbitration and enforcement costs, and other transaction costs.[12]
>
> —*Nick Szabo, Smart Contracts*

A canonical real-life example, which we might consider to be the primitive ancestor of smart contracts, is the humble vending machine. Within a limited amount of potential loss (the amount in the till should be less than the cost of breaching the mechanism), the machine takes in coins, and via a simple mechanism, which makes a beginner's level problem in design with finite automata, dispense change and product fairly.

—*Nick Szabo, Smart Contracts:*
Building Blocks for Digital Markets[13]

Smart contracts are envisioned to be self-executing agreements among parties. They do not require intermediaries such as lawyers, and can reference variables in the contract programmatically. The promise, as with blockchains and software in general, is efficiency, reliability, and transparency.

While the topic as to whether smart contracts are actually legal contracts is hotly debated, in the context of DeFi the definition of smart contracts is more prosaic. Smart contracts are computer programs that run on a blockchain. They form the basis of DeFi applications.

Smart contracts are usually written by developers in high-level programming languages such as Solidity. High-level languages are more human-readable and require an intermediary step known as *compiling* to convert the code into low-level machine-oriented code.

Smart contracts have a few differences with regular computer programs. They are immutable: once deployed, smart contracts cannot be modified. Modification requires deployment of a new smart contract. In Ethereum, smart contracts can be deleted.

The most popular smart contract programming language is Solidity, which is similar in syntax to JavaScript and C++. Recently, Rust has gained popularity also, with usage in Solana and Polkadot.

Programming in smart contracts is a specialized skill set from regular programming, and requires an understanding of the blockchain system. Many aspects of security and other best practices must be adhered to, given the sensitivity of the applications and unforgiving nature of the blockchain. Smart contract programming requires rigorous software engineering methodologies as would be found in high-frequency trading firms and aerospace engineering. Many catastrophic losses have occurred due to hacks, bugs, and other cyberattacks. We will look deeper into risks in Chapter 4.

2.9   Clients and Nodes

Clients are the software applications that implement the specification of the blockchain. They allow for computers to act as nodes and communicate over the P2P network with other clients. They allow users to send transactions. There may be several clients for the same blockchain, giving diversity in options and functionality. Most wallets are *remote clients* that allow for creation, signing, and broadcasting of transactions without a large storage requirement.

Nodes make up the participants in the P2P network. They store the history of the blockchain, communicate with other nodes, and verify transactions. There are three types of nodes:

Full nodes participate in block validation and verify transactions. They store the most recent 128 blocks (Ethereum). Full nodes can be expensive and resource intensive to run because of the validation function.

Light nodes do not store a full copy of the blockchain and do not validate blocks, but are able to verify transactions. They store relevant information such as the block header, timestamps, and hash of the previous block. These are useful in mobile-devices such as smartphones.

Archive nodes maintain the complete copy of the blockchain data. This may take up a significant amount of storage – at the time of writing the Ethereum blockchain is 871GB. Archive nodes may not participate in validation and are used when a complete record of the chain is required, for example, by block explorers.

2.10 Block Explorers

Block-explorers are online tools that allow users to search, query, and look at the history of the blockchain in a human-friendly way. They display information on addresses, transactions, and tokens. Etherscan is the most popular Ethereum block explorer.

2.11 Custody

There are many ways to hold crypto-assets. They differ in security, connectivity to the internet and convenience (Figure 2.7).

Hot wallets are always connected to the internet. The key issue here is where the private key is stored. Hot wallets may be more convenient but they are also less safe. If a hacker manages to install malware or a keylogger on your local machine, or somehow access your seed phrase that was stored in plaintext anywhere other than your password manager, your crypto-assets are at risk. There exists an entire plethora of cyberattack vectors including phishing, scam software, and misinformation. Be vigilant and be careful! Always update your system software and do not click on dubious links. An example of a hot wallet is MetaMask, a browser extension and mobile app for Ethereum. Mobile wallets are also in this category.

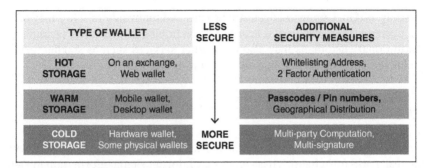

Figure 2.7 Custody types.
Source: Blockdata: Crypto Custody[14]

Multi-signature smart contract wallets offer customizable ownership settings and are compatible with both hot and cold storage solutions. Safe, previously known as Gnosis Safe, enables users to specify the number of required signatures for both ownership of a particular smart contract wallet and transaction approval. For instance, a wallet could be controlled by three separate keys, requiring at least two signatures for any outgoing ETH transfer. Frequently employed by DAOs seeking a trustless asset storage solution, multi-signature wallets are also suitable for individual users aiming to mitigate single-point-of-failure risks and thereby reduce the likelihood of hacks or losses. As of 31 August 2023, Safe holds more than US$50 billion in assets.

Exchange custody offers another option for users, essentially delegating asset custody to the trading platform. The benefits of this approach include seamless asset conversion to and from fiat currency (provided the exchange supports fiat-to-crypto transactions), the flexibility to trade at will, and potentially easier transfers across multiple blockchains. However, the key downside is the risk of asset loss due to exchange insolvency or failure to honor withdrawals, as exemplified by the Mt. Gox debacle.

While centralized exchanges have attracted many retail and institutional traders in the crypto realm, they deviate from the principles of decentralization and self-custody intrinsic to blockchain technology, thereby introducing often-overlooked risks. Centralized platforms exercise ultimate control over user funds, becoming potential single points of failure susceptible to hacks or scams.

The risks are even greater with unregulated exchanges. Such platforms frequently lack transparency regarding their security measures and have been known to misuse and co-mingle customer funds to earn yield, often without proper disclosure, as evidenced by Celsius and FTX. Legal battles involving these exchanges have also resulted in the unwelcome public release of sensitive data.

Institutional custody has become a key component for institutional adoption of crypto-assets. There are many players including Fireblocks, Coinbase

Custody, BitGo, Copper, Ledger, Anchorage, and many others. They may offer full custody solutions (with a license and technology) or just the technology. Institutional custodians may also offer other services such as staking, prime brokerage, settlement, lending, and accounting services.

2.12   Oracles

Oracles are data feeds that bridge the blockchain environment (on-chain) with the real world (off-chain). These feeds may inform pricing information in DeFi and be referenced in smart contracts. Examples of oracles include Chainlink (Ethereum) and Pyth (Solana).

2.13   RegTech

As DeFi becomes more mainstream and regulated, crypto RegTech solutions are increasingly becoming an integral part of DeFi infrastructure. Companies such as Chainalysis, Elliptic, CipherTrace (Mastercard), and TRM Labs offer a suite of services including compliance, risk management, investigation, fraud prevention, transaction monitoring, and on-chain analytics. They may help in satisfying AML (Anti-Money Laundering) and CFT (Combating the Financing of Terrorism) requirements for regulated crypto entities. The sophistication of law enforcement in understanding and investigating on-chain processes and transactions has also increased significantly, with the aid of these RegTech tools. This has been demonstrated by the largest financial seizure ever by the US Department of Justice of US$3.6b from the 2016 Bitfinex hack .

2.14   Identity

Decentralized identity, also known as self-sovereign identity, looks to enable individuals and organizations to manage their digital identities and credentials without reliance on governments and big tech companies such as Google or Facebook. In particular for DeFi, decentralized identity could be a major part in bridging loans between DeFi and the real world.

2.15   Bridges

Just like real-world bridges, blockchain bridges connect two different networks, enabling cross-chain transfer of assets and information. Wrapped tokens are bridged tokens. As multi-chain becomes more common, bridges become more important. Bridges can come in centralized and decentralized forms. Nonetheless, some have highlighted security issues with bridges[15] and this has been witnessed with the US$320m Wormhole hack in 2022. Examples of bridges include: WBTC, Wormhole, Celer, and Anyswap.

2.16   DeFi Instruments

In this section, we'll look at the various instruments that are used in DeFi. Crypto tokens are open-ended and can be designed to represent nearly anything: real-world assets like gold, fiat currencies, software access rights, or identity tokens. At last count, CoinMarketCap lists 20,691 different crypto-assets, with a market capitalization of US$1 trillion. In 2018, the Swiss Financial Market Supervisory Authority (FINMA) defined three types of tokens:

Payment tokens used for payments,
Utility tokens used for access to blockchain-based applications or services,
Security tokens which are representations of assets, such as debt or equity claim
    on the issuer.

Hybrid tokens with characteristics of two or more categories also could exist. This categorization is a representation of the legal and regulatory dimension of crypto-assets, which hinges around payment and securities laws.

I prefer the term "crypto-assets" to refer to the superset of tokens, as the more commonly used "cryptocurrency" suggests a purely monetary function. For example, Bitcoin is a cryptocurrency but Ether, having utility functions in Ethereum, would be a crypto-asset. The term "utility" is also open-ended, and other functions such as access, governance, staking, and so on would fall under utility, insofar as it pertains to the access and usage of the decentralized application.

We can further categorize crypto-assets into the following categories:

Pure Cryptocurrencies
- In the intent of BTC, to be internet-native, state-independent money
- For example, BTC, DOGE, SHIB, LTC, XMR
- Aim to have the three functions of money: Store of value, medium of exchange, and unit of account (mileage may vary)
- Payment tokens

L1 / L2 tokens
- Tokens issued in conjunction with L1 or L2, and can represent a variety of functions on L1 or L2, including
  - Gas fees on the platform
  - Governance
  - Staking

- For example, ETH, SOL, DOT, MATIC, AVAX, ATOM
- These tokens can be native-money for the L1 ecosystem, and are often utilized for payments for ICOs / token launches on the platform and other DeFi activities
- Utility tokens

DApp tokens
- Tokens issued by decentralized applications, which typically have utility and governance aspects, that allow for token holders to propose and vote on issues pertaining to the application / platform
- For example, UNI, LINK, AAVE, MKR
- Typically issued using the fungible standard specification of the native L1, for example, ERC-20

Liquidity Provider (LP) tokens
- These are specific tokens issued by DeFi protocols as holding receipts for providing, locking-up, or staking liquidity in liquidity pools
- For example, cETH (Compound), stETH (Lido)
- Typically issued using the fungible standard specification of the native L1, for example, ERC-20

Exchange tokens
- Tokens issued by exchanges, designed to incentivize trading activity
- For example, BNB, FTT, CRO
- May grant fee discounts for trading or free transactions with a certain number of exchange token staked
- Tokens may be bought-back and burned by the exchange to increase the value of the token

Stablecoins
- Stablecoins look to solve the volatility problem of cryptocurrencies. They seek to represent units of fiat currency, but on the blockchain
- For example, USDT, USDC, BUSD, DAI
- Stablecoins may be fiat-collateralized, crypto-collateralized, commodity-collateralized, or algorithmic
- Stablecoins are a key aspect of DeFi: more on stablecoins in a later section

Token standards are commonly used in DeFi for a few reasons. Standards uniformly define functions such as transfers or checking total token supply, token balances, and approvals. They allow for interoperability between applications and security best-practices. Unlike Ether, which is handled at the protocol level, tokens are handled at the smart contract level. Token standards are smart contract templates.

Fungible tokens
- The most common and well-known standard: ERC-20
- Frequently used for dApp tokens.

- Fungibility means interchangeable or replaceable. For example, a US$100 bill is fungible with five US$20 bills.
- The "Approve" function authorizes a recipient address (spender) to spend multiple times from the authorizing account (owner).
- The "Allowance" function authorizes the maximum amount the spender can withdraw from the owner.
- The above two functions allow for authorized DApps to execute transactions on behalf of the owner.

Non-fungible tokens
- Standard for NFTs: ERC-721
- For example, Bored Apes Yacht Club, CryptoPunks, ENS, Sandbox land
- NFTs may be collectible graphic art, virtual land, in-game items, and many other things.
- This is a broad definition and refers to the unique nature of NFTs. They can belong to certain sets within the NFT superset, and have different attributes and rarities.
- See OpenSea, the largest marketplace for NFTs, for an idea of what the universe of NFTs looks like.

Security tokens
- Representations of regulated real-world assets such as equities, bonds, or commodities
- Debt or equity claim against the issuer or third party
- For example, Securitize, Polymath

Wrapped tokens
- Wrapped tokens are proxy tokens whose value is pegged to the original token
- Usually happens on a separate chain, for interoperability purposes,
- For example, WBTC, WETH.
- WBTC is an ERC-20 version of Bitcoin. It allows for Bitcoin to be traded on Ethereum and is minted by a custodian, who safeguards the BTC until the opposite "burn" process is requested (destroying the WBTC and returning the BTC) (Figure 2.8).

2.17 Stablecoins

Stablecoins are cryptocurrencies whose value is pegged to a fiat currency. They look to solve the volatility of cryptocurrencies which make it unsuitable for merchants and users to use cryptocurrencies as a *store of value*. (Remember the three functions of money?) Cryptocurrencies such as Bitcoin are also not commonplace by any means, and this means that stablecoins are a much better *unit of account* for businesses to do their accounting with. As a *medium of exchange*, stablecoins generally excel in terms of cross-border transfers, but

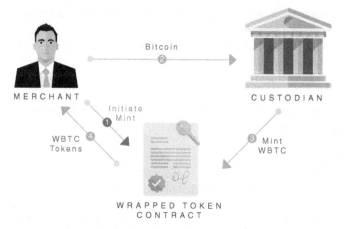

Figure 2.8 WBTC minting process.
Source: wbtc.network

may encounter different frictions with adoption of crypto-asset and blockchain infrastructure, and on-off fiat ramps.

Stablecoins have had incredible growth in the last three years, and have mirrored the growth of DeFi as a whole. Total stablecoin supply grew from US$5b to US$142b (Aug. 2019–Aug. 2022; Figure 2.9).[16] The vast majority of stablecoin issuance is in USD, with USD representing 99.4% of all stablecoin issuance. EUR represents 0.54% and GBP represents 0.03% of total stablecoin issuance.

The popularity of stablecoins is due to a few factors:

1. Stablecoins combine the best of both worlds – the stability of fiat and the cross-border, global nature of crypto.
2. If one does not want to hold crypto, it is much easier to store value in stablecoins than the alternative of converting into fiat, owing to frictions of cost and time between fiat–crypto on-off ramps.
3. Utilization of stablecoins in trading pairs in crypto–crypto exchanges (exchanges without fiat on-off ramps).
4. Stablecoin transfers are faster, simpler, and cheaper than bank transfers.
5. Opportunities for higher yields in DeFi than TradFi.

Stablecoins thus represent a major and growing crossover point between DeFi, FinTech, and TradFi. As with my suggestion on trying out USDC transfers on Solana or Polygon, it is entirely possible to transact in stablecoins without having significant crypto exposure (other than to pay for gas fees). One alternative way of thinking about DeFi could well be using stablecoins as value-transmission, on blockchain infrastructure. Other speculative crypto-assets may not even factor into this use-case, outside of L1 / L2 tokens supporting the infrastructure.

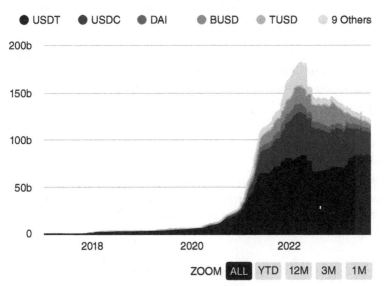

Figure 2.9 Total stablecoin supply.
Source: The Block, Coin Metrics

Many FinTech firms such as Stripe are actively looking into utilizing stablecoins for payments,[17] due to their global, internet-native nature.

> Making commerce more global is one of the most powerful ways we're going after our mission to increase the GDP of the internet. Because crypto protocols are global by default, they're a natural vector for doing this. With crypto payouts, platforms using Stripe can send money to verified recipients nearly anywhere in the world, instantaneously.
> —*Will Gaybrick, Chief Product Officer, Stripe*

Regulators and central banks worldwide have also begun to monitor developments in stablecoins closely, given their multiple implications on monetary policy, financial stability, consumer protection, and AML / CFT. In November 2021, the (US) President's Working Group, comprising of the Federal Deposit Insurance Corporation and the Office of the Comptroller of the Currency, released a report on stablecoins that recommended that Congress "act promptly to enact legislation to ensure that payment stablecoins and payment stablecoin arrangements are subject to a federal prudential framework on a consistent and comprehensive basis."[18]

Central banks are also looking at stablecoins for another reason: they serve as a pilot test for CBDCs and a possible adjunct to CBDCs. In particular, since

central banks are not in the business of having direct relationships with consumers and businesses (this is left to commercial banks), stablecoins may provide clues as to how the private sector would handle the technology and
distribution of CBDCs. More about CBDCs in Chapter 6.

While stablecoins may look and function similarly on the surface, they differ
in many ways in terms of their collateralization and stabilization mechanisms
under the hood. Let's examine the four different types:

1. Fiat-collateralized
2. Crypto-collateralized
3. Commodity-collateralized
4. Algorithmic

Fiat-collateralized stablecoins are issued by centralized entities who hold an
equal amount of cash and short-term debt instruments equivalent to the total
float of stablecoins (Figure 2.10). Typically, these entities publish audited
reports of their reserves on their websites (Figure 2.11).

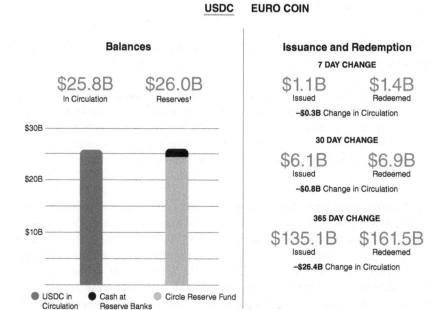

Figure 2.10 USDC reserves.
Source: Circle.com

Reserves Breakdown

■ 85.05%	■ 0.13%	■ 3.78%	■ 1.94%	■ 2.73%	■ 6.36%
Cash & Cash Equivalents & Other Short-Term Deposits	Corporate Bonds	Precious Metals	Bitcoins	Other Investments	Secured Loans (None To Affiliated Entities)

Cash & Cash Equivalents & Other Short-Term Deposits					
■ 75.86%	■ 12.09%	■ 0.78%	■ 11.06%	■ 0.12%	■ 0.09%
U.S. Treasury Bills	Overnight Reverse Repurchase Agreements	Term Reverse Repurchase Agreements	Money Market Funds	Cash & Bank Deposits	Non-U.S. Treasury Bills

Figure 2.11 USDT reserves.
Source: Tether.com

Since they do not pay depositors (i.e., parties who deposit fiat with the issuers to create the stablecoins) interest, the interest earned on short-term debt instruments is their profit (minus other expenses).

Other examples include: USDC, USDT, BUSD, GUSD, TUSD, PAX

Crypto-collateralized stablecoins are backed by other crypto-assets. Since the collateral base is constantly fluctuating, overcollateralization is the norm here. DAI, issued by MakerDAO, has the highest market cap among the various crypto-collateralized stablecoins of ~US$7b, and accepts various crypto-assets such as USDC and ETH as collateral. As of time of writing, the collateral ratio for DAI is 139.27%.[19]

Additional examples of crypto-collateralized stablecoins include Liquity and Gravita. Liquity is a protocol that solely accepts ETH as collateral, while Gravita is a collateral-debt-position (CDP) based protocol that accepts a range of collateral types, including liquid staking tokens such as stETH (Lido staked ETH) and rETH (Rocket Pool ETH).

Commodity-collateralized stablecoins are collateralized by commodities, typically gold.

PAXG (Paxos Gold) and XAUT (Tether Gold) are the two most popular ones in this category. The issuers may also make it possible to redeem for physical gold.

Algorithmic stablecoins represent the deep (and arguably, dark) end of crypto experimentation. Uncollateralized stablecoins rely on methods such as *seigniorage* and *rebasing*.

Seigniorage models consist of at least two tokens, the most infamous case being UST / LUNA, which had a spectacular collapse in May 2022. The stabilization mechanism utilized LUNA as the collateral for UST. If UST traded above US$1, arbitrageurs could sell UST in the market and buy UST from Terra using LUNA. (Terra guaranteed 1 UST = US$1 of LUNA.) If UST traded below US$1, arbitrageurs could buy UST in the market and sell UST to Terra using LUNA. This mechanism worked, until market conditions and various circumstances created negative feedback loops (aka the death spiral). UST also combined the seigniorage model with Anchor, a "savings" protocol promising 19.5%/yr, enabling UST to reach a peak of US$18b.

In *rebasing* models, the supply of the stablecoin is adjusted algorithmically according to the peg. If the stablecoin price trades over the peg, supply is increased. If the stablecoin price trades under the peg, supply is decreased. This will apply to all holders of the token. An example of a rebasing algo stablecoin is Ampleforth.

Fractional-reserve algo stablecoins maintain a less than 1:1 ratio of collateral, and may combine seigniorage mechanisms. An example is FRAX.

Examples: UST (collapsed), FRAX, ESD (collapsed), DSD (collapsed), Basis Cash (collapsed), AMPL

As with all crypto-asset activities, please take caution and be cognizant of the risks. Many people have lost a lot of money with algorithmic stablecoins.

Since stablecoins (and possibly CBDCs) look to be a key part of DeFi, we'll discuss this further in Chapter 9.

2.18 Derivatives

"Derivatives" refers to financial instruments whose value is derived from another financial instrument (the underlying instrument). Derivatives may also reference indices or other kinds of financial data such as interest rates. The derivatives market in TradFi is enormous: the BIS estimates the gross market value of all derivatives contracts at US$12.4 trillion (end 2021).[20] Common derivatives include futures, forwards, options, and swaps. Derivatives can be said to trade over-the-counter (OTC, off-exchange) or on an exchange.

Just as with TradFi, numerous derivative products in DeFi have evolved over the last few years. They are used for the same purposes in TradFi: hedging risk, gaining leverage, gaining financial exposure, and speculation. Cash settlement often entails less friction than physical settlement of the underlying instrument. Many DeFi derivatives are not tokenized and exist as contracts between the buyer and seller.

A common type of futures contract in DeFi are *perpetual futures contracts*. They do not expire and are cash-settled. Payments are settled periodically between the buyer and seller of the contract and are a factor of the funding rate and the change in the price of future. They were pioneered by BitMEX in 2016, but were first proposed by the economist Robert Schiller in 1992. Perpetual futures are common on centralized exchanges and are also available on decentralized exchanges such as dYdX, Mango Markets, and Drift.

Options are also starting to be more common in DeFi. The largest crypto options exchange currently is Deribit (a centralized exchange), with the majority of volume being ETH and BTC options. Decentralized options exchanges have also emerged, such as Opyn, Hegic, Zeta Markets, and PsyOptions. Even more advanced structured products, DeFi Options Vaults (DOVs) have also emerged, combining aspects of AMMs (automated market makers) and options.

Index products mimic ETFs in TradFi, and provide exposure to a basket of crypto-assets, usually grouped by a theme. One index that tracks the DeFi market is the DeFi Pulse Index, maintained by DeFi Pulse. Set Protocol maintains a token (DPI) that provides exposure to the index. Nonetheless, index products do not seem to have proven popular: the market capitalization of index products remains in the tens of millions.

2.19   Chapter Summary

This chapter has described the basics of blockchains, the infrastructure built on top of the blockchain, and the instruments that exist on blockchain-based infrastructure that makes DeFi possible. If you're completely new to crypto, and you made it through this whole chapter: congratulations! You now have a basic working knowledge of crypto / DeFi, and what most crypto professionals take for granted. In the next chapter, we'll look at the meat of what people consider to be DeFi – the financial activities and applications themselves. Let's go!

Notes

1. https://bitcoin.org/bitcoin.pdf
2. https://www.schneier.com/essays/archives/2004/08/cryptanalysis_of_md5 .html
3. https://bitcoin.org/bitcoin.pdf
4. https://en.wikipedia.org/wiki/Merkle_tree
5. https://usa.visa.com/run-your-business/small-business-tools/retail.html
6. https://vitalik.ca/general/2021/04/07/sharding.html
7. https://consensys.net/blog/press-release/metamask-surpasses-10-million-maus-making-it-the-worlds-leading-non-custodial-crypto-wallet/
8. https://medium.com/@arikan/a-comparison-of-heterogeneous-blockchain-networks-4bf7ff2fe279
9. https://twitter.com/VitalikButerin/status/1050126908589887488
10. https://www.fool.com/the-ascent/buying-stocks/articles/blockfi-accidentally-sends-users-millions-in-bitcoin/
11. https://www.bis.org/publ/bisbull58.pdf
12. https://www.fon.hum.uva.nl/rob/Courses/InformationInSpeech/CDROM/ Literature/LOTwinterschool2006/szabo.best.vwh.net/smart.contracts.html

13. https://www.fon.hum.uva.nl/rob/Courses/InformationInSpeech/CDROM/ Literature/LOTwinterschool2006/szabo.best.vwh.net/smart_contracts_2.html
14. https://download.blockdata.tech/BLOCKDATA-Crypto-Custody-The-Gateway-to-Institutional-Adoption-VF.pdf
15. https://old.reddit.com/r/ethereum/comments/rwojtk/ama_we_are_the_efs_ research_team_pt_7_07_january/hrngyk8/
16. https://www.theblock.co/data/decentralized-finance/stablecoins
17. https://stripe.com/newsroom/news/crypto-payouts
18. https://home.treasury.gov/system/files/136/StableCoinReport_Nov1_508.pdf
19. https://daistats.com/#/
20. https://www.bis.org/publ/otc_hy2205.htm#:~:text=The%20gross%20 market%20value%20of%20derivatives%20contracts%20%E2%80%93%20a%20 measure%20of,%248.6%20trillion%20at%20end%2D2021

3

Activities and Applications

This chapter shows what is possible in DeFi, in view of TradFi's tried-and-tested financial activities. As we leave familiar territory, you'll gain a new vocabulary. Case studies will illustrate novel mechanisms and innovations in the various categories. Once again, they do not represent the end-point of innovation by any means and many of the principles might change in the future. Nonetheless, these examples are some of the oldest and well-established DeFi protocols, so they are a good starting point.

From an implementation perspective, many of these protocols connect directly to the user's wallet, such as MetaMask or Coinbase Wallet, or use connecting protocols such as WalletConnect to connect to the user's wallet.

3.1   Trading / DEXs

3.1.1   Automated Market Makers (AMMs)

If you hadn't noticed by now, a lot of crypto and DeFi centers around the trading of tokens. A big breakthrough in facilitating trading of tokens was with decentralized exchanges, or DEXs. How are DEXs different from centralized exchanges? First, unlike centralized exchanges, DEXs do not require customers to identify themselves. This enables a private, frictionless, and permissionless trading experience. It enables DEXs to be composable and to allow for other platforms like aggregators to be integrated with many DEXs.

Second, many DEXs utilize what is known as an Automated Market Maker (AMM) model. Ethereum founder Vitalik Buterin first proposed AMMs in 2016[1] and they were subsequently implemented by Hayden Adams, founder of *Uniswap*. AMMs are a radical departure from the *centralized limit order book* (CLOB) model that the vast majority of exchanges are run on (both in TradFi

Decentralizing Finance: How DeFi, Digital Assets, and Distributed Ledger Technology Are Transforming Finance, First Edition. Kenneth Bok.
© 2024 John Wiley & Sons Ltd. Published 2024 by John Wiley & Sons Ltd.

and crypto exchanges). In CLOB models, traders post bids and offers with specific quantities on a centralized order book. Trades occur when participants decide to sell (or buy) "at market" – transacting with the highest bid (or lowest offer) on the order book.

Other than institutional and retail participants on CLOB exchanges, professional market makers play a role in providing liquidity for these markets. These market makers are commissioned by the exchange, the company of the asset, or independent. Market makers have the role of making sure that there is always a buyer or seller for markets. They make the spread between what they buy and sell. These are usually professional traders with large balance sheets and sophisticated technology.

AMMs change this dynamic completely. In contrast with CLOBs, where there is always a distinct counterparty in a trade representing the opposite and matching side, buyers and sellers in an AMM transact with a liquidity pool. The liquidity pool is made up of (usually) two assets that have been deposited from liquidity providers (LPs). When LPs deposit crypto-assets into a pool, they are issued LP tokens, which are pro-rated representations of claims on the total pool. LPs earn commissions on trading fees charged by the protocol, and may also earn other rewards such as the governance token of the AMM (yield farming).

AMMs typically use a *constant product function* that mathematically determines prices and quantities. Prices on AMMs are deterministic. Figure 3.1 illustrates this.

The quantity of token A in the pool is denoted by x, and the quantity of token B is denoted by y. The product of x and y is fixed at a constant, k. When a trader sells a certain quantity of token A (in exchange for token B) into the pool, the balance of token A in the pool increases, and the balance of token B decreases.

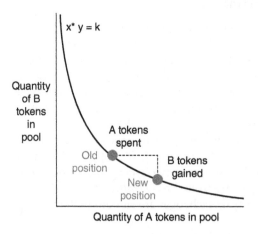

Figure 3.1 Constant production function in AMMs.
Source: CoinDesk https://www.coindesk.com/learn/2021/08/20/what-is-an-automated-market-maker/

The new state of the pool will determine the price that the next transaction will get, according to the curve. For the exact mathematics and implementation, please refer to the respective whitepapers and GitHub repo.

AMMs thus model for supply and demand in token markets, without the need for intermediaries like market makers. They crowdsource the liquidity required in market making and democratize the process. In practice, prices on AMMs for liquid tokens such as BTC and ETH stay mostly in line with centralized exchanges due to the action of arbitrageurs.

One key question here is: how much do LPs make providing liquidity? This brings us to what is known as impermanent loss. Impermanent loss occurs when the value of your deposited assets changes, relative to the value when you deposited them. ("Impermanent" refers to the fact that losses aren't actualized until one withdraws from the pool, in the same sense as paper losses.) This occurs because the composition of the pool changes due to the actions of traders who trade with the pool. In general, there can be a tendency for LPs to suffer impermanent loss because the pool is constantly negatively selected in trades with traders who are more price-informed than the pool (since the price function of the pool is purely algorithmic and does not reflect market information).

There are several consequences to the AMM model. Here are two:

The first is that execution and settlement occurs on-chain for DEXs, and not off-chain, as happens in centralized exchanges. This trade-off creates permissionless access to DEXs, and enables many of the DeFi features such as composability, interoperability, and decentralization. It shifts settlement to the L1, but slows down execution. It creates significant opportunities for MEV and risks for front-running and other "invisible taxes,"[2] which are unregulated and not easily visible to retail users.

Second, this enables practically any token to be listed on DEXs and for liquidity to be created, without going through what can be expensive and time-consuming processes with centralized exchange listing. The upside of this is permissionless innovation. The downside is the possibility for low-quality tokens to enter the market, many of which might be outright scams.

Since Uniswap pioneered the AMM model, there have been many other AMM-DEXs that have innovated upon the basic AMM model, and created on other blockchains outside of Ethereum. Let me highlight a few which I think are noteworthy:

Curve is an AMM specifically designed for fungible assets: stablecoins, and different wrapped versions of crypto-assets such as BTC and ETH. Curve utilizes a more linear function curve, especially in the trading ranges of the assets, so that slippage is minimized.

Balancer allows for multi-asset pools (up to eight), and allows for pool creators to set the trading fees and asset weights.

SushiSwap is an interesting case that illustrates the competitive dynamics of the DeFi space: it is one of the most well-known examples of a vampire attack. In August 2020 a pseudonymous developer forked the code of Uniswap and encouraged users to deposit assets into SushiSwap, but with Uniswap LP tokens. It issued its own governance token for incentives, and catalyzed Uniswap into issuing one as well.

Serum is an on-chain DEX on Solana that runs on a centralized limit order book model. It has the function of a liquidity protocol across Solana and connects DEXs for trade matching.

Mango Markets, also on Solana, is a DEX that allows for cross-margined positions, perpetual futures, as well as spot trading. Many interesting capabilities are possible on Solana due to the faster block time. (If it can stay stable!)

3.1.2 Aggregators

Aggregators enable users to source for liquidity across multiple DEXs, to get the best price. They may also employ other smart routing algorithms that take into account market depth and gas fees. Some of the most popular aggregators are *1inch*, *Cowswap*, *Paraswap*, and *Matcha*.

3.2 Overcollateralized Lending / Borrowing

Credit markets underpin a fundamental part of any financial system, and this is where DeFi is also looking to solve. DeFi lending and borrowing protocols have similarities with P2P lending platforms in FinTech as they both match lenders with borrowers, but utilize crypto-assets, stablecoins, may pool these assets in smart contracts, and decentralized governance.

Lending and borrowing also occurs in a unique environment as compared to TradFi. We don't know who is borrowing (unless the borrowers willingly identifies themselves), but we can see their transaction history and what they hold. Any penalties for default must be done on-chain and we can't use legal means of debt collection. Pseudonymous borrowers may also borrow more than once.

Out of this set of characteristics has emerged the predominant type of loan DeFi lending / borrowing: overcollateralized loans. Two of the most popular lending / borrowing platforms are *Aave* and *Compound*, with outstanding debt of US$2.71b and US$0.95b respectively.[3] *MakerDAO* is also in this category, but is slightly more complicated as it issues its own stablecoin, DAI. How do they work?

Let's look first at Aave, the largest lending / borrowing platform.

In Aave, depositors can lend to the protocol for a specified interest rate. They are issued interest-bearing aTokens (cTokens in Compound) that can be redeemed for the original deposit at any time. As with DEXs with LPs, governance tokens may also be issued to reward depositors. Interest is paid pro rata based on the total interest paid by borrowers in the asset pool, on a block-by-block basis. aTokens can also be traded on DEXs such as Uniswap.

Borrowers must supply collateral to borrow. The amount they are able to borrow is defined by a loan-to-value (LTV) ratio. If they supply US$100 USDC and the LTV is 0.75, they are able to borrow US$75 USDC (or equivalent in other crypto-assets). If their overall collateral-to-debt ratio falls below a certain threshold (health factor), third parties known as liquidators are able to purchase the user's collateral for a discount (liquidation bonus). The protocol thus ensures that net assets are greater than net liabilities by incentivizing liquidators to execute liquidations, and by adjusting the various parameters.

To be more specific, each asset in Aave has specific risk parameters: the loan-to-value (LTV) ratio, liquidation threshold, liquidation bonus, and a reserve factor. The health factor is a function of the total collateral multiplied by the respective liquidation thresholds, divided by the total debt.

$$H_f = \frac{\sum Collaterall_i \times Liquidation\ Threshold_i}{Total\ borrow}$$

These parameters can be adjusted via the governance mechanism / process.

The interest rate is derived by the utilization rate of each asset pool. The utilization rate is the ratio of assets being borrowed vs lent. The model is designed to encourage borrowing when the utilization rate is low, by lowering interest rates; and encouraging lending when the utilization rate is high, by raising interest rates. Interest rate models in Aave are linear functions as illustrated in Figure 3.2. The model is designed to keep the utilization rate below a defined optimal point, above which the interest rate rises sharply to encourage lending.

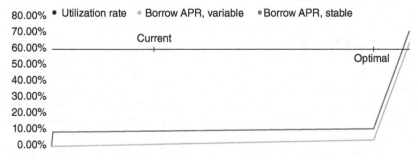

Figure 3.2 Interest rate model in Aave.
Source: Aave.com

You might also note that there is a variable and stable rate. This choice between variable and stable rate is for borrowers only. Both rates are determined by parameters in the protocol, with the stable rate being higher as a trade-off for certainty.

At this point, one might ask: why would anyone want to do this? If I had US$100, why would I deposit US$100 to borrow US$80? Unlike in the real-world, where loans can be undercollateralized (as with credit cards), crypto-loans are predominantly used to gain exposure to crypto-assets, leverage up on positions, and earn interest.

Let's take an example of Bob, who holds 10 ETH. Let's assume the price of ETH is US$2,000, and the LTV of ETH is 0.8. He's thus able to borrow up to US$16,000. He doesn't want to sell his ETH but needs to pay some household expenses. He decides to take a loan in Aave, depositing his 10 ETH and borrows US$10,000 in USDC (for some cushion so he doesn't get liquidated). He still gets risk exposure to ETH (both up and down), but is able to use the cash to pay off expenses (or whatever he chooses to use the cash for).

Alternatively, Bob might be very bullish on the market and decides to lever up on his positions. He deposits the ETH and borrows a further 8 ETH. He now has a total position of 18 ETH long, having originally owned 10 ETH, for a leverage ratio of 1.8.

The third case is where Bob doesn't feel so bullish, but still wants to earn some interest on his ETH as it just "sits there." He decides to deposit his ETH, and earns 1% APY. He still holds his ETH but now is earning some passive income.

It might also occur to you if it is possible to lend out the borrowed crypto-assets, in order to gain even more leverage. The answer is yes. Recursive loans are possible with these platforms that reach a mathematical limit of $1/(1-r)$, r being the collateral ratio. Using the same example with Bob, this makes it possible to borrow US$100,000 / lend US$80,000 (in any available crypto-asset on the platform) with 10 ETH of collateral. One reason why you might want to do this is if the interest being paid on the long leg is more than on the short leg. This is just economic exposure and not true ownership – the platforms will not allow you to withdraw the long position without unwinding.

Another interesting function, unique to DeFi and pioneered by Aave, are *flash loans*. Flash loans allow for uncollateralized loans up to practically any amount (limited by the size of the reserve), provided they are repaid, with interest, in the same transaction block. If any part of the transaction fails, the flash loan does not go through, guaranteeing safety for the protocol. Flash loans are typically used for arbitrage, swapping, and other complex transactions in DeFi.

MakerDAO is one of the oldest DeFi platforms. It's a combination of a lending / borrowing platform, and a crypto-collateralized stablecoin called DAI. The governance token is called MKR. DAI is currently the fourth most popular

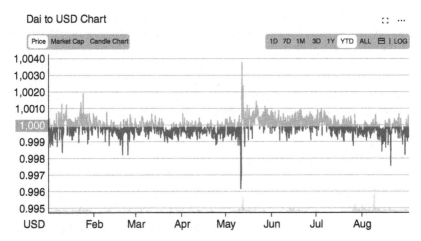

Figure 3.3 DAI / USD price history in 2022.
Source: CoinMarketCap

stablecoin after USDT, USDC, and BUSD, and the most popular crypto-collateralized stablecoin with a market cap of US$7b. Its exchange rate in 2022 with USD is shown in Figure 3.3. The difference here with Aave and Compound is that you can lend several types of crypto-assets, but can only borrow DAI. You can trade DAI for other crypto-assets subsequently, since DAI is liquid. Many of the capabilities of MakerDAO and its associated ecosystem of DApps have similar functions with Aave and Compound, enabling leverage, borrowing in alternative crypto-assets, and earning yield.

DAI is created when crypto-asset collateral is locked up in "vaults." The value locked always needs to exceed the borrow, just as with the LTV ratios always needing to be below 1 in Aave. Currently, borrowing DAI using ETH requires a 1.7× collateralization ratio (0.59 LTV).[4] Conversely, DAI is destroyed when the debt is repaid to the vaults.

There are two key interest rates with DAI: the Stability Fee, charged for borrowing DAI; and the Dai Savings Rate (DSR), paid for lending DAI. Both rates are decided by the governance process and the MKR token holders, and calibrate the level of demand and supply for DAI accordingly.

MakerDAO also outsources liquidation by third-parties, called keepers. Keepers also perform monitoring of vault positions, market making, and arbitrage (on DAI and related pairs). MakerDAO also utilizes an auction model with liquidations in their latest version.

In a black swan situation when there is insufficient collateral to cover the debt, a debt auction is initiated, minting MKR tokens and selling them for DAI: recapitalizing the system. MKR holders thus are the final backstop for the MakerDAO system.

Lending and borrowing activities are not limited to fungible tokens like Wrapped Bitcoin and Ethereum; they can also occur with non-fungible tokens (NFTs). NFTfi is a peer-to-peer lending platform that allows borrowers to use their NFTs as collateral, while enabling lenders to earn interest on their principal. The use of NFTs as collateral opens the door to unique use cases that are difficult to replicate with fungible tokens. For example, NFTfi recently facilitated a loan that was backed by a borrower's on-chain income stream.

3.3 Governance / DAOs

Remember the narrow definition of DeFi? *Blockchain-based finance that is self-custodial, uncensorable, and community-driven.* The community-driven aspect is also known as governance, and these processes and mechanisms are a key aspect of many DeFi protocols. These processes are implemented via voting functions enabled by token holders. The more tokens you have, the larger number of votes you have. This is in-line with the decentralized ethos of allowing stakeholders to have a say in the running of these platforms.

As an example, the governance tokens of Uniswap, Aave, Compound, and MakerDAO are UNI, AAVE, COMP, and MKR respectively. Many of these protocols will have their own governance forums and voting portals that allow for stakeholders to discuss and vote on proposals relating to the function of the protocol. There are off-chain and on-chain governance processes – just as with real-world political processes, there is a substantial amount of discussion and debate before the issue is tabled for voting. In most cases, a simple majority of 50% of votes is sufficient to execute a new proposal. Figure 3.4 shows MakerDAO's governance structure and process.

Proposals may be on any issue related to the operation of protocols. These may be changes to key parameters, onboarding of new counterparties, listing of new tokens, and many other operational issues based on the results of the discussions and votes. In many cases, protocols have substantial funds held in on-chain treasuries and grant programs are often instituted to foster the growth of the ecosystem. Proposals may be made by community members for these grants according to the intent of the protocol, along with deliverables.

Not everyone has the time to read through every proposal and keep current with the details of each protocol. This is where delegation comes in. Like a republic political system, this allows token holders to delegate their voting power to one or more chosen delegates. Delegates don't have ownership of delegated tokens, only the voting power.

Tally and Snapshot are voting aggregators that allow token holders to keep track of multiple DeFi / Web3 platforms, and have some interesting features that allow one to save gas, for example.

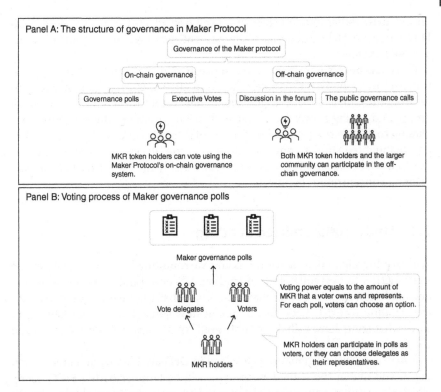

Figure 3.4 MakerDAO governance structure and process.
Source: https://arxiv.org/pdf/2203.16612.pdf

Some of the largest holders of tokens are VC funds, and crypto-sophisticated funds such as a16z have also articulated their philosophy behind crypto governance. According to their article "On crypto governance,"[5] a16z is in favor of delegating votes, grant programs, and early adopter rewards.

Another term that is frequently used in crypto / DeFi governance is *DAO*. So what's a DAO?

To quote Wikipedia, a Decentralized Autonomous Organization (DAO) is "an organization constructed by rules encoded as a computer program that is often transparent, controlled by the organization's members and not influenced by a central government."[6] The first DAO, simply called "The DAO," was launched on Ethereum in 2016. It was one of the highest profile projects on Ethereum at that time and raised a significant amount of ETH (US$150m, or 15% of all ETH circulating at that time). The intent was to be a new type of VC fund, but was hacked and drained of US$60m three months after its launch.[7]

As some names suggest, some protocols consider themselves DAOs (MakerDAO). For others, it is not so clear. Formal definitions of what DAOs do do not exist either. Nonetheless, the evolution of DAOs is also rapid, with DAOs beyond DeFi extending to investment, venture, social, philanthropic, and NFT themes.

There has been some analysis that suggests that the voting in DAOs is centralized.[8] In an analysis on MakerDAO from 2019 to 2021, a team of researchers from the University of Glasgow found that "voters are centralized in a small group, and voting power is unequally distributed among these voters," concluding that "governance in Maker protocol is highly centralized." The BIS has also highlighted similar concerns, citing that the "decentralization illusion" is due to the fact that "some features in DeFi, notably the consensus mechanism, favour a concentration of power."[9]

3.4 Undercollateralized Lending

We have highlighted some of the issues surrounding lending in DeFi in the introduction to overcollateralized lending. We noted that pseudonymity, the default design of public blockchains, makes it challenging for undercollateralized lending to exist. Let's take a look at how some startups are looking to solve what some have called the "holy grail" of use-cases: undercollateralized lending.

Two key issues that remain to be solved in DeFi are identity and credit scoring. If you live in the United States, you will be familiar with a FICO score, which determines your creditworthiness and your ability to obtain a credit card. Your FICO score is shared amongst various credit issuers such as banks. If you miss on your loan payments or default on debt, you may not be able to get credit again. Assuming you do not do identity fraud, this system is reasonably effective in deterring abuse. There currently is no widely adopted identity standard or system, let alone a credit scoring system in DeFi.

It is certainly possible to mint a token with one's identity data, with a third party identity verification service. For this system to be effective, the identity token must be nontransferable. This is the idea behind soul-bound tokens (SBTs) described in a whitepaper from Glen Weyl, Puja Ohlhaver, and Vitalik Buterin,[10] that articulates the possibility of a much richer web3 space that can support undercollateralized lending, among other things.

Goldfinch has taken some steps along this approach to identification. Goldfinch partners with an identity verification company, Persona, to mint a nontransferable ERC-1155 Unique Identity (UID) token. This is used for KYC on the Goldfinch platform. According to Goldfinch, "no personally identifiable data is stored on-chain," implying that the PII (personally identifiable information) is stored with Persona. UIDs are interoperable, but are not currently adopted outside of Goldfinch's platform (as far as I know).

There are a number of startups in the undercollateralized lending space that cater to different niches. Let's look at the segments.

3.4.1 Uncollateralized Lending to Real-world Borrowers

Goldfinch and Credix (Figure 3.5) describe themselves as credit platforms or credit marketplaces. Using USDC in both cases, they allow lenders to lend to pools that invest in loans issued by third-party companies. Goldfinch uses Ethereum and Credix uses Solana. The USDC stablecoin is converted into fiat by an on-off ramp. In the case of Goldfinch, some of these third parties are Aspire (SME neobank in SEA), Almavest (debt investment firm) and Cauris (debt investment firm). Most of the debt is deployed in developing regions / countries such as Asia, Latin America, Africa, and India. Credix is currently focused in Latin America across a variety of lenders: Tecredi (Auto financing), a55 (SME), Adiante Recebíveis (invoice factoring), and others.

In Goldfinch, lenders have two options to lend: (1) as a "backer," lending to specific "borrower pools" with a specific third party debt issuance for a higher yield (12–18.75%) and higher risk (being first-loss capital / junior tranche); (2) as a "liquidity provider" supplying second-loss capital to the senior pool, which

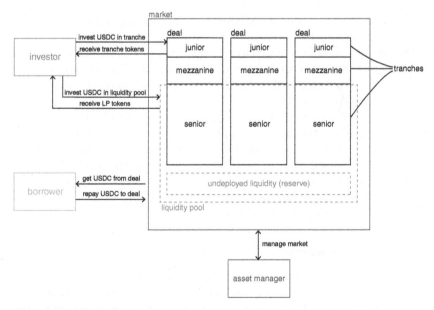

Figure 3.5 Credix market and process.
Source: Credix https://docs.credix.finance/product/markets-and-deals

automatically allocates across all borrower pools. The "liquidity provider" is a safer and more diversified option for a lower yield (~7.8%).

The GFI token, the "core native token," is used for governance voting, auditor staking, protocol incentives, community grants, and several other functions. The FIDU token represents a liquidity provider's deposit to the senior pool.

The task of credit scoring the end-borrower is thus shifted to the third party debt issuer. Both Credix and Goldfinch have processes that perform due diligence on these third parties / borrowers. Goldfinch has a separate class of participants, Auditors, who stake GFI and whose function is to evaluate the legitimacy of borrowers. They review documents sent by borrowers, perform due diligence checks, and then vote on the borrowers being able to raise capital on the platform. In the case of Credix, this due diligence on borrowers is currently carried out by the core team.

At time of writing, Goldfinch has US$99m of credit outstanding at an average lender APY of 17%. Credix has US$23m of credit outstanding with an average lender APY of 14%.

3.4.2 Uncollateralized Lending to Crypto Institutions

Maple, TrueFi, and Clearpool represent a more crypto-native undercollateralized lending play. They focus on lending to crypto-native institutions such as market makers / OTC desks and hedge funds. This capital is typically used for capital-intensive activities such as high-frequency trading and market making. Table 3.1 shows how they compare.

The process for onboarding borrowers is similar to Goldfinch and Credix. Institutions looking to borrow must go through a due diligence process managed by "pool delegates," "stakers," or the core team. Borrowers are institutional-only (so far) and not retail.

The native token is used for launching pools, becoming a "staker," participating in governance, earning fees, and providing pool cover. Due to the crypto-native nature of the borrowers, the loan issuances on these platforms are likely to be more correlated with the bull and bear market crypto cycles than those lending to real-world borrowers. Since the CeFi contagion of 3AC, Celsius, Voyager, and BlockFi in June 2022, the total outstanding loans on both Maple and TrueFi have declined (Figure 3.6).

3.4.3 Real World Assets

One of the promising directions for DeFi is in representing regulated, real-world assets on-chain. This has the potential to enable the enormous set of assets to benefit from the innovative features of DeFi to be traded and settled on a global, internet-native infrastructure. This is also where regulation comes into play more heavily, and more trade-offs between regulatory friction and

Table 3.1 Uncollateralized lending to crypto institutions – comparisons.

	Maple	TrueFi	Clearpool
Total Outstanding Loans	$287m	$207m	$117m
Total Cumulative Loans	$1,686m	$1,710m	$253m
Token	MPL	TRU	CPOOL
Token Market Cap	$82m	$33m	$9m
Token FDV	$187m	$89m	$51m
Borrowers	Maven 11, Orthogonal Trading, Celsius, Alameda Research	WOO Network, USDC.homes, Alameda Research, Caruis	Amber Group, Auros, Folkvang, Wintermute, FBG Capital
L1s	Ethereum, Solana	Ethereum, Optimism	Ethereum, Polygon
Offered APYs	1.2–8.4%	9–14%	9–12%

Source: Dune Analytics, CoinMarketCap, Maple, TrueFi, Clearpool, Accessed 7 September 2022

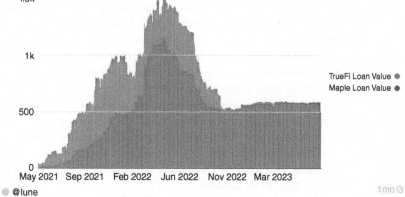

Figure 3.6 Maple and TrueFi total loan outstanding.
Source: https://dune.com/lune/Maple-and-TrueFi-Dashboard

consumer protection become obvious. In many jurisdictions, including the United States and European Union, security tokens are subject to the same laws as traditional securities.

The first wave of interest in blockchain technology as it relates to regulated assets focused on Security Token Offerings (STOs). Platforms like Securitize and Polymath enabled companies to leverage tokens for capital-raising. This also provided investors with an avenue for liquidity to buy and sell equity. So why not simply use a traditional stock exchange? The barriers to entry, including stringent listing requirements and high costs, make it a less viable option. Additionally, investors must qualify as accredited and undergo Know Your Customer (KYC) procedures. Another limitation is the lack of interoperability; if you complete the onboarding process for one security token exchange, you would need to repeat the process for any additional platforms.

This is an adjacent category to undercollateralized loans to real-world borrowers, and opens up using the rest of the asset classes beyond fixed income as collateral for on-chain loans.

3.4.4 Centrifuge

Centrifuge is a real-world assets (RWA) platform that currently offers a variety of fixed income pools, including commercial real estate, trade receivables, and consumer loans. Where the RWA part comes in is with companies being able to finance these assets with loans sourced from the platform. Loans to companies are collateralized by the RWA.

Centrifuge utilizes DAI as the native stablecoin, and the total value of all asset pools is currently US$87m. To be precise, Centrifuge is an L1, and Tinlake is Centrifuge's investment app.

After going through an onboarding process that involves submitting a proposal to the community, Asset Originators tokenize their real-world assets into NFTs. The NFTs are used as collateral in their Tinlake pool by Asset Originators to finance their assets. Investors invest in pools via two classes of tokens: TIN and DROP. TIN represents shares in the riskier junior tranche, and DROP represents the less risky senior tranche (with a lower yield). There is a specific TIN and DROP NFT token for each pool, which are not fungible across different pools.

The introduction of idiosyncratic real-world assets presents several challenges. How are the assets valued? How will buyers and sellers of the tokenized asset pool create and redeem? Pricing is easy for Bitcoin when there is deep liquidity with multiple 24/7 markets. Without adequate liquidity, other methods of valuing assets need to be utilized.

Net asset value (NAV) is a common term used in finance, especially in the valuation of open-ended funds. It's the net assets of the fund: assets minus liabilities. NAV can differ from the market price (i.e., the price that the buyer and seller agree on), and is an estimate of the asset value. In the case of Centrifuge, NAV is based on *discounted cash flow* (DCF) calculations. DCF models are common in finance, and an example from Centrifuge is illustrated in Figure 3.7. DCF models are a sum of the future expected cash flows, adjusted for the time value of money.

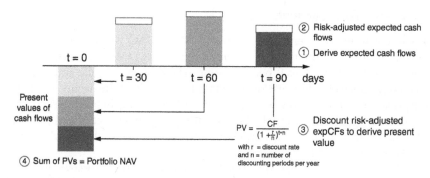

Figure 3.7 NAV model.
Source: https://docs.centrifuge.io/learn/pool-valuation/

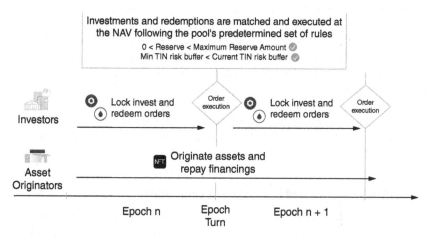

Figure 3.8 Tinlake epochs – investment and redemption execution.
Source: https://docs.centrifuge.io/learn/epoch/

Valuation parameters are provided from the documentation / prospectus underlying the NFT, and a smart contract uses parameters from an oracle in order to calculate the NAV.

The matching of buyer and sellers takes place in *epochs*. On two pools that I viewed, the maximum epochs are about 5 days. Creation and redemption orders of TIN and DROP NFT tokens are held and only executed at the end of an epoch (Figure 3.8). The smart contract also takes into account the risk parameters preset by the pool, that is, the ratio of TIN to DROP.

Centrifuge appears to allow companies to obtain debt financing using collateral posted to the pools, and not equity.

A similar platform, RWA Markets, is a tie-up between Centrifuge and Aave. It utilizes USDC instead of DAI as the stablecoin.

3.4.5 MakerDAO and RWA

The other tie-up that Centrifuge has is with MakerDAO. MakerDAO has been looking to diversify the types of collateral that backs DAI, its stablecoin, outside of crypto-assets. This is because using crypto-assets as collateral in a stablecoin issuance / lending platform tends to be *procyclical*: during bull markets, the prices of crypto-assets rise, encouraging more lending; in bear markets, the prices of crypto-assets can fall sharply, prompting margin calls and liquidations that can exacerbate "death spirals," or negative feedback loops, which can quickly destroy confidence in these platforms.

MakerDAO has also been spearheading some interesting crossover projects with commercial banks that are breaking new ground in DeFi–TradFi capital markets.

In August 2022, MakerDAO announced a 100 million DAI "participation facility" with Huntingdon Valley Bank (HVB), a US commercial bank, in what looks to be the first commercial loan participation between a US regulated financial institution (HVB is regulated by the FDIC, Federal Reserve, and the SEC) and a DeFi protocol / stablecoin. Although MakerDAO has stated that it is "not a borrower-lender relationship,"[11] the facility (which is complex in structure and I will not go into detail here) essentially allows HVB to access DAI liquidity in exchange for "participation interests" in loans originated by HVB. HVB's loan portfolio consists mainly of commercial and residential mortgages. HVB will be required to retain a minimum of 50% of each loan, and MakerDAO a maximum of 50%.

3.4.6 SocGen Pilots and MakerDAO Collaboration

The digital assets arm of French multinational bank Société Générale (SocGen), SG-Forge has also been involved with MakerDAO in drawing down on DAI for liquidity, using bonds as collateral. SG-Forge has been running a few projects that have some meaningful crossovers between bonds issued on the blockchain (smart bonds), CBDCs, and RWA. Let's take a chronological look.

In April 2019, Société Générale SFH, the covered bond vehicle of SocGen, had previously issued EUR 100m of "OFH tokens" (Obligations de Financement de l'Habitat, i.e., home loans) as security tokens (smart bonds) on the Ethereum blockchain. OFH tokens have been rated Aaa / AAA by Moody's and Fitch and were fully subscribed by SocGen. Payment was made via traditional methods.

In May 2020, Société Générale SFH issued a further EUR 40m of OFH tokens to SocGen, using digital euros / CBDC issued by the Banque de France to settle the delivery versus payment (DvP) (i.e., simultaneous) transaction.

In July 2022, the MakerDAO community voted to approve the creation of a RWA vault dedicated to SG-Forge and OFH tokens (Figure 3.9). By using OFH

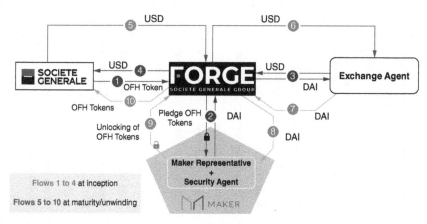

Figure 3.9 SocGen – MakerDAO vault structure.
Source: https://forum.makerdao.com/t/
security-tokens-refinancing-mip6-application-for-ofh-tokens/10605

tokens as collateral, SG-Forge is able to borrow up to 30m DAI. This arrangement also allows MakerDAO to use these real-world assets as collateral for the issuance of DAI, according to the prescribed limits and requirements as decided by MakerDAO.[12]

3.4.7 Smart Bonds

The aforementioned OFH token is an example of one of many pilots done by banks, central banks, stock exchanges, and corporations on the issuance of bonds on the blockchain, or smart bonds.

The issuance of bonds involves many intermediaries, is a lengthy and technical process, and has high transaction costs. All of these factors make blockchain technology well-suited to addressing these problems. According to Elisabeta Pana and Vikas Gangal from Central Connecticut State University, blockchain technology and smart contracts have the potential to "yield significant gains in operational efficiency and resilience by automating a previously manual process"[13] in the bond issuance process. They further note that "blockchain applications have reached a mature stage only in the area of bond structuring, registration, sales, and distribution. Blockchain technology has been partially applied in the area of bond transfer of ownership, payment and settlement and is yet to be applied in benchmarking and reporting."[14]

The International Capital Market Association (ICMA) keeps a helpful running list[15] of fixed income applications with blockchain technology, across primary, secondary, and repo markets, as well as "cross-cutting" (CBDCs) categories (Table 3.2).

Table 3.2 Smart bond issuances (as of August 2021).

Issuer	Sale Date	Par Amount (USD Millions)	Issuance	Blockchain	Country
Commonwealth Bank of Australia	January, 2017	N/A	N/A	Private Ethereum	Australia
Daimler AG	June 28, 2017	111	1-year Bond	Private Ethereum	Germany
Fisco	August 10, 2017	0.813	3-year Bond	Private Ethereum	China
Sberbank	May 18, 2018	12	Commercial Bond	Hyperledger Fabric	Russia
World Bank	August 24, 2018	108	2 Tranche "bond-i"	Private Ethereum	Australia
Société Générale	April 18, 2019	112	5-year Covered Bond	Public Ethereum	France
Santander	September 12, 2019	20	1-year Bond	Public Ethereum	Spain
INVAO	September 27, 2019	20	10-year Bond	Public Ethereum	Lichtenstein
Bank of China	December 3, 2019	2,800	2-year Bond	Proprietary Blockchain	China
Bank of Thailand	September 11, 2020	1,600	Savings Bond	IBM Blockchain	Thailand
Union Bank of the Philippines	December 7, 2020	190	3 and 5.25 year Dual Tranche Bond	Proprietary Blockchain	Philippines
Vonovia Investment Bank	January 13, 2021	24	3-year Bond	Stellar Blockchain	Germany
Société Générale	April 15, 2021	6	Autocall, Euro Medium Term Notes	Tezos Public Blockchain	France
European Investment Bank	April 27, 2021	121	2-year Bond	Public Ethereum	France

Source: Wikipedia / ICMA

Pana and Gangal also cite "lack of awareness, lack of standardization, issues related to privacy, and lack of regulatory clarity" as hurdles to large-scale implementation of blockchain in bond markets. In the issuance of EIB's first smart bond using Ethereum, Matthew McDermott, Global Head of Digital Assets at Goldman Sachs, cited the choice of French law as a "natural fit" as France had passed a law that allowed the registration of digital securities to be recognized as financial securities, permitting the registration and transfer of unlisted securities using blockchain technology, removing the need for central securities depositary (CSD) and a custodian.[16]

In May 2022, the Monetary Authority of Singapore (MAS) announced the inception of Project Guardian, whose aim is to "test the feasibility of applications in asset tokenisation and DeFi while managing risks to financial stability and integrity."[17] It looks to develop and pilot uses cases in four areas: open networks, trust anchors, asset tokenization, and institutional grade DeFi protocols. The first industry pilot will be led by DBS Bank, JP Morgan, and Marketnode, which involves the creation of a permissioned liquidity pool comprising of tokenized bonds and deposits.

3.4.8 Credit Scoring

As mentioned earlier, undercollateralized lending in DeFi will very likely require an identity layer – without which, it would be possible to borrow and default on loans without significant repercussions due to the anonymous nature of public blockchains. Nonetheless, some startups are looking to build credit scoring systems based on on-chain activity. A few startups that are looking to crack this puzzle are Cred Protocol, CreDA (Credit Data Alliance), RociFi, Bird, and Masa. All of these startups are at early stages and don't have significant traction as yet.

In the real world, a FICO score is calculated using a weighted set of credit factors such as amounts owed, payment history, new credit, length of credit history, and credix mix. Newer FinTech lenders have also taken to using alternative data for credit scoring. This is especially applicable in the era of big data and machine learning. This could include the plethora of data generated by usage of smartphones, social media behavior, and other purchasing patterns.

So how does this translate to the on-chain world? *CreDA* looks to be the "first trusted decentralized credit rating service that links the on-chain and traditional financial systems to create a universal credit score for Web3.0."[18] It calculates a credit score based on:

- User assets: size of assets on each blockchain and the length of holding;
- Activity: on-chain transactions;
- On-chain behavior: participation in DeFi programs; and
- Loan participation: loan repayment behavior, liquidations, and value of collateral.

CreDA also looks to create an interoperable identity layer using DIDs (decentralized identity), combining on-chain and off-chain data.

3.5 Investing

The classic *A Random Walk Down Wall Street* by Burton Malkiel, published in 1973, set the stage for low-cost, buy-and-hold passive investing strategies through diversified asset products such as mutual funds and ETFs. In recent years, robo-advisor platforms such as Betterment and Wealthfront have taken this to the next level by utilizing algorithms to tailor and implement portfolio management strategies for retail clients. What was formerly a high-touch service only available to wealthy clients is now made available, albeit in a diluted form, to the masses by the power of software. According to Statista, assets under management in the robo-advisor category are projected to reach US$1.66 trillion in 2022.[19]

3.5.1 Index Products – Spot

Whether or not one can utilize a buy-and-hold (hodl?) strategy for crypto is a subject of debate, given the volatility of crypto. Nonetheless, there are some startups that are looking to solve diversification through ETF-like products, and other kinds of dashboards that enable portfolio management. Let's take a look.

Set Protocol allows for the construction of customizable baskets of crypto-assets, represented as ERC-20 tokens. The Set Token smart contracts support external integrations with exchanges, lending platforms, automated market makers, and asset protocols.

Set Protocol allows "Managers" to create their own Sets (baskets), choosing their own tokens, metadata (such as description, symbol, and start price), and fees. Set Protocol limits the selection of tokens to ERC-20, and has some other criteria such as no rebasing tokens, no transfer fees, and "liquidity against WETH on a DEX."

As with ETFs, Sets can be created and redeemed with the issuer in a "primary issuance." This is a process where Set Protocol will lock up the specified proportion of the ERC-20 token basket in the smart contract and mint the Set basket token, or vice-versa. Approvals for all the ERC-20s are required with your wallet and this can be done directly with Set Protocol. This can be a gas-intensive process as there will be as many transactions as there are underlying tokens in each basket.

Set basket tokens can also be bought and sold in the secondary market. This is much less gas-intensive as it only involves transfer of the basket token.

Trading of Sets basket tokens can be done on the Set Protocol website, centralized exchanges, and decentralized exchanges.

The two most popular Set basket tokens are "DeFi Pulse Index" (DPI) and the "Metaverse Index" (MVI), maintained by DeFi Pulse and MetaPortal respectively. They both charge a 0.95% / yr "streaming fee" and have market capitalizations of ~US$28m and ~US$5m respectively as of time of writing (September 2022).

Beyond passive indices, Set Protocol allows for the creation of many types of baskets, including actively managed, inverse, and leveraged strategies.

3.5.2   Index Products – Perpetual Futures

As mentioned in Chapter 2, perpetual futures are popular methods to gain long or short exposure to crypto-assets. Perpetuals also allow the use of leverage. This also extends to index products, the majority of which are indices that are maintained in-house by respective centralized exchanges. There are no standardized or widely adopted index providers at this point such as S&P as yet.

Binance maintains a DeFi index[20] available for spot and futures trading on its platform.

At present, there do not seem to be perpetual futures index products trading on decentralized futures exchanges.

3.5.3   Dashboards

The Open Banking movement in TradFi started in earnest in the European Union, with the introduction of PSD2 (Payment Services Directive 2) in 2015. This required banks to open their APIs for customer-account information to third-party providers, paving the way for the creation of new types of personal finance management applications that allow consumers to look at multiple bank balances on one application, and to manage their finances in an integral manner.

This has parallels in DeFi, as DeFi was built from the ground up with interoperability in mind. Three examples of aggregators are Zapper, Zerion, and DeBank. These applications allow for users to look at multiple positions in various DeFi applications that may be staked, lent, or borrowed, in one application. This can be very useful for active DeFi users as it can be hard to keep track of everything – many active DeFi users use spreadsheets to keep track of all the wallets and positions they are running. Dashboards pull in transaction data from the blockchain for the given address and present the information in an easily readable format. They can also aggregate a user's positions for the same address across multiple EVM-compatible blockchains.

In addition, these dashboards may also allow users to swap, bridge, and trade directly from application.

3.6 Payments

When you pay for a cup of coffee at your local coffee shop, have you ever thought about what happens when you use your Visa or Mastercard at the terminal? What exactly happens during those few seconds between you tapping your card on the point of sale device and the approval notification? There's a whole world of payments intermediaries underneath that most consumers don't see.

Payments is an exciting, complex, and rapidly evolving area of FinTech, and DeFi is fast becoming an integral part of next generation payment services. On the whole, while national payment systems are efficient, DeFi excels with cross-border payments. DeFi also opens up merchants to accepting payments and storing value in crypto or stablecoins.

In recent years, the field of payments in e-commerce has accelerated greatly. Payment processors like Adyen, Stripe, and PayPal fill a gap in the payments ecosystem that could not be done by banks. In 2021, the top five payment processors processed US$6 trillion.[21] They allow merchants, which may be e-commerce websites and mobile applications, to accept payments via credit cards and mobile payment methods. They provide fraud detection, chargeback protection, and for businesses to manage their finances. They enable large omnichannel (physical and online shops) brands like Nike and McDonald's (who use Adyen) who have customers all over the world and have different payment preferences to simplify their payments operations and reduce costs.

In Chapter 1 of this book, I suggested using USDC on a gas-light blockchain like Solana or Polygon to try DeFi out for yourself. The natural extension to this of course, is whether or not one can make payments to retailers using crypto or stablecoins. The beauty of crypto is being able to accept payments easily. While this may be easy for "mom and pop" merchants, it may not scale for larger organizations that have different requirements. Invoicing, processing refunds, and providing insightful data for business are part of what payment service providers help solve.

Let's take a look at how crypto is being used in the vast area of payments.

3.6.1 Crypto Payment Gateways

A payment gateway is a front-facing interface that the end customer interacts with. Merchants looking to accept payments using crypto can use these companies to integrate payment solutions on their website or at physical stores via their point-of-sale terminals. Three companies that are in this category are Coinbase Commerce (Figure 3.10), BitPay, and Coingate.

Coinbase Commerce allows for integrations with e-commerce platforms such as Shopify and WooCommerce, API integrations, invoicing, and business

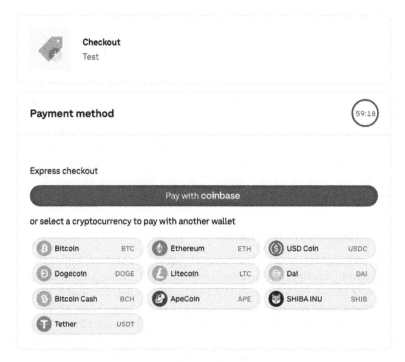

Figure 3.10 Example checkout from Coinbase Commerce.

reporting. It charges 1% on transactions, and the crypto assets are self-managed by the merchant with private keys.

BitPay also charges 1%, and offers settlement of funds via local bank transfers. BitPay also allows businesses to send crypto as payments, without handling the crypto themselves.

3.6.2   Big Payments and Crypto

Let's take a look at how the large payment companies are incorporating crypto with their product lineups. Both Stripe and PayPal have integrations with crypto.

In April 2022, Stripe announced a partnership with Twitter to pay out creators in USDC on Polygon. This is part of Stripe's Connect program, which onboards, manages, and performs the payments to the users / creators of the platform. Stripe also handles the KYC and compliance requirements for platforms and marketplaces. In a blog post by Stripe, it cited the use of cryptocurrencies as being able to help address the problem that "many countries remain out of reach in part due to the intrinsic complexity involved in supporting heterogeneous local payments systems,"[22] and that "the prospect of 'open-access global financial rails' as being at least equally compelling" as the store of value functions of cryptocurrencies. Creators will be able to manage account details, track their earnings, and see upcoming payouts on the Stripe Express app. Stripe had previously supported Bitcoin payments but closed the function, citing that there was less demand from customers and expensive fees.[23]

PayPal also allows the use of crypto for payment of goods and services, having introduced "Checkout with Crypto" in March 2021. PayPal's feature requires users to maintain a crypto balance with PayPal during checkout, selling the crypto for fiat during the purchase. Since August 2022, PayPal also allows for US customers to transfer Bitcoin, Ethereum, Bitcoin Cash, and Litecoin in and out of their PayPal crypto accounts.

3.6.3   Crypto Debit / Credit Cards

Many exchanges have started offering crypto debit cards. These cards allow you to spend directly from your exchange account, converting at the point of sale. Cards issued by Visa include Crypto.com, Coinbase, and Binance; and those issued by Mastercard include Gemini and BitPay. Some of these cards allow for cashback rewards in the native token of the issuer: Binance offers up to 8% in BNB, and Crypto.com offers up to 5% in CRO, both depending on the tier of the card. Recently, Gnosis launched Gnosis Pay, a self-custodial Visa debit card that builds on top of Safe, a self-custody protocol, and Gnosis Chain, an EVM chain.

The two payments giants, Visa and Mastercard, have not been standing still when it comes to crypto.

In March 2021, Anchorage, an institutional crypto custody provider, announced "the first crypto-native settlement transaction made to Visa,"[24] via a pilot with Crypto.com (a centralized crypto exchange). Crypto.com has a Visa debit card program, and utilized Anchorage's APIs to settle payments with Visa, on Ethereum. In other words, Visa is utilizing Anchorage as the back-end settlement rails for crypto, since it does not have that expertise.

Visa has created a number of in-house crypto programs, including "Visa FinTech Fast Track," which allows for "fast, easy issuance of Visa credentials, so that crypto holders can quickly and securely pay with Visa at over 100 million merchants worldwide,"[25] and "Digital Currency Innovation Hub," a consulting arm that allows partners to "gain access to industry insights and work closely with our Product, Visa Consulting & Analytics, and Innovation Center subject matter experts."[26]

In a post by Mastercard in February 2021, they state their "straightforward" philosophy on cryptocurrencies:

> It's about choice. Mastercard isn't here to recommend you start using cryptocurrencies. But we are here to enable customers, merchants and

businesses to move digital value – traditional or crypto – however they want. It should be your choice, it's your money.

Doing this work will create a lot more possibilities for shoppers and merchants, allowing them to transact in an entirely new form of payment. This change may open merchants up to new customers who are already flocking to digital assets, and help sellers build loyalty with existing customers who want this additional option. And customers will be able to save, store and send money in new ways.

We want to help these concepts flourish and reach their potential, while also developing and encouraging the necessary guardrails.[27]

Mastercard also announced a "proprietary virtual testing environment for central banks to evaluate CBDC use cases" in September 2020, stating that "The platform enables the simulation of issuance, distribution and exchange of CBDCs between banks, financial service providers and consumers."[28]

3.6.4 On-off Ramps

Another category in crypto payments are "on-off ramps" such as MoonPay, Wyre, Simplex, and Transak. These companies allow for FinTechs and wallet applications to integrate buying (and selling) crypto inside their application, with fiat. Trust Wallet, for example, one of the more popular crypto wallets, directs users to a choice of different on-off ramp providers (which may have different prices). The on-off ramp provider then handles the payment processing, depending on the user's choice of preferred payment method.

3.6.5 Solana Pay and Circle

Solana Pay is a payments framework built on Solana, which aims to facilitate fast, scalable, inexpensive, and energy efficient transactions. Announced in February 2022, Solana's vision for payments is centered around merchants accepting stablecoins as payments. Circle, the issuer of USDC, is one such partner with stablecoins. Here's them describing their vision:

A new customer walks into your store looking for the latest hot sneaker release. You have it in stock, and she's thrilled. She pulls out her phone and scans the QR code on your point-of-sale for a seamless transaction. The funds hit your merchant account at the speed of sending an email, at near-zero cost, and immediately begin earning high-yield interest.

Before the customer leaves the store, two tokens appear in her digital wallet. The first is an NFT version of her new sneakers, usable in any game or virtual world she chooses. The second is an authenticated NFT receipt, which admits her into your exclusive online community of verified sneaker-lovers. She's now a customer for life.

Nine months later, the next version of her favorite sneaker drops. Her digital wallet has a new offer reminding her of their availability at your store, along with a personalized offer on new laces she can't find anywhere else.[29]

We'll cover NFTs in more detail and the possibilities for NFTs and the Metaverse later on, but Solana Pay has a vision that incorporates NFTs as loyalty tokens, that integrates natively with the crypto wallet. In a video demo[30] Solana showcased this function where the NFT automatically enabled a discount for a purchase at a retail outlet (which issued the NFT). As per the above example, NFTs can also be sent from the merchant to the customer's wallet, enabling receipts and other kinds of customer engagement that could involve online communities and metaverse versions of the physical item.

Solana also has plans for a phone that runs on Android, with "unique functionality and features tightly integrated with the Solana blockchain making it easy and secure to transact in web3 and manage digital assets, such as tokens and NFTs."[31] Some announced features include a "Seed Vault" for secure private key management, a "Mobile Wallet Adapter" for connecting web apps and Android apps to mobile wallets, and other Solana Pay integrations.[32]

The vision of Circle, along with being a stablecoin issuer, is that of a "dollar protocol." Circle has a suite of APIs that enable merchants to accept card and wire payments in USDC. Circle also has a treasury solution that enables merchants to invest their USDC balance to generate yield.

What Solana and Circle represent is a combination that could disintermediate the likes of Visa, Mastercard, Stripe, and large sections of the incumbent payments ecosystem. With this payment functionality, there is no need for credit cards or bank accounts. If a stablecoin can be used by a merchant to pay suppliers and employees – effectively an entire business can be run with stablecoins. With the growing adoption of NFTs by large consumer brands, this is a future-forward solution that enables companies to have more direct relationships with consumers, instead of the current payment system that gives this data to intermediaries.

3.6.6 Bitcoin Payments

I would be remiss if I did not mention Bitcoin payments. The major challenge with Bitcoin and merchant acceptance is that most merchants want to focus on running their business and do not want the volatility of Bitcoin. Bitcoin transaction fees are not exactly prohibitive (costing under a dollar at time of writing), but they can take a long time to settle. Many exchanges require at least 6 confirmations, and one confirmation can take a few minutes to just under an hour, depending on the network congestion.

In 2021, El Salvador became the first country to make Bitcoin legal tender, setting the stage for the largest experiment with using Bitcoin in a real-world setting. By a few accounts, it has not been particularly successful. Surveys show that only 20% of the population was using the Chivo Wallet, the national Bitcoin payment app, and only 14% of businesses were using Bitcoin for transactions.[33]

The Lightning network, a layer 2 network for Bitcoin, looks to solve the scalability and speed problems. Twitter has allowed users to send and receive Bitcoin tips, using Strike, a Bitcoin wallet app using the Lightning network.

3.7 Insurance

The earliest known insurance contracts date back to the fourteenth century in Genoa, Italy. These contracts were part of a broader practice of maritime loans, where merchants would secure their shipping ventures. The development of these contracts laid the foundation for modern insurance practices.[34] Insurance is an integral part of risk management and transfer in our modern world, and the possible application of blockchain in insurance has been frequently mentioned in the last few years.

A report done by ConsenSys in June 2019, "Blockchain and Insurance: New Technology, New Opportunities,"[35] cites numerous ways that blockchain can enhance existing and new insurance processes – including KYC / AML, fraud mitigation, P2P insurance, and claims handling. In general, it would seem that the immutable, traceable nature of the blockchain that is able to attest to a common truth that an event has *indeed* happened (with the aid of an oracle), combined with self-executing smart contracts that does away with cumbersome paper-based processes, would make blockchain an ideal technology to enhance the insurance industry.

So, where are we in 2023? The first sobering point as I started to look into this – was the dissolution of B3i, a blockchain insurance consortium established in 2017 by some of the largest insurance and reinsurance companies in the world. This consortium includes Swiss Re, Allianz, Liberty Mutual, Aegon, AXA, China Pacific Insurance, and many more. The reason cited for the dissolution by John Dacey, group CFO for Swiss Re, was that there was a lack of demand and that it "didn't seem like it was going to go forward in a profitable way."[36]

The challenge is the large-scale revamp of siloed IT infrastructure that would enable blockchain to truly unlock its potential as an end-to-end solution, and for large businesses to share data in ways that are compatible with their existing business model, legal compliance, and strategy.

In the permissionless DeFi space, this has also been somewhat true – the uptake has been muted and does not seem to have taken off as much as the

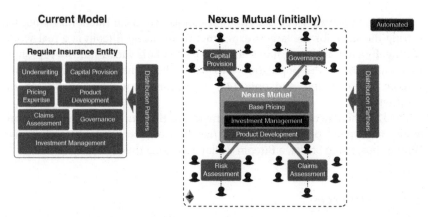

Figure 3.11 Envisioned model of Nexus Mutual.
Source: Nexus Mutual Whitepaper

other DeFi categories. There are three startups that I looked at – Nexus Mutual, InsurAce, and Etherisc. Let's take a brief look at how they work and what has been done.

Nexus Mutual and InsurAce look to insure native DeFi risks such as smart contract vulnerabilities, stablecoin de-pegging, and custodian risk. At time of writing, Nexus Mutual and InsurAce claim to have US$197.7m and US$345.8m of total value covered respectively.[37]

Nexus Mutual, design-wise, seems to be aligned with the ethos of DeFi: outsourcing and decentralizing the functions of risk and claims assessment (Figure 3.11). It does not tout itself as an insurance solution; rather, it models itself as a discretionary mutual (fund), a structure that is like a cooperative and whose payouts from claims are subject to the discretion of its members. The native NXM token has several functions. It is

- Designed to act as representations of membership rights. Members vote on claims and perform other governance functions.
- Used to purchase insurance.
- Used for staking against specific protocols / custodians. Members earn a percentage of the cover premiums in these risk pools, but may also have their stake burned if there is a claim against the pool.

InsurAce has a similar design. It also describes itself as a mutual, with membership rights also being represented by their INSUR token. Claim and risk assessment is "decentralized and governed by community voting and expert investigations."[38] On InsurAce's app, there's a wide range of cover on many of the leading blockchains and DeFi applications, with monthly costs mostly under 1%. The "cover wording" (what ostensibly is the policy wording equivalent) is

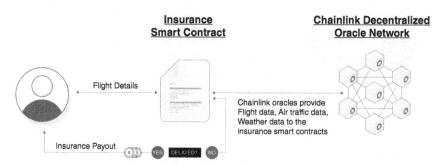

Figure 3.12 Etherisc flight delay insurance design.
Source: Chainlink website

also available for review for the various covers. InsurAce also has paid out US$11.6m of total claims.

Etherisc looks to provide real-world risk coverage with smart contracts. Two types of insurance that are available on its website are crop insurance and flight delay insurance (Figure 3.12). Etherisc's flight delay insurance product is an interesting proof-of-concept of parametric insurance based on smart contracts. Parametric insurance, which is less common in the insurance industry, offers prespecified payouts based on trigger events. It works by the smart contract being linked to the Chainlink oracle network, which provides data on the flight, air traffic, and the weather. In the event of a flight delay of 45 min or more, the claim is automatically paid without any further action from the insured.

Insurtech is also looking into the blockchain. Lemonade, is insurtech startup, established the Lemonade Crypto Climate Coalition through its nonprofit arm, the Lemonade Foundation in March 2022. The coalition, which includes Avalanche, Chainlink, DAOstack, Etherisc, reinsurance giant Hannover Re, Kenya-based insurtech Pula, and weather intelligence platform Tomorrow.io, aims to provide parametric weather insurance to subsistence farmers in emerging markets. In the event of a flood or drought, sensors detect the event and automatically makes the payout instead of requiring the farmers to submit claims. The removal of paperwork streamlines the process and makes the premiums more affordable.

3.8   Prediction Markets

Free markets are amazing things. They price in future expected scenarios of how the world economy will evolve, according to the sum of all known information at the present time. Through the power of the crowd and incentives, the collective intelligence of market participants can be harnessed to forecast events.

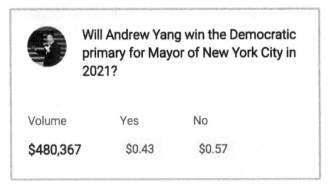

Figure 3.13 Example of a Polymarket outcome market.
Source: Polymarket website

Prediction markets take this to a more specific level, allowing participants to take financial positions on any kind of binary outcome, ranging from politics, markets, sports, and current events. The use of prediction markets has been the subject of much economic research and one of the earliest known examples is in 1503 with the papal election.

There have been a few attempts at creating prediction markets on the blockchain. Currently, Polymarket, SX Network, Azuro, and Augur are some of the more popular platforms.

Polymarket utilizes USDC and the Polygon blockchain. To bet on an outcome, one deposits USDC into their Polymarket wallet in order to buy "outcome shares" in a particular market. Outcome shares are priced between US$0.01 and US$1, reflecting the implied probability of the expected outcome (Figure 3.13). If you were right, your outcome shares will be worth US$1. If you were wrong, your outcome shares will be worth nothing. Outcome shares can also be sold before the market resolves. SX uses the Polygon chain, and Azuro is built on top of several chains such as Gnosis Chain, Arbitrum, and Polygon. Some of these markets are also variations of the AMM model (automated market makers, as covered in the example with Uniswap earlier in this chapter), allowing for participants to be liquidity providers for these markets.

3.9 Chapter Summary

This chapter is one of the longest in this book, as it presents the substance of what DeFi concretely is. We've categorized the broad financial activities as per the real world and applied the same lens to DeFi, examining what's novel in DeFi and how the technology works in this new environment. Generally speaking, these products are not regulated and adhere to the three characteristics of DeFi: self-custody, uncensorability, and community-driven.

All of the examples cited can be accessed with an internet connection and additional documentation is often made freely available for users to look deeper into if they wish. It's also inevitable that some of the examples will grow and others will fail. So I urge you to exercise your good judgment when interfacing with them, and taking any kind of financial action with them. They have been used insofar as I think they are helpful in articulating what the state-of-the-art in DeFi is in terms of the technology, design, and techniques and do not represent an endorsement on my part.

In the next chapter, we discuss a critical aspect of DeFi and one of the main challenges to its widespread adoption: risks.

Notes

1. https://www.reddit.com/r/ethereum/comments/55m04x/lets_run_onchain_decentralized_exchanges_the_way/
2. https://www.bis.org/publ/bisbull58.pdf
3. https://www.theblock.co/data/decentralized-finance/cryptocurrency-lending (Accessed 30 August 2022)
4. https://oasis.app/borrow
5. https://a16z.com/2021/02/05/on-crypto-governance/
6. https://en.wikipedia.org/wiki/Decentralized_autonomous_organization
7. This was also the incident that caused Ethereum to be hard forked, creating ETC.
8. https://arxiv.org/pdf/2203.16612.pdf
9. https://www.bis.org/publ/qtrpdf/r_qt2112b.pdf
10. https://papers.ssrn.com/sol3/papers.cfm?abstract_id=4105763
11. https://twitter.com/MakerDAO/status/1537462756508585985?s=20&t=2kdKvUwpLxKOc8nbAVrRhw
12. https://mips.makerdao.com/mips/details/MIP21#sentence-summary
13. https://articlegateway.com/index.php/JABE/article/view/4064/3869
14. https://articlegateway.com/index.php/JABE/article/view/4064/3869
15. https://www.icmagroup.org/market-practice-and-regulatory-policy/fintech-and-market-electronification/new-fintech-applications-in-bond-markets/
16. https://www.goldmansachs.com/insights/pages/from_briefings_10-june-2021.html
17. https://www.mas.gov.sg/news/media-releases/2022/mas-partners-the-industry-to-pilot-use-cases-in-digital-assets
18. https://creda-app.gitbook.io/creda-protocol/

19. https://www.statista.com/outlook/dmo/fintech/digital-investment/robo-advisors/worldwide
20. https://www.binance.com/en/support/faq/53a02affc6dd481aa1c53c9eae480e94
21. https://www.globenewswire.com/en/news-release/2022/03/31/2413950/0/en/Top-Five-Payments-Companies-Processed-6-Trillion-in-2021-Payment-Card-Volume.html
22. https://stripe.com/blog/expanding-global-payouts-with-crypto
23. https://stripe.com/blog/ending-bitcoin-support
24. https://medium.com/anchorage/anchorage-apis-power-visa-crypto-native-settlement-63bb73d1b979
25. https://usa.visa.com/solutions/crypto.html
26. https://usa.visa.com/solutions/crypto/digital-currency-innovation-hub.html
27. https://www.mastercard.com/news/perspectives/2021/why-mastercard-is-bringing-crypto-onto-our-network/
28. https://www.mastercard.com/news/press/press-releases/2020/september/mastercard-launches-central-bank-digital-currencies-cbdcs-testing-platform/
29. https://solana.com/news/solana-pay-announcement
30. https://www.youtube.com/watch?v=5uABl49jknk
31. https://solana.com/news/saga-reveal
32. https://solana.com/news/solana-mobile-stack-reveal
33. https://theconversation.com/one-year-on-el-salvadors-bitcoin-experiment-has-proven-a-spectacular-failure-190229
34. https://www.jstor.org/stable/251881
35. https://consensys.net/blockchain-use-cases/finance/insurance/
36. https://www.insurancejournal.com/news/international/2022/07/29/677926.htm
37. https://nexustracker.io/
38. https://docs.insurace.io/landing-page/documentation/overview/what-is-insurace

4

Risks and Mitigation

This chapter will unpack the risks associated with DeFi. DeFi is a highly complex system involving multiple layers of technology, financial arrangements, and human behaviors. Things can and do go wrong in crypto for a wide variety of reasons, many of which may be baffling for the average person, as they involve details that are very specific to blockchains, the protocols that are built with smart contracts, and the unique environment they operate in.

With the billions of dollars at play in crypto, it is also inevitable that this concentration of wealth on the internet attracts criminal activity, including fraud and other kinds of activity that most legal systems safeguard against. Having no legal jurisdiction, DeFi remains a wild west with little recourse if one gets hacked. The nature of cybercrime can be sudden, esoteric, and opaque.

Not a week seems to go by without a high profile hack or exploit, with losses numbering in the millions. It seems to be par for the course for DeFi, and has unfortunately been associated with DeFi for the general consumer and regulators. The tongue-in-cheek site "Web3 is Going Great" counts a whopping US$11b in losses in DeFi.[1]

I have some personal experience with cyberattacks. In 2020, I was personally targeted for a call forwarding attack (a variation of a SIM swap attack), where my mobile phone provider was maliciously convinced to forward my calls and messages to the attacker in order to take over my Telegram account. As much as I could do with my own personal cybersecurity there was not much I could do with my mobile phone provider and their internal processes. Law enforcement in my country did not manage to find the attackers. Thankfully, I noticed the warning signs on Telegram and with my phone early on, and the attacker did not succeed in the take-over attempt.

Beyond the risks associated within DeFi (*endogenous* risks), there are also risks associated with the growing interconnectedness of DeFi with TradFi and FinTech. These are the risks that many international bodies such as the IMF are concerned with, as there could be effects on financial stability, money

Decentralizing Finance: How DeFi, Digital Assets, and Distributed Ledger Technology Are Transforming Finance, First Edition. Kenneth Bok.
© 2024 John Wiley & Sons Ltd. Published 2024 by John Wiley & Sons Ltd.

laundering, and organized crime. We'll also take a look at these risks, which we'll call *exogenous* DeFi risks.

On a broader level, the mainstream adoption of DeFi is fundamentally tied to the mitigation of these risks. What can be done to mitigate these risks? Are they structural in nature and can they be mitigated at the root? Or will they remain, hindering DeFi's adoption indefinitely?

We'll take a high-level view of what types of risks there are associated with DeFi and look at some of the high profile failures that have happened in the history of DeFi. Many of these moments have been watershed moments for crypto as a whole, so they are worth taking note.

As with Chapter 2, many of these examples will be Ethereum-based, as Ethereum has had the most amount of adoption.

4.1 Types of Losses

How can I lose thee? Let us count the ways.

Users can be exposed to financial losses in DeFi in a number of ways. One could lose crypto-assets in self-custody, stored on an exchange, or staked in a DeFi protocol. One could send crypto-assets erroneously to the wrong address, click on a malicious link from a phishing attack, or authorize a compromised DeFi protocol to access one's wallet. One could experience a devaluation in the crypto-assets due to the specific project becoming compromised or hacked, as many holders of UST and LUNA experienced in the collapse of Terra.

Recovery of stolen crypto-assets is difficult, if not impossible in many cases. This is due to the unregulated, anonymous, and cross-border nature of DeFi that makes it difficult for law enforcement to trace, track, and apprehend cyber criminals.

Nonetheless, blockchain analytics solutions such as Elliptic, Chainalysis, and TRM Labs have made parsing the blockchain easier for law enforcement. In February 2022, the US Department of Justice seized over US$3.6b in stolen Bitcoin during the 2016 hack of Bitfinex, a crypto exchange. A cursory look at the "Statement of Facts"[2] released by the DOJ reveals the high degree of awareness and sophistication that law enforcement possesses on crypto.

4.2 Basic Terminology

As we get deeper into cybersecurity territory, we encounter yet another universe of terminology. So perhaps it is worthwhile defining some key terms here.

Hack: Unauthorized access and / or control over a computer system for an illicit purpose. Hackers can be white-hat or black-hat. White-hat hackers seek to improve security systems by discovering vulnerabilities. Black-hat hackers do it for profit and malicious purposes.

Exploit: This can be a noun or a verb. Sometimes used interchangeably with "hack" or "bug." Exploits in DeFi are usually some means of causing unintended or unanticipated results due to taking advantage of a bug or vulnerability in the system.

Bug: An error, flaw or fault in the software that causes unintended results.

Vulnerability: Similar to "bug." A weakness in the system that enables an attacker to access or control the system for illicit purposes.

4.3   Endogenous DeFi Risks

In Chapter 1, we defined the DeFi stack with the aid of a diagram (Figure 1.4) consisting of five layers: settlement, asset, protocol, application, and aggregation. Each layer of the stack builds on top of one another and all five layers are interconnected through the smart contract code that runs on the blockchain, the assets that are maintained and transferred in the network, and the DeFi applications themselves.

In visualizing endogenous DeFi risk, this diagram is again useful, for the simple reason that failures can occur at *any* level of the stack. This is further complicated by the involvement of the key individuals / actors at each level. Regardless of the aspirational goals of blockchain to disintermediate human beings, some of the highest profile failures in DeFi have been due to dishonesty and unethical behavior by key individuals.

Nick Carter and Linda Jeng have produced a similar diagram, tailored towards a lens on risk, in their excellent paper "DeFi Protocol Risks: the Paradox of DeFi" (Figure 4.1). In electronic (paper) versions blue (dark) boxes refer to centralized functions and parties, and green (light) boxes refer to decentralized, blockchain-based operations.

We'll use Figure 4.2 as we start unpacking the specific types of risk within DeFi.

A 2022 report from Elliptic, a blockchain analytics company, has indicated that the top three types of exploits are code exploits (US$5.5b), economic (US$5.3b) and admin key exploits (US$1b).

Code exploits refer to logic errors and vulnerabilities in smart contract code that make it prone to theft, hacks, and losses.

DeFi applications are interconnected. For instance, a lending / borrowing platform might determine how much a user can borrow based on the valuation of the collateral posted. If the price of the collateral can be manipulated in some way, for instance via an oracle or by cornering the market – this can be exploited by a black-hat hacker.

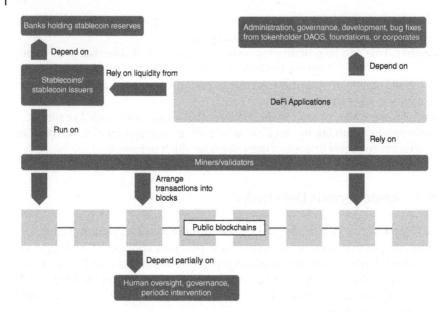

Figure 4.1 Map of interconnected DeFi risks.
Source: DeFi Protocol Risks, Nic Carter and Linda Jeng https://papers.ssrn.com/sol3/papers
.cfm?abstract_id=3866699

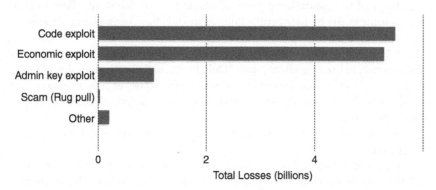

Figure 4.2 Total losses by exploit type.
Source: Elliptic, 'DeFi: Risk, Regulation, and the Rise of DeCrime'

Economic exploits thus refer to design flaws within DeFi applications that enable attackers to steal crypto-assets via economic or financial methods, as opposed to hacking the code directly.

Administrative key exploits refer to lapses in access control within the operation and administration of DeFi applications. Since these pertain to the operations of the project, I'll refer the general category as *operational exploits*. Another example of an operational exploit would be the colloquial "rug pull."

Due to the unregulated nature of DeFi, the original deployers of the smart contracts utilized by the DeFi application have the final say as to *how* the funds are stored, and the architecture of safeguarding the private keys. They could include multi-signature or hardware solutions for cold storage. Teams decide by themselves who are the key executives holding these keys.

4.3.1 Smart Contract Risks: Code Exploit Example: The DAO Hack

Launched in 2016, "The DAO" was one of the highest profile projects launched on Ethereum at the time. Having raised 11.5m ETH (~US$150m, nearly 14% of total ETH circulation), it sought to be an innovative form of venture capital fund. On 17 June 2016, the DAO was attacked using a *reentrancy* exploit that resulted in a third of the funds being stolen. Eventually, this resulted in the first ever hard fork of the Ethereum network, resulting in the network becoming split into two: the original unforked network (Ethereum Classic) and the forked network (Ethereum).

While this hack is unusual in that it caused a hard fork in Ethereum (also testing the "code is law" dictum), it illustrates the vulnerabilities of smart contracts and the difficulty of getting them right. Unlike programs that run on a local server or a cloud, smart contracts are deployed on the blockchain. Their immutability, usage of gas to deploy, and low tolerance for error make smart contract programming challenging. The specific nature of smart contract languages also set them apart from more common programming languages and software development processes such as Python and JavaScript, requiring specialized knowledge from developers.

In a reentrancy attack, the attacker calls the vulnerable smart contract multiple times, draining the smart contract using a "fallback function." This works because the vulnerable smart contract fails to update its balance before sending the next round of withdrawals as called by the attacker.

Reentrancy exploits are just one example of a common weakness in smart contracts. The Smart Contract Weakness Registry[3] maintained by the MythX team (a security analysis service from ConsenSys) lists over 30 types of common weaknesses with smart contracts, with examples of Solidity code, as well as relationships with other known software weaknesses in another registry known as the Common Weakness Enumeration.

4.3.1.1 Mitigation

There are many resources that developers can use to mitigate smart contract vulnerabilities. ConsenSys maintains a helpful website on best practices for developers writing smart contract code.[4] These principles of "General Philosophy" include

- Preparing for failure
  - Having circuit breakers to pause the contract when things go wrong
  - Managing the crypto-assets at risk with rate limits and caps

- • Having a upgrade path for bug fixes and improvements
- Keeping up to date with developments in security
  - • Checking contracts as soon as new bugs are discovered
  - • Upgrading to latest versions of tools and libraries
  - • Adopting new security techniques
- Keeping smart contracts simple
  - • Using pre-written tools and code
  - • Optimizing for clarity and simplicity
  - • Only using the blockchain when decentralization is needed
- Quality Assurance, Control, and Testing
  - • Testing contracts thoroughly, adding tests when new vulnerabilities are discovered
  - • Providing bug bounties
  - • Rolling out production in phases, with increasing usage and testing

Smart contract auditing is a big market for smart contract auditing firms such as CertiK, ConsenSys Diligence, Quantstamp, OpenZeppelin, Trail of Bits, and Least Authority, just to name a few. These companies review and test the code, inspect and highlight vulnerabilities, model threats, and suggest remediation.

There also exist a wide variety of tools that assist in auditing code. Many of them are created and maintained by ConsenSys Diligence. Examples include:

- • MythX / Mythril: Security analysis service and tool (ConsenSys Diligence)
- • VS Code extensions: Syntax highlighting in Visual Studio Code to assist developers (ConsenSys Diligence)
- • Securify: Security analysis scanner (Ethereum Foundation / ChainSecurity)
- • Slither: Security analysis scanner (Trail of Bits)

The usage of standardized smart contracts is also a good practice. For example, OpenZeppelin maintains a popular implementation of the ERC20 token contract that has been audited and utilizes best practices.

Bug bounty programs reward hackers for finding vulnerabilities in software systems. White-hat hackers have financial incentives to work and projects protect their customers from catastrophic exploits. On a popular bug bounty website, Immunefi, over US$62m in bounties have been paid out and over US$140m of bounties are available to claim. Rewards are paid out according to the severity of the vulnerability and the likelihood of the vulnerability causing loss. Bug bounty programs exist for both L1s / L2s and DeFi applications.

4.3.2   Economic Exploit Example: Mango Markets

On 12 October 2022, Mango Markets, a DEX on Solana, was drained of US$114m by an attacker using an economic exploit. The attacker utilized two accounts for the exploit. MNGO is the native token of Mango Markets. In the first account, he deposited US$5m USDC and shorted 483m MNGO perpetual futures. In the second account, he deposited US$5m USDC and went long the equivalent MNGO perpetual futures at the same price. He subsequently bought MNGO spot, a thin market, on FTX and Ascendex to force the price of MNGO up. The second account became in-the-money and he was able to withdraw US$114m of spot tokens, using the MNGO perpetuals as collateral.

The attacker subsequently self-identified as Avraham Eisenberg[5], who claimed that his actions were legal. The Mango Markets DAO later passed a proposal allowing Avraham to keep US$47m as a bug bounty, returning the rest (~US$67m).

The Mango Market exploit is just one example of an economic exploit. In February 2020, another DeFi application bZx suffered an economic exploit utilizing flash loans, collapsing the platform.

In the Mango Markets example, the exploit could have been mitigated by having limits on the perpetual position and leverage. The MNGO-PERP value was also marked using oracles (Pyth / Switchboard) which took a simple average from FTX, Ascendex, and Serum. Even though they performed as designed and were not at fault, using more exchanges could have helped. The ETH Chainlink oracle, for example, uses 31 feeds from exchanges, with a minimum of 21 to be able to calculate a trusted answer.

Economic audits are also available using financial modeling solutions such as Gauntlet. Using agent-based simulation, Gauntlet assists DeFi protocols in optimizing key parameters, improving capital efficiency, and reducing risk. Gauntlet has worked with many leading DeFi protocols such as Sushiswap, Compound, Balancer, Aave, and others.

As with code exploits, there are many ways in which economic exploits can happen in systems as complex as DeFi protocols. Teams should examine past failures of DeFi projects and patch accordingly.

4.3.3 Operational Exploit Example: Ronin Bridge Hack

In March, Ronin, an L2 built for the popular play-to-earn NFT game Axie Infinity was hacked for 173,600 ETH and 25.5m USDC, for a combined value of over US$600m. This remains one of the largest hacks in DeFi history. According to Chainalysis, the North Korean "Lazarus" cybercriminal group was behind the hack.[6] This ETH address was subsequently added to OFAC's (US Office of Foreign Assets Control) SDN (Specially Designated Nationals) list. Here's how the hack happened, from a blog post by the Sky Mavis (the project team):

> "Sky Mavis" Ronin chain currently consists of 9 validator nodes. In order to recognize a Deposit event or a Withdrawal event, five out of the nine

validator signatures are needed. The attacker managed to get control over Sky Mavis's four Ronin Validators and a third-party validator run by Axie DAO.

The validator key scheme is set up to be decentralized so that it limits an attack vector, similar to this one, but the attacker found a backdoor through our gas-free RPC node, which they abused to get the signature for the Axie DAO validator.

This traces back to November 2021 when Sky Mavis requested help from the Axie DAO to distribute free transactions due to an immense user load. The Axie DAO allowlisted Sky Mavis to sign various transactions on its behalf. This was discontinued in December 2021, but the allowlist access was not revoked.

Once the attacker got access to Sky Mavis systems they were able to get the signature from the Axie DAO validator by using the gas-free RPC.[7]

The Block also reported that the hack involved a social engineering / phishing attack involving a fake job application that a senior engineer at Axie Infinity was duped into applying.[8]

The Ronin hack is a case of an application-specific blockchain, having few validators (likely for the benefits of centralization), experienced a takeover due to an employee's computer getting compromised via a sophisticated social engineering attack. The attacker, a state-level threat, was sophisticated, organized, and well-funded.

Admin keys enable project teams to control the DeFi application and the smart contracts: shutting them down, pausing, upgrading, and moving crypto-assets. The existence of admin keys in the first place seems antithetical to the tenets of DeFi. To place control in a few hands is a clear centralization risk. Nonetheless, for some fast moving software startups, this seems to be a compromise teams are willing to take. Some projects delegate these key functions and controls to their governance token holders and require voting. The downside of a more decentralized approach is that in a crisis situation such as an active exploit, a rapid response might not be possible.

Again, given the lack of standards and regulation, DeFi applications have no obligation to declare if admin keys exist at all. It's not easy to find out either, assuming the team has declared it in their public documentation in the first place. Chris Blec has written on this topic on a blog post "The Trustlessness of DeFi's Top 10 Richest Products"[9] where he looked at the top 10 (by TVL) DeFi protocols and ranked them by trustlessness and decentralization.

The more insidious, "rug pulls," are exit scams where a DeFi project team has the premeditated intent to defraud users of a DeFi platform. This could happen by disappearing with the crypto-assets contributed during a crowdsale or deposited in a DeFi application. The project team could do a pump-and-dump scheme on its token holders or other unsuspecting buyers, selling the native token and cashing out in an alternative crypto-asset. The commonality of anonymous project teams does not help either. Certain VCs funds have even gone so far as to fund anonymous teams.

Timelocks are built in delays that are hard-coded into the smart contracts that enable for reaction time from the project teams in the event of a hack or exploit.

Good cyber hygiene, cybersecurity, and InfoSec practices are essential for key personnel in DeFi projects. Best practices in access control such as the principle of least privilege should be applied and adopted accordingly.

4.3.4 CeFi Contagion / Systemic Risk

This pertains more to CeFi than DeFi. Nonetheless, given the interconnected nature of the crypto ecosystem as a whole, it is worth listing some events that have transpired in 2022.

Table 4.1 provides a timeline of DeFi contagion events.

Table 4.1 DeFi contagion events, 2022.

Date	Event	Companies / assets affected	Cause
May 2022	Terra / LUNA / UST collapse	3AC, stETH	Negative feedback loop aka "Death spiral"
June 2022	3AC collapse	Voyager, Blockchain.com, BlockFi, Genesis, BitMex, FTX	Terra collapse, stETH, adverse market conditions
June 2022	Celsius collapse	Various	Adverse market conditions, stETH
July 2022	Babel Finance collapse	Zipmex	Trading losses
July 2022	Vauld collapse	Various	3AC, Terra collapse
July 2022	Zipmex collapse	Various	Babel Finance collapse, Celsius collapse
July 2022	Voyager bankruptcy	Various	3AC collapse
August 2022	Hodlnaut collapse	Various	Terra collapse
November 2022	FTX suffers bank run	Various	Coindesk article on Alameda / FTX assets

While not DeFi related, systemic risks in CeFi can have many effects on DeFi. Many of these major incidents such as the collapse of FTX actually support the case for DeFi, but this is not obvious to the average consumer. Through the volatility of 2022, DeFi has actually held up well with no major DeFi protocol going under.

4.4 Exogenous DeFi Risks

In this section, we'll take a look at the risks that DeFi poses to the broader financial system and society as a whole. In doing so, we might as well put on our regulatory hats, since these two domains are closely related. Let's imagine for a moment that it is our mission to be the overseer of the entire financial system. What do we make of this DeFi phenomenon? In what ways does it pose risks to the public good? How does it fit within our well-established frameworks around risk management? What can go wrong with the broader financial system and society if DeFi works as designed? What if it doesn't?

These are the key exogenous DeFi risks:

- Financial Stability
- Market Integrity
- Consumer Protection
- Money Laundering / Illicit Activity
- Environmental Issues

This section will also tie in nicely with our next chapter on regulation, as these risks will translate to the ways in which regulators will set policy. On the whole, regulators don't think DeFi has serious systemic risks, due to its current size. Nonetheless, they note that the trajectory of growth has been very fast, and thus change could be unexpected.

Here we also get into some territory which can be quite arcane for most individuals: the regulation of finance at the international level. While financial professionals might be aware of the regulator in their local jurisdiction, international bodies such as the BIS, IMF, FSB, IOSCO, and others may be less familiar to them. Table 4.2 shows the key institutions, their objectives, and the reports that are relevant to DeFi.

Regulators face significant challenges in regulating DeFi. If you've made it through Chapters 2 and 3, and maybe played around with how these applications work, you will have a sense of how different this financial system is. Decentralization, anonymity, and the technical complications of DeFi make enforcement, supervision, and regulation challenging. In TradFi, most financial institutions and financial intermediaries have substantial "skin in the game." They require licenses to operate, pay licensing fees, maintain collateral, have directors and key executives that can be financially and legally censured, and so forth.

Table 4.2 International finance regulators and key DeFi reports.

Institution	Objectives	Key DeFi Reports
BIS	Support central banks' pursuit of monetary and financial stability through international cooperation, and to act as a bank for central banks.	Prudential treatment of cryptoasset exposures, June 2021 DeFi risks and the decentralisation illusion, December 2021 Miners as intermediaries: extractable value and market manipulation in crypto and DeFi, June 2022 DeFi lending: intermediation without information?, June 2022
IOSCO	Brings together the world's securities regulators and is recognized as the global standard setter for the securities sector. Develops, implements, and promotes adherence to internationally recognized standards for securities regulation. Works intensively with the G20 and the Financial Stability Board (FSB) on the global regulatory reform agenda.	Decentralized Finance Report, March 2022
FSB	Promotes global financial stability by coordinating the development of regulatory, supervisory, and other financial sector policies and conducts outreach to nonmember countries.	Assessment of Risks to Financial Stability from Crypto-assets, February 2022 Regulation, Supervision and Oversight of Crypto-Asset Activities and Markets, October 2022 Review of the FSB High-level Recommendations of the Regulation, Supervision and Oversight of "Global Stablecoin" Arrangements, October 2022

(Continued)

Table 4.2 (Continued)

Institution	Objectives	Key DeFi Reports
G20	Intergovernmental forum comprising 19 countries and the European Union (EU). It works to address major issues related to the global economy, such as international financial stability, climate change mitigation, and sustainable development.	See FSB
CPMI	Promotes the safety and efficiency of payment, clearing, settlement and related arrangements, thereby supporting financial stability and the wider economy. The CPMI secretariat is hosted by the BIS.	See BIS
OECD	Intergovernmental organization with 38 member countries to stimulate economic progress and world trade	Why Decentralised Finance (DeFi) Matters and the Policy Implications, January 2022
IMF	Foster global monetary cooperation, secure financial stability, facilitate international trade, promote high employment and sustainable economic growth, and reduce poverty around the world	Regulating the Crypto Ecosystem, September 2022

Source: Institution websites

All of this radically changes in DeFi. To start, public blockchains are not built with linkages to identity. One may choose to link one's real world identity with one's on-chain identity, but this is an opt-in choice. Some crypto advocates also point to the risks of KYC. Transactions are visible and transparent, which aids in the tracing of funds that have been stolen.

One important caveat with this section and the following chapter, as we cover the exogenous DeFi risks, is that the regulatory view is mostly a traditional view. It mostly views anonymity and decentralization as bugs, and not features. When the regulator says a DeFi product is "non-compliant," it is making a value judgment that is based on how compliance has historically been done with financial products.

DeFi advocates will disagree with many of these positions, and argue that anonymity and decentralization are features. Areas of using technology to regulate and supervise DeFi (RegTech and SupTech) are also new areas which do not feature much in these reports from international regulators.

4.4.1   Financial Stability

Regulators are understandably concerned about DeFi's impact on financial stability, as the linkages between DeFi and TradFi increase. These linkages occur in a multitude of ways. Perhaps more importantly than even consumer adoption is institutional adoption of DeFi. This is the gateway to significant volumes being transacted.

> If financial institutions continue to become more involved in crypto-asset markets, this could affect their balance sheets and liquidity in unexpected ways. As in the case of the US subprime mortgage crisis, a small amount of known exposure does not necessarily mean a small amount of risk, particularly if there exists a lack of transparency and insufficient regulatory coverage.
> —FSB[10]

The OECD has also highlighted the risks that the increasing interconnectedness of DeFi and TradFi poses. Here's an excerpt from a report that summarizes their point of view:

> Increased participation of institutional investors in digital asset markets can give rise to investor risks at the micro-level, while it may also create channels of potential contagion between decentralised finance and traditional finance. Growing involvement of institutional investors in cryptoasset markets may in the future lead to increased interconnectivity between traditional finance and decentralised finance through many avenues, and risks of spillovers to the traditional financial system and the real economy may emerge. Stablecoins constitute the key bridge linking the decentralised finance with the traditional financial markets. Other points of possible linkage between decentralised finance and traditional markets include institutional versions of DeFi protocols and the pledging of tokenised assets on DeFi protocols instead of crypto-assets or the potential future use of CBDCs in DeFi protocols. Growing institutionalisation of digital assets could bring a number of potential benefits to financial markets and their participants that should not be underestimated or overlooked.
> —"Institutionalisation of crypto-assets and DeFi-TradFi interconnectedness," p. 34, OECD

Consumers and businesses may start to hold crypto-assets as part of their portfolio. If crypto prices start to fall, they may sell off other holdings in their portfolios to compensate. An OECD report[11] goes on to elaborate on the systemic behavior of the crypto market as a whole, highlighting its *procyclical* nature, which means that feedback loops are exacerbated in crypto. (Its reverse, countercyclical behaviors, are systemic mechanisms that counterbalance the broader trend, slowing down these feedback loops.)

Much of DeFi's credit creation is based on overcollateralization of highly volatile crypto-assets. When the market is going up, more credit is extended on lending protocols. When the market falls, and often sharply, this can go the other way very quickly, as forced liquidations in lending protocols occur to maintain collateralization ratios. This forced selling can lead to liquidity cascades. Unlike stocks and commodities, which are traded on highly regulated exchanges, crypto has no circuit breakers, and trades 24/7.

The unrestricted use of leverage in DeFi is also a concern for regulators. Perpetual futures are an easy way for users to take long or short leveraged positions on both centralized exchanges and decentralized exchanges. On Binance, for example, it's possible to take 20× leverage. This new limit was brought down from 100× in July 2022,[12] in what was seen as a pre-emptive response to regulatory concerns. On dYdX, a perpetuals DEX, the leverage limit is also 20× for BTC and ETH. The use of leverage can amplify the volatility of the crypto-asset markets.

The number of institutional investors in crypto has been increasing since the rise of crypto, tracking its growing acceptability as an alternative asset class. Although this has mainly been in specialized hedge funds and VC funds, many traditional FinTech companies such as PayPal have been offering access to crypto. In November 2022, Fidelity, one of the largest brokerages in the world, announced "Fidelity Crypto," which will allow retail investors to buy and sell BTC and ETH, and allow clients to use custodial and trading services provided by its subsidiary Fidelity Digital Assets.[13]

The subject of crypto-asset ETFs and other BTC products available on the traditional securities market is also one of large contention. One of the earliest and largest BTC products on the securities market is GBTC, from Grayscale. GBTC holds over US$10b of BTC, making it one of the largest holders of BTC, with just over 3% of the total market capitalization of BTC. Nonetheless GBTC is not an ETF but is a closed-end fund. The ProShares Bitcoin futures ETF, BITO, was the first US-based Bitcoin ETF based on CME futures. The US SEC has not approved any "physical" spot ETF products as yet.

The benefit of products such as GBTC and BITO is that users do not have to handle custody, already use existing brokerage relationships, and don't take on the risk of getting hacked.

More crypto companies are also accessing the broader capital markets via an IPO. Coinbase went public in April 2021 with much fanfare. USDC stablecoin issuer Circle has also announced plans to go public via a SPAC IPO, as well as an application to become a US chartered bank.

The BCBS has issued two consultative documents on the "Prudential Treatment of Cryptoasset Exposures," one in June 2021 and another in June 2022. This looks to be a key framework in shaping the requirements placed on banks that look to provide access to crypto-asset services. They note:

> While the cryptoasset market remains small relative to the size of the global financial system, and banks' exposures to cryptoassets are currently limited, its absolute size is meaningful and there continue to be rapid developments. The Committee (BCBS) believes that the growth of cryptoassets and related services has the potential to raise financial stability concerns and increase risks faced by banks. Certain cryptoassets have exhibited a high degree of volatility, and could present risks for banks as exposures increase, including liquidity risk; credit risk; market risk; operational risk (including fraud and cyber risks); money laundering / terrorist financing risk; and legal and reputation risks.
>
> —BCBS[14]

We will look further into the BCBS framework around cryptoassets as it is being introduced via "SC060: Cryptoasset Exposures" into the Basel Framework in the next chapter. The Basel Framework is the international standard for the prudential regulation of banks.

Finally, one method of measuring linkage between crypto-assets and the traditional financial markets is the correlation between crypto and other asset

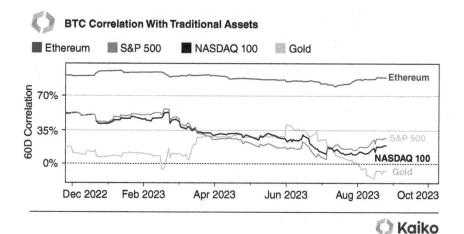

Figure 4.3 Bitcoin's correlation with traditional assets.
Source: Kaiko

classes. Figure 4.3 shows the 60 day rolling correlation of BTC with the S&P 500, Nasdaq, Gold, and ETH from December 2022–September 2023. Unsurprisingly, BTC and ETH are highly correlated.

Correlations between BTC and the Nasdaq 100, S&P 500, and gold mostly vary between 0 to 0.7, indicating weak to moderate correlation. In recent months, the correlation between BTC and the stock markets has decreased, strengthening the case for including BTC as a diversifying asset in a balanced portfolio.

4.4.2 Pronounced Risks in Developing Countries

The FSB also notes that financial stability risks from crypto could be pronounced in "emerging market and developing economies where crypto-assets may in some situations replace the domestic currency, or offer opportunities to circumvent exchange restrictions, and capital account management measures."[15]

In a policy brief, the UNCTAD (United Nations Conference on Trade and Development) notes that in 2021, 15 of the top 20 economies by crypto ownership were emerging market and developing economies (Figure 4.4). UNCTAD cites two reasons. First, during the pandemic, crypto was a useful channel to send remittances, due to low cost and speed. Second, crypto was held by middle-income individuals in countries facing currency depreciation and rising inflation. As a result, crypto was seen as a means of protecting household savings.

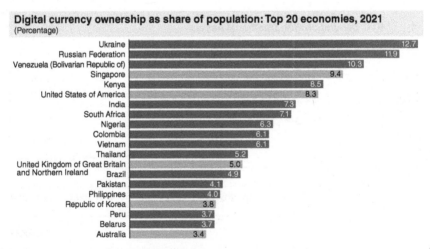

Figure 4.4 Digital currency ownership as share of population.
Source: UNCTAD, Triple A

In addition to financial stability risks, cryptocurrencies may undermine the effectiveness of capital controls, an essential instrument in developing countries in protecting their economies.

This substitution risk is most pronounced with stablecoins denominated in foreign currencies (e.g., USD) that may well be a compelling form of money and payment, much like what the US dollar already is in many developing countries, albeit in cash.

Both the Central African Republic and El Salvador have adopted Bitcoin as legal tender. In February 2022, the IMF issued warnings against the use of Bitcoin as legal tender in El Salvador, citing financial stability, financial integrity, consumer protection, and contingent liability risks.[16]

4.4.3 Banking-to-Crypto Concentration Risks

Many banks do not serve cryptocurrency clients due to the compliance risk. For a certain set of banks though, cryptocurrency clients are seen as a business opportunity. This includes Silvergate Bank, Provident Bancorp Inc., Metropolitan Commercial Bank, Signature Bank, and Customers Bancorp Inc.

In particular, Silvergate Bank, a publicly traded US bank, has been one of the most active banks in serving the cryptocurrency industry. As of 30 September 2022, Silvergate's total deposits from digital asset clients totaled US$11.9b.[17]

The Silvergate Exchange Network (SEN) has been a key enabler for cryptocurrency exchanges and institutional investors in the digital asset space to transfer and settle USD and EUR 24/7 between Silvergate accounts and clients. In Q3 2022, SEN volume reached US$112.6b.[18]

Silvergate has also been in the spotlight in the wake of the FTX collapse. In December 2022, Democrat Senator Elizabeth Warren, member of the US Senate banking committee, Republican Senator John Kennedy, and Roger Marshall of Kansas sent Alan Lane, CEO of Silvergate, a letter requesting for information relating to Silvergate's relationship with FTX.

Silvergate and other similar centralized points of contact between the crypto and fiat world are possible risk factors for DeFi and crypto.

4.4.4 Stablecoins

Stablecoins are fast becoming a substantial point of linkage between DeFi and TradFi. The risk here is the stability and behavior of stablecoin issuers. As covered at the end of Chapter 2, stablecoins vary significantly in design. Without in-depth research and understanding, consumers will find it difficult to differentiate and assess risk between stablecoins.

Regulation is fast coming for stablecoins (to be covered in the next chapter), but has not caught up with issuers as yet. As such, the backing, auditing, and transparency of stablecoins differ between issuers.

The concentration risk of stablecoins is high, with the top three stablecoins (USDT, USDC, and BUSD) making up 91.5% of total market capitalization (US$143b) of all stablecoins.[19]

Key risks for users and holders of stablecoins are the potential devaluation of their stablecoin holdings and the inability to redeem at par due to design flaws, governance issues, or otherwise some form of misconduct by the stablecoin issuer.

On the "back-end," stablecoin issuers hold cash, cash equivalents, and short-term debt securities in the money markets. Regulators are concerned that in the event of a "bank run," stablecoin issuers could be forced to sell these short-term debt securities quickly, causing disruption to these markets.

Given that stablecoins are issued by private companies, regulators have suggested that stablecoin issuers should be "required to be insured depository institutions, which are subject to appropriate supervision and regulation."[20] A failure of a large stablecoin could have run-on effects on traditional financial markets.

Notably, the last attempt by Meta (previously Facebook) to create a stablecoin Diem (previously Libra) was met with fierce opposition from governments and financial regulators, over concerns around financial stability, monetary sovereignty, privacy, and antitrust issues.

4.4.5 Market Integrity

Market integrity refers to the fair and proper function of markets, enabling all participants to have equal access without unmerited unfair advantage. With regards to DeFi, the most serious issue that challenges market integrity is the MEV / frontrunning issue. The other issue is market manipulation in the largely unregulated and difficult-to-regulate DeFi market.

4.4.6 Frontrunning

Front running in TradFi is generally considered to be a form of market manipulation in most regulated markets. In contrast, the possibility of being front-run is nearly inevitable in many DeFi transactions. This is a serious problem as it may be a form of "invisible tax" paid by the uninformed user, as the BIS has stated.[21]

We covered the mempool (memory pool) briefly in Chapter 2: the mempool is a waiting area for transactions that are looking to be included in a block that is validated by validators. These transactions are unconfirmed. The mempool, like the rest of the blockchain, is publicly visible and transparent by design.

Validators are not obligated to validate transactions in the order that they were submitted. Validators can choose to include, exclude, and / or change the order of transactions in a block. This gives rise to a unique phenomenon in permissionless blockchains: MEV, or Maximal Extractable Value, which refers to "the maximum value that can be extracted from block production in excess of the standard block reward and gas fees by including, excluding, and changing the order of transactions in a block."[22]

One of the most common ways this can happen is in a DEX. Let's take an example of a retail user who decides to execute a large trade on a DEX. Since transactions submitted to a DEX are on-chain (unlike a transaction on a centralized exchange that is off-chain), what can happen is a "searcher" (a term for participants that specialize in capitalizing on MEV opportunities) will detect the trade, and execute the trade (by incentivizing validators with higher gas fees) *before* the retail user's trade. The retail user experiences slippage and a poorer execution. After the retail user's trade, the searcher can also execute a reverse order, capitalizing on the price movement caused by the retail user's trade. This is known as a "sandwich" trade.

Other types of MEV phenomena include arbitrage, liquidations, and generalized frontrunning.

4.4.6.1 Mitigation

The Flashbots project is a project working on "mitigating the negative externalities" of MEV and "avoiding the existential risks MEV could cause to state-rich blockchains like Ethereum."[23] Their approach is to bring MEV out into the open by making the tools and information on MEV opportunities publicly available, instead of to a select, knowledgeable few. One of their solutions is "Flashbots Auction," a private communication channel between Ethereum users and validators. Flashbots recently introduced an order flow auction protocol that makes incoming user transactions private by default, which reduces potentially malicious front-running.

There are also startups such as Eden Network, Manifold, Blocknative, and bloXroute that look to mitigate MEV risk in private channels. Eden Network incentivizes use of its native EDEN token to prioritize transactions. These relay networks connect to DeFi applications through RPC (remote procedure call) connectors. MEVboost.org gives details on the usage of these relays.

As an extension of moving transactions away from the public mempool and into private channels, order flow auctions attempt to pass on MEV created by technical actors to the order flow source, which is in most cases either a normal user, or a party (wallet, app) facilitating the transaction. This theoretically creates a perfect competition market that drives MEV profits for technical actors such as arbitrageurs towards zero. Examples include CowSwap's MEVBlocker solution, and Merkle.

4.4.7 Market Manipulation

In TradFi, stock exchanges are highly regulated institutions, with clear rules governing market conduct. Market participants can be disciplined for misconduct as both trades and identity are known to the centralized exchange.

Regulators have oversight and surveillance over centralized exchanges. Similar developments are occurring in crypto centralized exchanges, with regulators requiring the same standards and norms as in TradFi.

DeFi markets can be quite different due to built-in pseudonymity. Why and who is moving the price level for any given crypto-asset market can be difficult or impossible to ascertain. This unfortunately paves the way for the preponderance of pump-and-dump schemes, insider trading, wash trading, whale wall spoofing, and other forms of market misconduct which are rife in crypto.

The Mango Markets exploit covered earlier is one such example of market manipulation. In that case, the hacker made himself known. It could have been even harder to track if he had remained anonymous.

In general, tokens with smaller market capitalizations are easier to manipulate than those with large ones. Investing in the more well-known crypto-assets such as BTC and ETH is one way to mitigate these risks.

4.4.8   Money Laundering, Funding of Illicit Activity and Terrorism

This is yet another topic that comes up all too frequently in discussions around crypto. It doesn't help that the early history of crypto was tied up with darknet illicit marketplaces such as the Silk Road, or that ransomware operators have a predilection for getting paid in Bitcoin.

Chainalysis has done good work in analyzing data and trends related to crypto crime. In their 2022 Crypto Crime Report,[24] they note that while the total value received by illicit addresses has increased from 2017 to 2021 (Figure 4.5), illicit activity in percentage terms has actually reduced (Figure 4.6).

In my opinion, this point about relative usage of DeFi for criminal activity is worth bearing in mind whenever the media plays up this narrative. Fiat is also

Figure 4.5 Total cryptocurrency value received by illicit addresses.
Source: Chainalysis, 2022 Crypto Crime Report

Figure 4.6 Illicit share of all cryptocurrency transaction volume.
Source: Chainalysis, 2022 Crypto Crime Report

used for criminal activity, and it's certain that any kind of medium for value exchange will inevitably be used for illicit activity.

In contrast, the United Nations Office on Drugs and Crime estimates that money laundering accounts for 2–5% of global GDP, or US$800b to US$2 trillion.[25] By this measure, it's fair to say that crypto is within or lower than the norms in the fiat world.

Nonetheless, the use of DeFi by organized crime, darknet marketplaces, and even nation-states looking to evade sanctions are serious issues that need to be addressed. Let's take a brief look at some of this activity.

Cyber criminals use a variety of tools to obfuscate the money trail left on the blockchain. Mixers, tumblers, and bridges can be used to muddy the trail and make it harder for law enforcement to trace funds. They generally work by combining the identifiable crypto-assets with others for a random period of time, and later transferring them out to a destination address.

In August 2022, the US Treasury's Office of Foreign Assets Control (OFAC) sanctioned the Ethereum smart-contract mixer Tornado Cash for its role in assisting money laundering operations for the North Korean-linked hacking organization Lazarus Group. This is the same group as mentioned earlier in the chapter as the group behind the Ronin hack.

Lazarus Group and other North Korean Government sponsored groups are some of the most sophisticated and systematic "advanced persistent threats" in the cryptocurrency industry.

The UN Security Council has noted that "in addition to attacks on fiat currency, cyberattacks involving cryptocurrencies provide the Democratic People's Republic of Korea with more ways to evade sanctions given that they

Table 4.3 Cryptocurrency-focused malware types.

Type	Description	Example
Info stealers	Collect saved credentials, files, autocomplete history, and cryptocurrency wallets from compromised computers.	Redline
Clippers	Can insert new text into the victim's clipboard, replacing text the user has copied. Hackers can use clippers to replace cryptocurrency addresses copied into the clipboard with their own, allowing them to reroute planned transactions to their own wallets.	HackBoss
Cryptojackers	Make unauthorized use of victim device's computing power to mine cryptocurrency.	Glupteba
Trojans	Virus that looks like a legitimate program but infiltrates victim's computer to disrupt operations, steal, or cause other types of harm.	Mekotio banking trojan

Source: Chainalysis, 2022 Crypto Crime Report.

are harder to trace, can be laundered many times and are independent from government regulation."[26]

Ransomware is a type of malware that denies access to a victim's data by encrypting it, and demanding a ransom payment to decrypt it. Payment in Bitcoin has been a popular choice for these cybercriminals.

One of the more well-known ransomware attacks was the Colonial Pipeline incident in May 2021. Colonial Pipeline is an American pipeline system that supplies 45% of gasoline and jet fuel to the Southeastern United States. Due to the cyberattack, operations were halted for a week. The ransom of 75 bitcoin (US$4.4m) was paid to the hacker group, Darkside. In June 2021, the US Department of Justice announced that it had recovered 63.7 bitcoin from the original ransom payment.

New classes of malware have also emerged due to the profitability of crypto-related cybercrime (Table 4.3).

In general, DeFi is becoming a popular choice for cyber crime because unlike centralized exchanges, DeFi does not need KYC and is self-custodial. In the increasingly regulated centralized exchange landscape, regulators can request exchanges to freeze funds and disclose identifiable information about clients.

I should also note here that stablecoins such as Tether and Circle are required by regulators to have a function that enables blacklisting and freezing of funds / addresses.

4.4.8.1 Mitigation

Elliptic, Chainalysis, and TRM Labs provide tools for tracing, flagging, and investigating illicit activity on-chain. These tools were not available just a few years ago. It's very likely that with the pace of innovation we've experienced in the last few years, these tools will only get better with time.

It's also clear that the ability for law enforcement to seize stolen assets is growing, as evidenced by the DOJ's seizure of the Bitfinex hack and partial recovery of the Colonial Pipeline ransom. This is important as it is a deterrent for cyber criminals looking to use DeFi for illicit purposes.

Performing illicit activity on-chain is getting harder, for the obvious reason that activity is transparent, immutable, and visible to anyone with an internet connection. Compare this to cash, the preferred method for most illicit activity, which is difficult to trace and completely offline.

4.4.9 Consumer Protection

This is another big area in which DeFi faces a gap due to its largely unregulated nature. Suffice to say, there is a dire lack of consumer protection in DeFi.

Let's take requirements from US securities law as a means of comparison for what constitutes best practices for consumer protection. According to a website from the SEC,[27] the Securities Act of 1933 has two basic objectives:

1. Require that investors receive financial and other significant information concerning securities being offered for public sale
2. Prohibit deceit, misrepresentation and other fraud in the sale of securities

4.4.10 Disclosure, or the Lack Thereof

The disclosure of important financial information enables investors to make informed decisions whether to purchase a company's securities. Investors also have recovery rights if they can prove that there was incomplete or inaccurate information disclosure.

A common refrain in crypto is "Do your own research" (DYOR). Nonetheless, DYOR doesn't really help if the token issuer has no requirement to disclose "important" information. While what is deemed "important" might be codified and standardized in securities, equivalent standards do not exist in crypto. Simply put, disclosure requirements don't exist in crypto – let alone recovery or recourse rights. Given the cross-border nature of crypto – it's also difficult to pursue legal recourse in the event of fraud or other misconduct.

There are attempts to introduce disclosure standards in crypto. A study from Liebau and Krapels suggests minimum disclosure requirements for cryptocurrency and token issuers.[28] They suggest two categories of disclosure: financial and nonfinancial. Financial disclosures include token issuer information, cash positions, as well as token treasury information. Nonfinancial disclosures include contact information, project progress updates, and open-source software components.

One of my personal observations with DeFi applications is that consumers, especially those new to crypto, don't necessarily spend the time to research and perform due diligence before putting funds on the platform. This has likely gotten better since there is so much media coverage around the high-profile failure of FTX, Terra, and others. A substantial amount of reliance is on social heuristics: "if many others are doing it, it must be safe."

From a cosmetic point of view, many DeFi applications (that may well be on iOS, Android, or a web app) look indistinguishable from a FinTech app. Many consumers may not know the difference between what has been vetted by a regulatory agency and what is not. Requiring DeFi apps to declare the regulatory status of the company behind the application is one possible way to address this.

4.4.11 Data Protection

This is yet another area that is already fairly robust in FinTech, but DeFi has yet to catch up. There's hardly any discussion around data protection standards such as GDPR. DeFi has a tendency to shun KYC, but there should be optionality for KYC to enable important functions such as lending. If and when DeFi gets there, standards and technologies around data protection and privacy in an on-chain environment will be pivotal.

4.5 Chapter Summary

This chapter has covered the major categories of risk in DeFi. We've examined them from the lens of endogenous risk, which may be code-related, economic, or operational in nature. We've also examined exogenous risk – risk that DeFi poses to society as a whole. This is a lens that regulators are familiar with applying in TradFi. In the next chapter, we'll look at regulation and how regulators are setting crypto and DeFi policy.

Notes

1. https://web3isgoinggreat.com
2. https://www.justice.gov/opa/press-release/file/1470211/download
3. https://swcregistry.io/

4. https://consensys.github.io/smart-contract-best-practices/
5. https://twitter.com/avi_eisen/status/1581326197241180160?s=20&t=vvBHfM rMMOZo512sazpv8g
6. https://twitter.com/chainalysis/status/1514645221027594245
7. https://roninblockchain.substack.com/p/community-alert-ronin-validators?s=w
8. https://www.theblock.co/post/156038/how-a-fake-job-offer-took-down-the-worlds-most-popular-crypto-game
9. https://survivingdefi.substack.com/p/the-trustlessness-of-defis-top-10
10. Assessment of Risks to Financial Stability from Crypto-assets, FSB
11. https://www.oecd.org/finance/why-decentralised-finance-defi-matters-and-the-policy-implications.htm
12. https://www.coindesk.com/markets/2021/07/26/binance-says-its-cutting-leverage-limit-to-20x-a-day-after-ftx-announces-the-same/
13. https://www.cnbc.com/2022/11/03/fidelity-to-open-commission-free-crypto-trading-to-retail-investors.html
14. https://www.bis.org/bcbs/publ/d519.pdf
15. https://www.fsb.org/2022/02/assessment-of-risks-to-financial-stability-from-crypto-assets/
16. https://www.imf.org/en/News/Articles/2022/02/15/cf-el-salvadors-comeback-constrained-by-increased-risks
17. https://ir.silvergate.com/news/news-details/2022/Silvergate-Provides-Statement-on-FTX-Exposure/default.aspx
18. https://www.theblockcrypto.com/data/crypto-markets/public-companies/sen-transfer-volume
19. https://coinmarketcap.com/view/stablecoin/ (Accessed and calculated 1 December 2022.)
20. Report on Stablecoins, President's Working Group on Financial Markets https://home.treasury.gov/system/files/136/StableCoinReport_Nov1_508.pdf
21. https://www.bis.org/publ/bisbull58.pdf
22. https://ethereum.org/en/developers/docs/mev/
23. https://docs.flashbots.net/
24. https://go.chainalysis.com/2022-Crypto-Crime-Report.html#:~:text=Our%20 latest%20report%20has%20original,and%20how%20it%20affects%20exchanges
25. https://www.unodc.org/unodc/en/money-laundering/overview.html
26. https://www.securitycouncilreport.org/atf/cf/%7B65BFCF9B-6D27-4E9C-8CD3-CF6E4FF96FF9%7D/s_2019_171.pdf
27. https://www.investor.gov/introduction-investing/investing-basics/role-sec/laws-govern-securities-industry
28. https://papers.ssrn.com/sol3/papers.cfm?abstract_id=3607821

5

Regulation

DeFi presents a panoply of opportunities. However, it also poses important risks and challenges for regulators, investors, and the financial markets. While the potential for profits attracts attention, sometimes overwhelming attention, there is also confusion, often significant, regarding important aspects of this emerging market. Social media questions like "Who in the U.S. regulates the DeFi market?" and "Why are regulators involved at all?" abound. These are crucial questions, and the answers are important to lawyers and non-lawyers alike. - Commissioner Caroline A. Crenshaw, SEC, Statement on DeFi Risks, Regulations, and Opportunities

5.1   Introduction

I hope you've been convinced enough to think that DeFi has merit and significant potential, despite its risks. As an emergent technology, public blockchains enable a tremendous leap forward in global connectivity and value transfers, but also pose many questions and implications for how finance has been run in our modern era. While the technology may be different, human behavior largely remains the same. Market manipulation, insider trading, and other types of financial fraud were not invented by crypto. Much of the regulation that governs the financial industry has been a response to the various lessons learnt throughout history.

Some proponents of DeFi believe that regulation goes against the industry's fundamental principles. They argue that DeFi should remain free, internet-based, and be allowed to innovate and grow without interference. While I can understand this perspective, I believe that it does not address the issue of how to achieve the objectives of regulation without relying on centralized regulation.

Decentralizing Finance: How DeFi, Digital Assets, and Distributed Ledger Technology Are Transforming Finance, First Edition. Kenneth Bok.
© 2024 John Wiley & Sons Ltd. Published 2024 by John Wiley & Sons Ltd.

Although I believe that fair and orderly markets, consumer protection, and financial stability can be achieved without centralized intervention, the industry currently lacks ethical standards for conduct and the means to enforce them. In the absence of such coordination, regulation from centralized authorities may be necessary. The key question is who should implement these rules: an international regulator, a national regulator, the industry itself, or some programmatic method?

In my view, regulation is a necessary step for DeFi to become mainstream and accessible to a wider audience, beyond just crypto-natives and early adopters. To achieve this, DeFi products and services need legal clarity for businesses that want to use them. For example, if a retail store accepts stablecoins as payment, what protections exist for them to hold the stablecoins? Are they considered legal tender? How can businesses manage their accounts alongside their regular bank accounts?

I believe that DeFi can significantly improve financial inclusion in developing countries. However, the reality is that developing countries usually adopt legal standards from developed countries, which can be a barrier to DeFi adoption if there is no legal clarity. This is especially problematic for reaching the last-mile users in these countries.

Regulators often follow the principle of "same activity, same risk, same regulation," which means that if crypto-assets and DeFi perform similar economic activities as in traditional finance, they should be subject to equivalent regulation. However, the challenge is determining which category crypto-assets fall into, whether they are securities, commodities, currencies, or something else entirely.

5.2 Global Nature of Crypto and DeFi

The global nature of crypto presents a challenge for DeFi regulation. Crypto startups typically deliver their products and services over the internet, through browser-based DeFi apps that interface directly with wallet-native browsers. This poses a challenge for regulators who are used to regulating brick and mortar institutions or app stores that can be restricted by Apple or Google.

Regulatory arbitrage, the practice of exploiting regulatory standards in different jurisdictions to circumvent regulation, is a substantial issue for crypto and the DeFi industry. Many exchanges operate offshore to avoid the higher cost of compliance. However, for regulation to be effective, regulators need to coordinate their efforts and establish a unified global set of standards. While national regulators have control over local licensing, most do not prohibit their citizens from accessing offshore exchanges through IP bans or other means of control.

For example, Binance, at the time of writing, maintains that it does not have a headquarters. In line with the decentralized ethos of crypto, Binance CEO Changpeng Zhao has stated that its operations are globally distributed.[1] However, the more likely reason for not explicitly naming a geographical HQ is to avoid being pinned down by any one regulatory authority. Nonetheless, in June 2022, Binance France was granted a Digital Asset Service Provider (DASP) registration by the French securities regulator with the approval of the French banking regulator. This effectively paves the way for Binance to legally serve the entire EU market with the upcoming European Union MiCA (Market in Crypto-assets) regulations.

In the aftermath of the FTX collapse, many called for more regulation due to the lack of clear jurisdiction between securities, commodities, and banking regulators in the United States. Some in the crypto industry cited the lack of legal clarity as a factor pushing crypto companies offshore. As a result, many crypto exchanges have shifted towards an offshore approach to their operations. For example, FTX.com was incorporated in Antigua and Barbuda and headquartered in the Bahamas, while FTX.us was available only to US residents.

Chapter 4 briefly covered standard-setting bodies (SSBs) and international regulators such as the IMF, BIS, FATF, FSB, and IOSCO, which have published various reports and guidance documents for crypto and DeFi. Although they may not have the authority to set laws in national jurisdictions, these bodies codify standards and best practices that guide policy. The relevant set of SSBs and reports that pertain to DeFi is described in Table 4.2 in Chapter 4.

5.2.1   How this Chapter Is Organized

We'll organize this chapter in three parts. First, we'll cover a few key topics in crypto regulation to get our feet wet. We'll take a whirlwind tour to answer these four key questions: What do regulators want? Are tokens securities? What is the travel rule? Can banks hold crypto?

Second, we will examine how regulation is being influenced globally by SSBs and their efforts to define regulation for the industry. We will look at the European Union's MiCA, being a key piece of legislation that will be the first cross-jurisdictional regulatory and supervisory framework for crypto-assets. We'll also cover the key issues for crypto regulation in the United States.

Third, we'll take a specific look at DeFi regulation. We will explore how two major categories in DeFi, DEXs and stablecoins, are being regulated and what discussions are taking place.

It is important to note that much of the ongoing work with crypto regulation is focused on CeFi, or centralized crypto. This is a logical starting point, as exchanges are a big on-ramp for consumers into the crypto world. Since the key personnel involved in CeFi are known, it is also much easier to regulate.

DeFi regulation is a subset of the larger field of crypto regulation, which is currently undergoing significant changes and developments. As the field of crypto regulation continues to evolve, DeFi regulation is likely to catch up and become more clearly defined.

5.3   What Regulators Want

Does that legitimize something that's inherently purely speculative? And in fact, slightly crazy? Or are we better off just providing ultra clarity as to what's an unregulated market and if you go in, you go in at your own risk. I lean a bit more towards the latter view. And then if crypto or blockchain or any of the parts of that ecosystem would like to do things that traditional finance is doing, you apply exactly the same regulations to that. Capital, liquidity, reserve backing, exactly the same regulations. So people are very clear. There is one regulatory system for everything. And if you're outside of the regulatory system, buyer beware.

—Tharman Shanmugaratnam, Past Chairman, Monetary Authority of Singapore[2]

The above quote from Mr. Shanmugaratnam sums up the challenge of regulators efforts to regulate crypto. Regulating crypto legitimizes it, but not regulating it drives it offshore and outside the oversight and control of regulators.

Of course, DeFi is more than just speculative activity. Stablecoin regulation, for instance, paves the way for FinTech applications to incorporate stablecoins and other forms of digital money.

Regulators have a significant role to play in balancing innovation and preventing financial misconduct while making policy decisions that shape the future of the financial industry. They must keep up with an industry that innovates at breakneck speed and find ways to draft policies that accommodate future innovation. They also have to monitor the global regulatory environment and make sure that their policies are aligned with other countries.

Crypto presents an ideology that directly opposes the authority and legitimacy of central banks, which can cause a spirited form of innovation that does not buy into the norms of central banking, regulation, and authoritarian forms of government.

Before crypto, regulators were already aware of FinTech, and the Bali FinTech Agreement is a high-level vocalization of how regulators view FinTech and how policy should be implemented. However, crypto takes FinTech to a deeper level with potentially greater consequences. While FinTech focused on accepting online payments and performing banking transactions through applications, crypto delved into the essence of money itself.

In other words, pre-crypto FinTech apps stored money on centralized ledgers, but crypto enabled money to be stored on decentralized ledgers, introducing various potentials and risks.

Regulators are paying closer attention to the growing involvement of private sector companies in building payment systems in a society that is increasingly cashless. In China, the PBOC has stated that the e-CNY has been developed to serve as a backup for Alipay and WeChat Pay, which collectively hold 98% of the mobile payments market. To promote competition and offer consumers more options, FinTech infrastructure systems must be open and interoperable to private sector companies. Blockchain-based systems could play a major role in these FinTech infrastructure systems.

Regulators need to determine their jurisdictions. In the United States, securities, commodities, and banking regulators have jurisdiction at the federal or state level. Due to the multifaceted nature of crypto-assets that span characteristics of securities and commodities, various regulatory bodies in the United States have jurisdiction over crypto. This complex web of regulation and lack of clarity has been identified by some[3] as part of the problem that led to the FTX collapse and subsequent losses from crypto consumers.

In March 2022, US President Biden signed the Executive Order on Ensuring Responsible Development of Digital Assets, which outlined a whole-of-government approach to consumer protection, financial stability, illicit finance, and digital asset innovation. The Executive Order provides for an interagency process to coordinate between the various regulatory bodies and relevant agencies.

In contrast, other countries like Singapore have only one regulator. The Monetary Authority of Singapore (MAS) has been able to move quickly to create a clear regulatory framework around crypto-assets, making Singapore a popular jurisdiction for crypto companies.

5.4   Are Tokens Securities?

The Howey test was established by a US Supreme Court case in 1946 and consists of four criteria to determine whether an investment contract exists. The four criteria are

1. An investment of money,
2. A common enterprise,
3. Expectation of profit, and
4. Derived from the efforts of others.

For an instrument to be considered a security, all four criteria must be fulfilled. In June 2018, William Hinman, the Director of the Division of Corporation

Finance at the SEC, gave a speech that delves into how securities laws apply to digital assets. He discussed the decentralized nature of digital assets and how they impact the Howey test and securities law.

> But this also points the way to when a digital asset transaction may no longer represent a security offering. If the network on which the token or coin is to function is sufficiently decentralized – where purchasers would no longer reasonably expect a person or group to carry out essential managerial or entrepreneurial efforts – the assets may not represent an investment contract. Moreover, when the efforts of the third party are no longer a key factor for determining the enterprise's success, material information asymmetries recede. As a network becomes truly decentralized, the ability to identify an issuer or promoter to make the requisite disclosures becomes difficult, and less meaningful.
>
> And so, when I look at Bitcoin today, I do not see a central third party whose efforts are a key determining factor in the enterprise. The network on which Bitcoin functions is operational and appears to have been decentralized for some time, perhaps from inception. Applying the disclosure regime of the federal securities laws to the offer and resale of Bitcoin would seem to add little value. And putting aside the fundraising that accompanied the creation of Ether, based on my understanding of the present state of Ether, the Ethereum network and its decentralized structure, current offers and sales of Ether are not securities transactions.[4]

This speech was effectively an announcement that the SEC would not be treating Bitcoin or Ether as securities. Hinman also provided a list of questions that analyze in greater detail this material point around "from the efforts of others" and decentralization.

The ongoing high-profile case on XRP is also illustrative of this issue. In December 2020, the SEC sued Ripple Labs, alleging that the firm raised over US$1.3b through "an unregistered, ongoing digital asset securities offering." The SEC claims that XRP is a security because it has not been used as a currency, there was no non-investment use for XRP, and that it was being generated and distributed by Ripple Labs in a centralized manner. Ripple Labs, on the other hand, argues that XRP is a utility token, citing parts of Hinman's speech.

5.5 The Travel Rule

The travel rule is a significant regulation in the realm of crypto-assets and its implementation globally is currently ongoing. But what is the travel rule exactly?

In 1995, the US Federal Reserve and FinCEN (Financial Crimes Enforcement Network) issued a rule that required financial institutions to collect, retain, and transmit identifying information of senders and recipients of fund transfers, including names, addresses, national identification numbers, place and date of birth, and account numbers. This rule was related to information required with fund transfers and is commonly known as the travel rule.

The information "travels" with the transaction from bank to bank until the funds reach the final recipient, hence the name. In the banking network, the SWIFT system, along with messaging standards such as ISO 15022/20022, is used to comply with this requirement.

The Financial Action Task Force (FATF) is an intergovernmental body established by the G7 to combat money laundering and illicit financing. In October 2018, the FATF updated its standards to Virtual Assets (VAs) and Virtual Asset Service Providers (VASPs) to comply with existing Anti-Money Laundering/Combating the Financing of Terrorism (AML/CFT) requirements.

As per the FATF guidance document,[5] a "virtual asset" is defined as:

> a digital representation of value that can be digitally traded or transferred and can be used for payment or investment purposes. Virtual assets do not include digital representations of fiat currencies, securities, and other financial assets that are already covered elsewhere in the FATF Recommendations.

"Virtual asset service providers" are defined as:

> any natural or legal person who is not covered elsewhere under the Recommendations and as a business conducts one or more of the following activities or operations for or on behalf of another natural or legal person:
> i. Exchange between virtual assets and fiat currencies;
> ii. Exchange between one or more forms of virtual assets;
> iii. Transfer of virtual assets;
> iv. Safekeeping and/or administration of virtual assets or instruments enabling control over virtual assets;
> v. Participation in and provision of financial services related to an issuer's offer and/or sale of a virtual asset.

Under these guidelines, most fiat–crypto and crypto–crypto exchanges would be considered VASPs. Custodial wallets, token issuers, payment facilitators, and Bitcoin ATMs would also be considered as VASPs.

With DeFi applications, the FATF says:

> A DeFi application (i.e. the software program) is not a VASP under the FATF standards, as the Standards do not apply to underlying software or technology (see paragraph 82 below). However, creators, owners and operators or some other persons who maintain control or sufficient influence in the DeFi

arrangements, even if those arrangements seem decentralized, may fall under the FATF definition of a VASP where they are providing or actively facilitating VASP services. This is the case, even if other parties play a role in the service or portions of the process are automated.

The travel rule will require most crypto exchanges to comply with AML/CFT requirements in the near future. However, there is currently no equivalent to SWIFT for crypto. Some solutions in the market include OpenVASP, TRP, TRUST, TRNow, Sygna Bridge, TRISA, Shyft, TransactID, VerifyVASP, and Notabene. Complying with the travel rule will be challenging for both exchanges and their customers due to increased costs and the requirements for obtaining and safeguarding sensitive customer data.

The travel rule applies to transactions over US$1,000 or EUR 1,000 under the current FATF guidelines. The travel rule also doesn't apply to unhosted wallets, that is, wallets that are not maintained by VASPs and / or financial institutions.

Another issue is the "VASP Discovery Problem," where the originating VASP needs to identify whether the beneficiary is also a VASP based on their address. Since each VASP may use different technical solutions or networks, some have proposed a global database of VASPs to address this problem.

5.6 Prudential Treatment of Crypto-asset Exposures

The question of whether banks can hold crypto-assets has led to concerns about how holding crypto-assets fits into the existing regulatory and risk controls that banks currently operate under. The Basel Committee on Banking Supervision (BCBS) is the primary global standard setter for the prudential regulation of banks and provides a forum for regular cooperation on banking supervisory matters. Its members comprise central banks and bank supervisors from 28 jurisdictions. The framework that governs banks globally is called Basel III, which is the third iteration of the Basel Accord. This framework sets international standards for the regulation, supervision, and risk management of banks worldwide.

In December 2022, the BCBS published its finalized prudential standard on crypto-asset exposures for banks, SCO60. This standard provides guidance to banks on the prudential treatment of crypto-asset exposures. It sets out capital and liquidity requirements for banks that hold crypto-assets, as well as outlining how banks should manage the risks associated with holding crypto-assets.

The standard requires banks to assign risk-weightings to their crypto-asset exposures, which will determine the amount of capital they need to hold against these exposures. Banks are also required to have robust risk management systems in place to identify, assess, and manage the risks associated with holding crypto-assets.

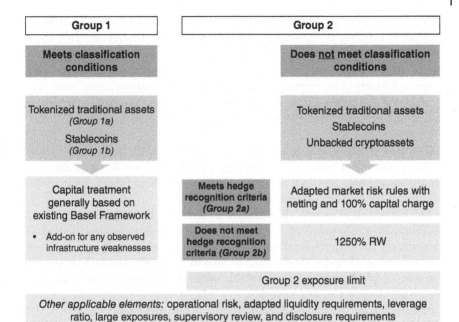

Figure 5.1 Crypto-asset classification under SCO60.
Source: https://www.bis.org/bcbs/publ/d533.pdf

Figure 5.1 is a high-level overview of SCO60 and its classification and treatment of crypto-assets.

Crypto-assets are categorized into two groups. Group 1 includes tokenized traditional assets and stablecoins, which are generally treated based on the existing Basel framework. Group 1 crypto-assets must meet classification conditions. On the other hand, Group 2 consists of everything else that does not meet the classification conditions, and they may be subject to the highest risk weight in the Basel framework, which is 1250%.

Group 1 crypto-assets comprise of Group 1a (Tokenized traditional assets) and Group 1b (Stablecoins). Group 1 crypto-assets must meet all four classification conditions, which are:

Classification condition 1: The crypto-asset is either: (i) a tokenised traditional asset; or (ii) has a stabilisation mechanism that is effective at all times in linking its value to a traditional asset or a pool of traditional assets (i.e. reference asset(s)).

Classification condition 2: All rights, obligations and interests arising from the crypto-asset arrangement are clearly defined and legally enforceable in all the jurisdictions where the asset is issued and redeemed. In addition, the applicable legal framework(s) ensure(s) settlement finality. Banks are required to conduct a legal review of the crypto-asset arrangement to ensure this condition is met, and make the review available to their supervisors upon request.

Classification condition 3: The functions of the crypto-asset and the network on which it operates, including the distributed ledger or similar technology on which it is based, are designed and operated to sufficiently mitigate and manage any material risks.

Classification condition 4: Entities that execute redemptions, transfers, storage or settlement finality of the crypto-asset, or manage or invest reserve assets, must: (i) be regulated and supervised, or subject to appropriate risk management standards; and (ii) have in place and disclose a comprehensive governance framework.[6]

Group 1a crypto-assets, tokenized traditional assets, are "digital representations of traditional assets using cryptography, DLT or similar technology to record ownership," and "pose the same level of credit and market risk as the traditional (non-tokenised) form of the asset."[7]

The definition of Group 1b, Stablecoins, specifies the requirements of the stabilization mechanisms of the stablecoins. They must be designed to be redeemable for a predefined amount of a reference asset (peg value) and be "effective at all times." Banks must be able to "verify the ownership rights of the reserve assets upon which the stable value of the crypto-asset is dependent," with a monitoring framework.

Stablecoins must also pass a redemption risk test and a basis risk test.

The redemption risk test ensures that "the reserve assets are sufficient to enable the crypto-assets to be redeemable at all times, including during periods of extreme stress, for the peg value." The value of the reserve assets must equal or exceed the aggregate peg value of all outstanding crypto-assets at all times. If there are additional credit, market or liquidity risks arising from the reserve assets, the value of the reserve assets must be overcollateralized.

Reserve assets must be managed and invested with an explicit legally enforceable objective of ensuring all crypto-assets can be redeemed promptly at the peg value. A robust operational risk and resilience framework must ensure the availability and safe custody of the reserve assets. The reserve assets must be subject to an independent external audit at least annually.

The basis risk test monitors the deviation of the stablecoin from the peg value over time. This is defined by [(peg value − market value) / peg value] in basis points. To fully pass the basis risk test, the stablecoin must not deviate more than 10bps more than 3 times in the last year. If the deviation exceeds more than 20bps over 10 times in the last year, it is deemed to have failed.

Issuers of stablecoins must also be supervised and regulated by a supervisor that applied prudential capital and liquidity requirements.

Algorithmic stablecoins are not considered stablecoins under Group 1.

As mentioned earlier, Group 2 consists of crypto-assets that do not fulfill the classification conditions of Group 1.

Group 2a allows for a specific set of capital requirements (specified in detail in 60.61–60.87), provided it meets three criteria which stipulate derivatives, minimum liquidity, and sufficient data. (60.60).

Group 2b crypto-assets are subject to a 1250% risk weight (RW) to either the absolute value of the long positions or the short positions in the crypto-asset, whichever is greater. Based on a 10% capital adequacy requirement, a bank will be required to hold US$125 of capital against an exposure of US$100 to a Group 2b crypto-asset.

A bank's total exposure to Group 2 crypto-assets must not be higher than 1% of the bank's Tier 1 capital at all times.

The implementation of SCO60 is targeted by 1 January 2025.

5.7 SSBs, United States and European Union

The Financial Stability Board (FSB) is an international organization established by the G20 to monitor and make recommendations about the global financial system. In October 2022, the FSB published a document called "Regulation, Supervision and Oversight of Crypto-Asset Activities and Markets." The document contains nine high-level proposed recommendations for the regulation, supervision, and oversight of crypto-asset activities and markets. It also includes a summary of the crypto-asset-related initiatives undertaken by other SSBs, such as the BCBS, CPMI, IOSCO, and FATF, and a survey of the current state of crypto-asset regulation from 24 FSB members and 24 RCG (regional consolidated group) members.

Overall, the FSB report provides a good starting point for understanding crypto-asset regulation from a top-down perspective. The report identifies the challenges and issues related to the implementation of crypto-asset regulation and supervision, including:

• Regulatory powers and their reach;
• Gaps and challenges in the application of regulatory powers;
• Challenges involving decentralized technology;
• Cross-border challenges;
• Risks relating to wallets, custody; and
• Risks relating to trading, lending and borrowing activities.

The nine proposed recommendations are as follows:

1. Authorities should have the appropriate powers and tools, and adequate resources, to regulate, supervise, and oversee crypto-asset activities and markets, including crypto-asset issuers and service providers, as appropriate.
2. Authorities should apply effective regulation, supervision, and oversight to crypto-asset activities and markets – including crypto-asset issuers and service providers – proportionate to the financial stability risk they pose, or potentially pose, in line with the principle "same activity, same risk, same regulation."

3. Authorities should cooperate and coordinate with each other, both domestically and internationally, to foster efficient and effective communication, information sharing and consultation in order to support each other as appropriate in fulfilling their respective mandates and to encourage consistency of regulatory and supervisory outcomes.

4. Authorities, as appropriate, should require that crypto-asset issuers and service providers have in place and disclose a comprehensive governance framework. The governance framework should be proportionate to their risk, size, complexity, and systemic importance, and to the financial stability risk that may be posed by the activity or market in which the crypto-asset issuers and service providers are participating. It should provide for clear and direct lines of responsibility and accountability for the functions and activities they are conducting.

5. Authorities, as appropriate, should require crypto-asset service providers to have an effective risk management framework that comprehensively addresses all material risks associated with their activities. The framework should be proportionate to their risk, size, complexity, and systemic importance, and to the financial stability risk that may be posed by the activity or market in which they are participating. Authorities should, to the extent necessary to achieve regulatory outcomes comparable to those in traditional finance, require crypto-asset issuers to address the financial stability risk that may be posed by the activity or market in which they are participating.

6. Authorities, as appropriate, should require that crypto-asset issuers and service providers have in place robust frameworks for collecting, storing, safeguarding, and the timely and accurate reporting of data, including relevant policies, procedures, and infrastructures needed, in each case proportionate to their risk, size, complexity, and systemic importance. Authorities should have access to the data as necessary and appropriate to fulfill their regulatory, supervisory and oversight mandates.

7. Authorities should require that crypto-asset issuers and service providers disclose to users and relevant stakeholders comprehensive, clear and transparent information regarding their operations, risk profiles, and financial conditions, as well as the products they provide and activities they conduct.

8. Authorities should identify and monitor the relevant interconnections, both within the crypto-asset ecosystem, as well as between the crypto-asset ecosystem and the wider financial system. Authorities should address financial stability risks that arise from these interconnections and interdependencies.

9. Authorities should ensure that crypto-asset service providers that combine multiple functions and activities, for example crypto-asset trading platforms, are subject to regulation, supervision, and oversight that comprehensively address the risks associated with individual functions as well as

the risks arising from the combination of functions, including requirements to separate certain functions and activities, as appropriate.[8]

The key SSBs and their crypto-asset policy initiatives were highlighted:

5.7.1   BCBS: Prudential Treatment on Banks' Crypto-asset Exposures

The BCBS, as covered earlier in this chapter, with SCO60 and prudential treatment of banks crypto-asset exposures.

5.7.2   CPMI – IOSCO: PFMI and Stablecoins

The Bank for International Settlements' Committee on Payments and Market Infrastructures (CPMI) and the International Organization of Securities Commissions (IOSCO) and their joint standards on financial market infrastructures: the Principles for Financial Market Infrastructures (PFMI).

The PFMI are the international standards for FMIs, financial market infrastructures, that is, payment systems, central securities depositories, securities settlement systems, central counterparties, and trade repositories. In particular, in July 2022, the CPMI and IOSCO published guidance on the application of the PFMI to stablecoin arrangements (SAs).[9] The guidance looks to provide clarity to stablecoin arrangements that may be considered systemically important financial market infrastructures. It provides guidance on various principles and key considerations on SA operations including governance, risk management, settlement finality, and money settlements.

It also articulates four factors that authorities should consider in assessing the systemic importance of a stablecoin issuer:

1. Size of the SA;
2. Nature and risk profile of the SA's activity;
3. Interconnectedness and interdependencies of the SA; and
4. Substitutability of the SA.

5.7.3   IOSCO

IOSCO established a board-level FinTech Task Force in March 2022 to develop, oversee, deliver, and implement its regulatory policy agenda in crypto-assets. The FinTech Task Force has two workstreams: a Crypto and Digital Assets workstream, and a DeFi workstream. Both workstreams focus on investor protection and market integrity. The DeFi workstream looks specifically into DeFi, stablecoins, crypto-asset trading, lending and borrowing platforms, as well as interactions of DeFi with broader financial markets.

5.7.4 FATF – AML / CFT

The FATF is the international SSB for AML / CFT issues. We have covered this earlier in the chapter with the Travel Rule.

5.7.5 Survey of Jurisdictions on the State of Crypto-asset Regulation

With reference to Figure 5.2, the majority of jurisdictions (49) surveyed apply existing regulatory standards to crypto-asset activities based on economic functions (e.g., payments, securities, commodities, derivatives). Fewer jurisdictions (21) have in place or will put in place a specific regulatory framework for crypto-assets. It was also found that authorities use different terminology, including "digital asset," "crypto-asset," "virtual asset," and "virtual currency."

Figure 5.3 shows the application based on eight common regulatory themes divided by the four economic functions of crypto-assets. We observe that AML/CFT is the most applied theme, followed by investor protection.

Figure 5.4 from PwC's Global Crypto Regulation Report 2023[10] also is helpful for looking at the status of various jurisdictions globally. China, Qatar, and Saudi Arabia have banned crypto. AML/CFT is the most applied category of regulation, tallying with the FSB survey.

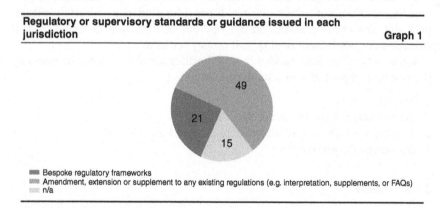

Regulatory or supervisory standards or guidance issued in each jurisdiction   Graph 1

- Bespoke regulatory frameworks
- Amendment, extension or supplement to any existing regulations (e.g. interpretation, supplements, or FAQs)
- n/a

Figure 5.2 Regulatory standards of FSB members.
Source: https://www.fsb.org/2022/10/
regulation-supervision-and-oversight-of-crypto-asset-activities-and-markets-consultative-report/

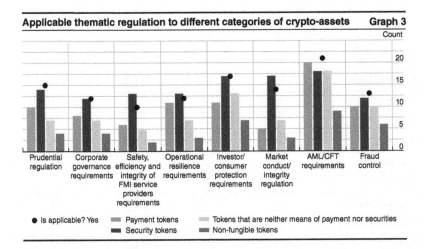

Figure 5.3 Applicable thematic regulation to different categories of crypto-assets.
Source: https://www.fsb.org/2022/10/
regulation-supervision-and-oversight-of-crypto-asset-activities-and-markets-consultative-report/

Jurisdiction	Regulatory framework	AML/CTF	Travel rule	Stablecoins (used for payments)
Jordan	⚠	✅	⚠	⚠
Kuwait	⚠	⚠	⚠	⚠
Luxembourg	◐	✅	◐	◐
Malaysia	✅	✅	✅	⚠
Mauritius	✅	✅	✅	✅
New Zealand	◐	◐	⚠	◐
Oman	⚠	⚠	⚠	⚠
Panama	◐	◐	⚠	⚠
Qatar	⊠	⊠	⊠	⊠
Saudi Arabia	⊠	⊠	⊠	⊠
Singapore	✅	✅	✅	◐
South Africa	◐	✅	◐	◐
Switzerland	✅	✅	✅	✅
Taiwan	⚠	✅	✅	⚠
Turkey	⚠	✅	⚠	⚠
United Arab Emirates	✅	✅	✅	✎

✅ Legislation/Regulation in place   ✎ Pending final legislation ◐ Process initiated or plans communicated
⚠ Regulatory process not initiated ⊠ The country prohibits cryptocurrencies

Figure 5.4 (Continued)

Jurisdiction	Regulatory framework	AML/CTF	Travel rule	Stablecoins (used for payments)
United States	○	✓	✓	✎
United Kingdom	○	✓	✓	✎
Australia	○	✓	○	○
Austria	○	✓	○	○
Bahamas	✓	✓	✓	✓
Bahrain	✓	✓	⚠	⚠
Canada	○	✓	✓	○
Cayman Islands	✓	✓	✓	✓
China (Mainland)	✗	✗	✗	✗
Denmark	○	✓	⚠	⚠
Estonia	✓	✓	○	⚠
France	✓	✓	✓	⚠
Germany	✓	✓	✓	⚠
Gibraltar	✓	✓	✓	✓
Hong Kong	✓	✓	⚠	○
Hungary	○	✓	⚠	⚠
India	⚠	○	⚠	⚠
Italy	○	✓	○	○
Japan	✓	✓	✓	✓

✓ Legislation/Regulation in place   ✎ Pending final legislation   ○ Process initiated or plans communicated
⚠ Regulatory process not initiated   ✗ The country prohibits cryptocurrencies

Figure 5.4 International crypto regulation.
Source: https://www.pwc.com/gx/en/new-ventures/cryptocurrency-assets/pwc-global-crypto-regulation-report-2023.pdf

5.8   European Union – MiCA

The Market in Crypto-Assets Regulation (MiCA) is a pioneering regulatory framework that seeks to create a unified market for crypto-assets within the European Union. First proposed in 2020 as a response to Facebook's Libra stablecoin initiative, MiCA is a significant piece of legislation that will impact one of the largest markets in the world, covering the European Union's population of 450 million.

MiCA is expected to be ratified by the European Parliament in early 2023 and to come into force in 2024. This framework will introduce new rules and requirements for crypto-asset issuers, service providers, and traders operating within the European Union.

MiCA's scope is comprehensive, covering all business activities related to crypto-assets, including issuance, trading, custody, and other crypto-asset related services. This is similar to the approach taken by MiFID, a landmark financial regulation law that harmonized regulation across the European Union for financial services.

MiCA also applies to non-EU crypto-asset firms serving EU customers, with the exception of "reverse solicitation," where the EU customer takes the exclusive initiative of soliciting the firm. This means that firms based outside the European Union will need to comply with MiCA if they wish to offer their services to EU customers.

Crypto-asset issuers (CAIs) have to meet several obligations when issuing a crypto-asset, including

- Publishing a whitepaper (akin to a prospectus);
- Disclosing information on issuer, the crypto-asset project or token, risks and the rights and obligations attached to the crypto-asset;
- Disclose adverse environmental and climate-related impacts of the consensus mechanism used to issue the crypto-asset;
- Approved market communication;
- Legal entity registration, financial condition of last 3 years, details of natural / legal persons involved;
- Brief description of the project, characteristics of the token, key features on utility, tokenomics;
- Business plan and use of funds;
- Disclosures on risks; and
- Restrictions on transferability of tokens.

CASPs (Crypto-asset service providers) are defined as "any person whose occupation or business is the provision of one or more crypto-asset services to third parties on a professional basis."[11] CASPs must have a registered office in an EU member state and must have authorization to provide regulated crypto-asset services from an NCA (National Competent Authority).

Authorization obtained in one member state allows CASPs to passport its regulated activities across other member states.

CASPs must

- Abide by general conduct of business rules;
- Act fairly and in the interest of clients;
- Show prudential capital and governance, risk, compliance and internal organizational requirements;
- Maintain robust and secure standards of safekeeping of assets and funds;
- Provide prompt and equitable complaint handling procedures;

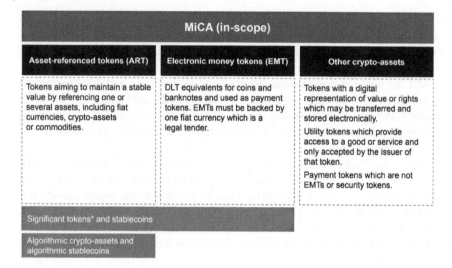

Figure 5.5 Crypto-asset categories in MiCA.
Source: https://www.pwc.com/gx/en/new-ventures/cryptocurrency-assets/pwc-global-crypto-regulation-report-2023.pdf

- Identify, prevent, and manage conflicts of interest promptly and fairly;
- Monitor outsourcing risk and comply with ongoing outsourcing requirements; and
- Comply with other policies including orderly wind-down and exits from markets.

CASPs offering custody must establish custody policy with segregated holdings, daily reporting of holdings, and have liability for loss of client's crypto-assets in the event of malfunctions or cyberattacks. They must also place client funds with a central bank or credit institution.

MiCA defines[12] three types of crypto-assets (Figure 5.5):

1. Asset-referenced tokens (ART)
   "a type of crypto-asset that purports to maintain a stable value by referring to the value of several fiat currencies that are legal tender, one or several commodities or one or several crypto-assets, or a combination of such assets."
2. Electronic money tokens (EMT)
   "a type of crypto-asset the main purpose of which is to be used as a means of exchange and that purports to maintain a stable value by referring to the value of a fiat currency that is legal tender."
3. Utility tokens
   "a type of crypto-asset which is intended to provide digital access to a good or service, available on DLT, and is only accepted by the issuer of that token."

ARTs and EMTs are variants of stablecoins. The definition of EMTs is narrower and must reference a single fiat currency, whereas ARTs can reference several fiat currencies, commodities, or crypto-assets. CAIs of EMTs are required to be authorized as credit institutions (banks) or electronic money institutions.

ARTs and EMTs may also be designated as "significant" by the European Banking Authority (EBA). This criterion includes: the number of holders, market capitalization, gatekeeper status of their issuer, and interconnectedness with the financial system.

Issuers of significant ARTs (sARTs) and EMTs (sEMTs) will be subject to more rigid rules such as capital requirements, and will generally be supervised by the EBA instead of national authorities.

What about DeFi and MiCA? Section 12a states:

> This Regulation applies to natural, legal persons and other undertakings and the activities and services performed, provided or controlled, directly or indirectly, by them, including when part of such activity or services is performed in a decentralised way. Where crypto-asset services as defined in this Regulation are provided in a fully decentralised manner without any intermediary they do not fall within the scope of this Regulation.

MiCA appears to make a distinction between centralized entities providing services and decentralized protocols providing services, the latter being out of scope. Tarik Roukny, Assistant Professor of Finance at the Faculty of Economics and Business, KU Leuven, has also weighed in on regulation and supervision of DeFi in a report[13] to the European Commission. Prof. Roukny suggests "new kinds of voluntary regulation" for DeFi, in view of MiCA largely leaving DeFi out-of-scope.

MiCA is an extensive piece of legislation and I can only scratch the surface here. Some other notable points include the prohibition of yield and interest on stablecoins.

MiCA also grants retail holders a right to withdraw from the purchase of such a token on the primary market within 14 days if the respective crypto-asset was not yet traded on a trading platform at the time of purchase.

It remains unclear whether NFTs are in or out of scope. The initial press release from the EC in June 2022[14] stated:

> Non-fungible tokens (NFTs), i.e. digital assets representing real objects like art, music and videos, will be excluded from the scope except if they fall under existing crypto-asset categories. Within 18 months the European Commission will be tasked to prepare a comprehensive assessment and, if deemed necessary, a specific, proportionate and horizontal legislative proposal to create a regime for NFTs and address the emerging risks of such a new market.

Nonetheless subsequent comments by Peter Kerstens, an EU official and adviser for technological innovation at the European Commission, have cast doubt on the exclusion.[15]

MiCA also looks to curb the market share of non-euro stablecoins where it has jurisdiction, with a particular view of US stablecoin dominance. Stablecoins not denominated in the euro will be limited to 1 million transactions and 200 million euros (US\$196m) in transaction value when marketed in the eurozone.[16]

Article 68 also looks to prohibit CASPs from trading "privacy tokens" such as Zcash, Monero, and Dash. It states:

> The operating rules of the trading platform for crypto-assets shall prevent the admission to trading of crypto-assets which have [an] inbuilt anonymisation function unless the holders of the crypto-assets and their transaction history can be identified by the crypto-asset service providers that are authorised for the operation of a trading platform for crypto-assets or by competent authorities.[17]

5.9 United States

The United States' global superpower status is evident in the world of cryptocurrency. This is exemplified by the fact that 98% of stablecoins by volume are denominated in US dollars. The direction that the United States takes in terms of crypto, DeFi, stablecoin, and CBDC policy has a significant impact on policies adopted by other countries worldwide. Many nations view the United States as a leader in the development of their own regulatory frameworks and often look to the United States for guidance.

Nonetheless, the regulatory landscape within the United States is by no means unified. According to a report on the US Financial Regulatory Framework,

> The financial regulatory system has been described as fragmented, with multiple overlapping regulators and a dual state-federal regulatory system. The system evolved piecemeal, punctuated by major changes in response to various historical financial crises. . . . To address the fragmented nature of the system, the Dodd–Frank Act created the Financial Stability Oversight Council (FSOC), a council of regulators and experts chaired by the Treasury Secretary.
>
> —"Who Regulates Whom? An Overview of the
> US Financial Regulatory Framework," Congressional
> Research Service[18]

This fragmentation has been particularly evident in the world of cryptocurrency, where an ongoing regulatory turf war appears to be taking place between the Securities and Exchange Commission (SEC) and the Commodity Futures Trading Commission (CFTC). In July 2022, CFTC Commissioner Caroline Pham criticized the SEC's approach in *SEC v. Wahi*, describing it as a "striking example of regulation by enforcement,"[19] and advocating for a more transparent process. The lack of regulatory clarity in the United States has led to a slow and muddled response, which has appeared to stifle innovation due to the uncertainty it creates. Some industry leaders, such as Coinbase CEO Brian Armstrong, have called for sensible regulation[20] to be created for centralized exchanges to prevent customers from moving to offshore companies with opaque and risky practices, such as the now-defunct FTX.com.

The United States has a dual banking system, with national banks being regulated at the federal level, and state banks regulated by respective states. The primary federal regulators include:

Securities: Securities and Exchange Commission (SEC)
Commodities: Commodity Futures Trading Commission (CFTC)
Banking: Office of the Comptroller of the Currency (OCC), Federal Deposit
   Insurance Corporation (FDIC), Federal Reserve
Anti-Money Laundering / Countering the Financing of Terrorism (AML/CFT):
   Financial Crimes Enforcement Network (FinCEN)

There are also notable state-level regulations, such as the BitLicense issued by the New York State Department of Financial Services (NYSDFS) and Wyoming's legislation allowing for DAO LLCs.

In June 2022, Senators Cynthia Lummis (Republican) and Kirsten Gillibrand (Democrat) introduced the Responsible Financial Innovation Act (RFIA), which seeks to establish a regulatory framework for digital assets in the United States. The RFIA would classify most crypto-assets as commodities, rather than securities, if it is passed by Congress. As a result, the CFTC would be the primary regulator for crypto in the United States, instead of the SEC. The proposed legislation covers a wide range of issues relating to crypto-assets, including taxation, securities, commodities, consumer protection, payments and stablecoins, banking laws, interagency coordination, and further agency research.

Another US Whole-of-Government approach to crypto is the Executive Order on Ensuring Responsible Development of Digital Assets signed by President Joe Biden in March 2022.[21] The Executive Order has six objectives:

1. Consumer and investor protection;
2. US and global financial stability;
3. Mitigation of illicit finance and national security risks;

4. US leadership in global financial system;
5. Access to safe and affordable financial services; and
6. Support of responsible technological innovation in digital assets.

The order calls for an interagency process that involves numerous members of the Executive Branch and relevant federal agencies to work together as necessary to achieve the specified objectives. These members include the Secretary of State, Secretary of the Treasury, Secretary of Defense, Attorney General, Board of Governors of the Federal Reserve System, SEC, CFTC, FDIC, and OCC, among others.

The Executive Order also specifies the Biden Administration's policy on a US CBDC. It includes:

- Prioritizing research and development efforts into potential design and deployment of a US CBDC;
- Showcasing US leadership and participation in international conversations and projects involving CBDCs; and
- Considerations of benefits and risks on interoperability between a US CBDC and other CBDCs.

As part of the EO, three reports[22] from the Secretary of the Treasury were published in September 2022. The EO sets out various timelines for actions, coordinations, and reports for the relevant members of the Executive Branch and federal agencies as part of the six objectives.

The Financial Stability Oversight Council (FSOC) had also published a report on "Digital Asset Financial Stability Risks and Regulation" in September 2022.[23] The report states:

> Crypto-asset activities could pose risks to the stability of the U.S. financial system if their interconnections with the traditional financial system or their overall scale were to grow without adherence to or being paired with appropriate regulation, including enforcement of the existing regulatory structure.

The FSOC report makes several recommendations to ensure appropriate regulation of crypto-asset activities, which include

- Legislation to be passed to allow for rulemaking authority for federal financial regulators over the crypto-asset non-security spot market;
- Steps to address regulatory arbitrage;
- Legislation regarding risks posed by stablecoins;
- Legislation relating to regulators to have visibility and supervision over activities of crypto-asset entities;
- Study of potential vertical integration of crypto-asset firms;

- Bolstering FSOC members capacities relating to data; and
- Enhancing capabilities on analysis, monitoring, supervision, and regulation of crypto-asset activities.

5.10   DeFi Specific Regulation

In this final section, we'll take a look at DEXs and stablecoins, two significant categories within DeFi, and examine some specific regulatory developments.

5.10.1   DEXs

Decentralized exchanges (DEXs) have received less attention from regulators in comparison to centralized exchanges. DEX founders argue that their applications are decentralized and protocol-based. However, regulators have indicated that DEXs are subject to the "same activity, same risk, same regulation" principle.

In January 2022, the Securities and Exchange Commission (SEC) proposed changes to the definition of "exchange" under Rule 3b-16 of the Exchange Act. The new definition would include "systems that offer the use of non-firm trading interest and communication protocols to bring together buyers and sellers of securities,"[24] potentially impacting DEXs and other DeFi applications. Venture capital firm Andreessen Horowitz (a16z) commented on the proposed changes, warning that if they were to apply to DeFi systems, they could have significant and negative consequences for these systems and web3 as a whole.[25] The SEC has previously taken regulatory action against DEX founders, such as in November 2018 when it charged Zachary Coburn, the founder of EtherDelta, for operating an unregistered securities exchange.

In a guidance document from the FATF regarding Virtual Assets and Virtual Asset Service Providers, it states:

> A DeFi application (i.e. the software program) is not a VASP under the FATF standards, as the Standards do not apply to underlying software or technology (see paragraph 82 below). However, creators, owners and operators or some other persons who maintain control or sufficient influence in the DeFi arrangements, even if those arrangements seem decentralized, may fall under the FATF definition of a VASP where they are providing or actively facilitating VASP services. This is the case, even if other parties play a role in the service or portions of the process are automated.[26]

The phrase "sufficient influence" may well be material for key members of the DEXs, and potentially governance token holders. As we've covered before in earlier chapters, governance token holders have an ability to vote on key parameters of these decentralized applications and propose changes to the governance of decentralized applications.

FinCEN's Customer Due Diligence (CDD) rules have four core requirements:

1. Identify and verify the identity of customers.
2. Identify and verify the identity of the beneficial owners of companies opening accounts.
3. Understand the nature and purpose of customer relationships to develop customer risk profiles.
4. Conduct ongoing monitoring to identify and report suspicious transactions and, on a risk basis, to maintain and update customer information.

It also stipulates that "financial institutions will have to identify and verify the identity of any individual who owns 25 percent or more of a legal entity."[27]

As part of these requirements, the CDD rules look to require beneficial owners of DEXs and governance token holders who own 25% or more of total voting power to disclose their name, date of birth, government ID numbers, and addresses.

In September 2021, the *WSJ* reported that Uniswap was being investigated by the SEC. In July 2021, about 100 tokens were delisted on Uniswap, in what appears to be a result of regulatory pressure[28] and the tokens in question being under the purview of the CFTC or the SEC. The delisting was made without a governance vote, causing some[29] to question the decentralized ideal of DEXs.

5.10.2 Stablecoins

The regulation of stablecoins has been one of the fastest evolving areas in DeFi, given its systemic importance, as we discussed earlier. Currently, stablecoins are predominantly used as a store of value and trading against other crypto-assets on exchanges. This is especially useful for crypto-exchanges that lack a fiat on-off ramp. However, if stablecoins start to be used for payments, their significance will grow.

The Libra project (later renamed to Diem) by Facebook (now Meta) sparked off a global regulatory response from the highest levels and catalyzed serious discussions around CBDCs. Even though Diem has since been shut down, parts of its architecture might be used in systems going forward. We will take a closer look at Libra in the beginning of the next chapter. The collapse of UST (a stablecoin backed by seigniorage of another crypto-asset, LUNA) was also a significant watershed event in stablecoins, prompting increased scrutiny of stablecoin issuance and types.

Among others, US Treasury Secretary and former Federal Reserve chair Janet Yellen called for regulation of digital assets[30] and governments and central banks are rapidly developing CBDCs.

Stablecoin regulation already exists by means of SCO60 (the BCBS prudential standard on crypto-asset exposures for banks), MiCA, and US-specific regulation (with the NYDFS and money transmitter licenses). The PFMI (Principles for Financial Market Infrastructures) has provided specific guidance on stablecoin issuers, in particular on systemically important stablecoins.

Singapore, a proactive regulatory mover, has finalized its regulatory approach for stablecoins as of August 2023.[31] The regulation will create a new "Single Currency Stablecoin (SCS) Framework," which complements the existing "Digital Payment Token Service Provider" regulatory framework. The SCS framework outlines the criteria that stablecoins must meet to be classified as an SCS. These include:

- They must be pegged to a single G10 currency or SGD;
- Reserve assets must be marked-to-market daily, be equivalent to 100% par value of stablecoins in circulation, and comprise of cash, cash equivalents, or debt securities (<3m tenure) issued by central bank or government of pegged currency or >AA- rated institution of governmental and international character;
- Regulated issuers must obtain a major payment institution (MPI) license with the MAS;
- Regulated issuers have to meet ML/TF requirements, tech and cyber risk management applicable to regulated payment service providers;
- Regulated issuers must honor redemptions in 5 business days; and
- Regulated issuers must publish a white paper on the stablecoin stipulating rights, risks, and other pertinent information.

At time of writing, there are three entities (Circle, Paxos, and StraitsX) who currently hold a Major Payment Institution (MPI) License with MAS for DPT and other payment services, though not specifically licensed yet for the activity of stablecoin issuance.

Upon a cursory observation of the criteria in SCO60 and Singapore's regulation, it is clear that stablecoin norms are developing. For example, there are emerging standards regarding redemption, reserve requirements, and what stablecoins can represent. This is a positive development in the post-Terra environment. As stablecoins become more regulated, they will become more clearly defined, with clearer labeling for consumers. Singapore's law will allow stablecoins regulated under MAS' stablecoin framework to be labelled as "MAS-regulated stablecoins," including by issuers and intermediaries such as exchanges, to differentiate stablecoins regulated for their value stability and those that are not.

It's also worth noting that algo stablecoins are not considered stablecoins at all. If algo stables continue to develop, they may well be limited to functioning only within the realm of cryptocurrency.

Most major stablecoin issuers such as Circle, Paxos, and Gemini are headquartered in the United States, particularly in New York, which is renowned for its reputation as a financial hub. In New York, the New York Department of Financial Services (NYDFS) has issued guidance on two possible options for regulating virtual currency issuers[32]: BitLicense or the limited purpose trust company provisions of the New York Banking law. Additionally, these issuers are regulated by the Financial Crimes Enforcement Network (FinCEN) for Anti-Money Laundering and Countering the Financing of Terrorism.

The Dodd–Frank Act was passed in the wake of the subprime mortgage crisis to prevent future crises. One of its key provisions is the designation of certain banks as "systemically important financial institutions" (SIFIs), subject to stricter regulations and oversight.

Under Dodd–Frank, banks with more than US$50 billion in assets are automatically designated as SIFIs. By this threshold, stablecoins such as USDT (market cap: US$71b) and USDC (market cap: US$43b) would be or close to being considered SIFIs, subject to additional capital and liquidity requirements, stress tests, and other regulations aimed at reducing the risk of their failure and minimizing the impact on the broader financial system if they do fail.

Among the major stablecoins, Tether stands out as the outlier. It currently has the most in circulation, and it has been at the center of numerous regulatory actions and accusations. These include allegations that its tokens are not fully backed by reserves, that reserves have been used to cover shortfalls in Bitfinex (its sister company), and that Tether has been used to manipulate the price of Bitcoin.

The fact that Tether is not regulated and still maintains a large float is intriguing. It raises the question of whether regulation is a bug or a feature. While most other USD stablecoin issuers are licensed in New York under the purview of the NYDFS, Tether is not regulated by US regulators in terms of deposits, although it is registered with FinCEN.

At present, USDT has the highest market cap amongst USD stablecoins. Therefore, USDT users are likely to view Tether's lack of regulatory presence in the United States as a feature, not a bug. Unlike Circle or Paxos, if US regulators decided to crack down on US stablecoins as a whole, USDT might be less risky. Nevertheless, the lack of regulatory supervision raises many questions about the stability of USDT as a whole. One can only surmise that to USDT users, the benefits outweigh the risks.

There have been several accusations against Tether in recent years, including the New York Attorney General's case against iFinex (Tether's parent company) in April 2019. The case alleged that reserves were lost with Crypto Capital

Corp, a now defunct Panama-based payments processor, and that Tether was used to cover up the shortfall. The case was settled in February 2021 with an US$18.5-million fine. Additionally, there have also been accusations that USDT is not fully backed by reserves and that Tether has been used to manipulate the price of Bitcoin. In March 2023, the Wall Street Journal reported that Tether had used falsified documents and shell companies in order to obtain bank accounts.[33]

The US banking regulator, the OCC, has issued guidance to clarify the rules around banks holding reserves for stablecoin issuers and hosting nodes in L1s / L2s as well as permissioned chains.

Stablecoin issuers often seek to hold assets in national regulated banks to provide assurance to users that the stablecoin is fully backed by sufficient assets. The October 2020 guidance clarified that "a national bank may hold such stablecoin 'reserves' as a service to bank customers."[34]

In January 2021, the OCC issued another guidance, stating that "National banks and Federal savings associations (collectively referred to as 'banks') may use new technologies, including INVNs (independent node verification networks) and related stablecoins, to perform bank-permissible functions, such as payment activities."[35]

INVNs refer to blockchains, and the OCC's definition does not distinguish between public and permissioned chains. These guidelines pave the way for banks to use stablecoins and blockchains for payments.

The Blockchain Association, a pro-crypto lobby group in the United States, hailed this as "a giant advance for crypto" as it paves the way for these networks to be a formal part of the US financial infrastructure. They also infer that the OCC's letter indicates that "blockchains have the same status as other global financial networks, such as SWIFT, ACH, and FedWire."[36]

The Bank for International Settlements (BIS) has also released reports regarding stablecoins and regulations. In "Stablecoins: Risks, Potential and Regulation," the BIS discusses the potentials of stablecoins and appropriate regulatory solutions for them, such as "embedded supervision." The report also raises questions about CBDCs being able to fulfill the same functions as stablecoins.

5.11   Chapter Summary

In conclusion, the regulatory landscape for DeFi is still evolving as regulators try to catch up with their understanding of this new field. While most regulators have a good understanding of crypto, they have yet to fully grasp the concept of DeFi. Unfortunately, the recent collapses of Terra, 3AC, and FTX have created a challenging regulatory environment for crypto. However, it is clear that the DeFi industry must work closely with regulators to ensure that innovative financial products can continue to emerge in a way that is responsible, compliant, and in the best interest of all stakeholders involved.

In the next chapter, we will shift our focus to the centralized world of central banking and explore central bank digital currencies (CBDCs). We will examine the similarities and differences between CBDCs and stablecoins, as well as the role of blockchain technology in the development of CBDCs.

Notes

1. https://decrypt.co/70045/cz-pressed-on-binance-headquarters-at-ethereal-summit
2. https://www.straitstimes.com/world/regulate-cryptocurrency-to-guard-against-money-laundering-davos-panel
3. https://twitter.com/brian_armstrong/status/1590511022104010753
4. https://www.sec.gov/news/speech/speech-hinman-061418
5. https://www.fatf-gafi.org/en/publications/Fatfrecommendations/Guidance-rba-virtual-assets-2021.html
6. https://www.bis.org/basel_framework/chapter/SCO/60.htm?inforce=20250101&published=20221216
7. https://www.bis.org/bcbs/publ/d545.pdf
8. https://www.fsb.org/2022/10/regulation-supervision-and-oversight-of-crypto-asset-activities-and-markets-consultative-report/
9. https://www.bis.org/press/p220713.htm
10. https://www.pwc.com/gx/en/new-ventures/cryptocurrency-assets/pwc-global-crypto-regulation-report-2023.pdf
11. https://www.europarl.europa.eu/doceo/document/CJ12-AM-719852_EN.pdf
12. https://eur-lex.europa.eu/legal-content/EN/TXT/?uri=CELEX%3A52020PC0593
13. https://op.europa.eu/en/publication-detail/-/publication/f689e5b2-4f55-11ed-92ed-01aa75ed71a1/language-en/format-PDF/source-272370364
14. https://www.consilium.europa.eu/en/press/press-releases/2022/06/30/digital-finance-agreement-reached-on-european-crypto-assets-regulation-mica/
15. https://setterwalls.se/en/article/the-upcoming-eu-crypto-asset-regulation-mica-are-nfts-to-be-regulated-like-crypto/#_ftn4
16. https://www.reuters.com/technology/eu-crypto-rules-set-cap-dollar-pegged-stablecoins-2022-10-07/
17. https://eur-lex.europa.eu/legal-content/EN/TXT/?uri=CELEX%3A52020PC0593
18. https://sgp.fas.org/crs/misc/R44918.pdf
19. https://twitter.com/CarolineDPham/status/1550159347984044033
20. https://twitter.com/brian_armstrong/status/1623459318476726272?s=20

21. https://www.whitehouse.gov/briefing-room/presidential-actions/2022/03/09/executive-order-on-ensuring-responsible-development-of-digital-assets/
22. https://home.treasury.gov/news/press-releases/jy0956
23. https://home.treasury.gov/system/files/261/FSOC-Digital-Assets-Report-2022.pdf
24. https://www.sec.gov/rules/proposed/2022/34-94062.pdf
25. https://a16z.com/wp-content/uploads/2022/04/a16z_comment_on_letter_on_file_number_S7-02-22.pdf
26. https://www.fatf-gafi.org/content/dam/fatf/documents/recommendations/Updated-Guidance-VA-VASP.pdf
27. https://www.fincen.gov/resources/statutes-and-regulations/cdd-final-rule#:~:text=The%20CDD%20Rule%20requires%20these,Rule%20has%20four%20core%20requirements
28. https://cointelegraph.com/news/uniswap-delists-100-tokens-from-interface-including-options-and-indexes
29. https://twitter.com/ChainLinkGod/status/1418700216144785410
30. https://www.barrons.com/articles/yellen-crypto-regulation-first-speech-digital-assets-51649328772
31. https://www.mas.gov.sg/publications/consultations/2022/consultation-paper-on-proposed-regulatory-approach-for-stablecoin-related-activities
32. https://www.dfs.ny.gov/virtual_currency_businesses
33. https://www.wsj.com/articles/crypto-companies-behind-tether-used-falsified-documents-and-shell-companies-to-get-bank-accounts-f798b0a5
34. https://www.occ.gov/topics/charters-and-licensing/interpretations-and-actions/2020/int1172.pdf
35. https://www.occ.gov/news-issuances/news-releases/2021/nr-occ-2021-2a.pdf
36. https://twitter.com/BlockchainAssn/status/1346233501604052992?s=20

Part II

DLT in Traditional Finance

6

Central Bank Digital Currencies

6.1 Introduction

CBDC as a new form of money and payment method could potentially facilitate enhancing the resilience of the retail payment system, contribute to a better financial system, improving efficiency of the central bank payment system, and promoting financial inclusion of the society.

—Changchun Mu, Director-General,
Digital Currency Institute of the People's Bank of China,
Theories and Practice of exploring China's e-CNY

Principle 1: Any CBDC should be designed such that it supports the fulfillment of public policy objectives, does not impede the central bank's ability to fulfill its mandate and "does no harm" to monetary and financial stability.

—Public Policy Principles for Retail
Central Bank Digital Currencies, G7 Nations

In this chapter, we will focus on the centralized world and explore how central banks plan to enhance the digital infrastructure that supports monetary policy and money issuance using Central Bank Digital Currencies (CBDCs). It's worth noting that some of these upgrades may not involve the use of blockchain technology. However, CBDCs are a critical topic that will be just as important as DeFi in the coming years. We will also examine the intersections between CBDCs and DeFi.

CBDCs have profound implications, as they can transform the banking and FinTech industries, introduce novel monetary policy tools, and combat illicit activities. They also have the potential to provide a secure and efficient payment system that is faster, less expensive, and more inclusive. They may allow

Decentralizing Finance: How DeFi, Digital Assets, and Distributed Ledger Technology Are Transforming Finance, First Edition. Kenneth Bok.
© 2024 John Wiley & Sons Ltd. Published 2024 by John Wiley & Sons Ltd.

for programmability and the use of smart contracts. CBDCs also could reduce transaction costs and increase the speed of cross-border payments. However, they also pose significant challenges regarding privacy, accessibility, and control.

So what's a CBDC? Let's start with some definitions of CBDCs:

> A digital liability of a central bank that is widely available to the general public.
>
> *—Federal Reserve Board[1]*

> A digital form of central bank money that is different from balances in traditional reserve or settlement accounts i.e., a digital payment instrument, denominated in the national unit of account.
>
> *—Group of central banks (2020)[2]*

A CBDC is essentially a form of money issued by a central bank that exists only in electronic form and can be used for payments and other transactions within an economy.

More technically, CBDCs are a new, third type of M0, after cash and deposits with the central bank.

Money issued by the central bank is considered the safest form of money due to the central bank's role as a lender of last resort and its ability to create fiat money without liquidity or credit risk. Among the three types of tokenized fiat, namely CBDCs, tokenized bank deposits, and stablecoins, CBDCs are the safest to hold, followed by tokenized deposits, and then stablecoins.

These unique characteristics have implications for CBDC designs. Where the three characteristics of money are concerned: CBDCs have little to no impact on the unit of account, but they significantly affect the medium of exchange and store of value functions. Central banks seek to promote the widespread adoption of CBDCs in commerce and payments while minimizing the destabilizing effects of flight-to-safety on commercial banks. That is, when consumers and businesses are presented with an option of either holding commercial bank or central bank money, the preference for the latter could cause capital to move out of commercial banks, causing financial instability and other deleterious effects.

The Bank for International Settlements (BIS) has been at the forefront of CBDC research, publishing several reports on the topic. In their report on foundational principles and core features, the BIS outlines the key characteristics of CBDCs, such as digitality, interoperability, and programmability, and the design choices that central banks need to make to ensure their successful implementation.

At time of writing, the central banks of 114 countries (representing over 95% of global GDP) are exploring CBDCs.[3] As per Figure 6.1, the interest in CBDCs

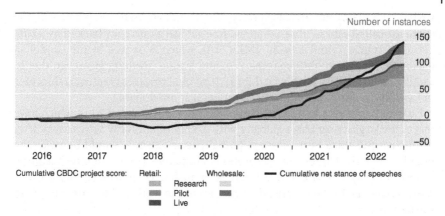

Figure 6.1 Number of CBDC projects by type and status.
Source: BIS, https://www.bis.org/publ/work880.htm

has increased dramatically since 2016. Some notable CBDC projects include the e-CNY by the People's Bank of China, the e-krona by the Sveriges Riksbank of Sweden, and the Sand Dollar by the Central Bank of the Bahamas.

Money is not just a technology but also a social construct, making discussions on CBDCs more complex than those on DeFi. These discussions must carefully negotiate issues around identity, privacy, data protection, and monetary and fiscal policies. Public–private partnerships are necessary to manage these vast systems involved in CBDCs. Additionally, CBDCs raise issues about fractional reserve banking and the relationship between central and commercial banks.

The issues surrounding CBDCs are relevant both domestically and internationally, and have geopolitical implications, particularly in the context of US–China relations and trade.

China is advancing its lead in FinTech, established originally with Alipay and WeChat Pay even further with e-CNY. Due to China's economic heft and its active policy direction on pushing its CBDC, the e-CNY appears to be the most significant CBDC in the coming years.

6.2 Prologue: Libra

The Libra project, later renamed Diem, by Meta (previously Facebook) was a significant catalyst for CBDCs, despite being subsequently canceled. First announced in June 2019, it was a litmus test for how global regulators view the combination of big tech and stablecoins.

Initially, Facebook aimed to create a consortium, which included major FinTech players like Mastercard, Visa, Stripe, PayPal, and Mercado Pago, as well as tech platforms such as Spotify, Uber, and Lyft, to develop a new digital currency called Libra. Libra 1.0 aimed to establish a currency backed by a basket of currencies, similar to the IMF's SDR, which is backed by the US dollar, euro, Chinese renminbi, Japanese yen, and pound Sterling. However, due to significant regulatory pushback, Libra 2.0 pivoted towards creating stablecoins in US dollars, euros, pound sterling, and Singapore dollars.

Facebook intended to integrate this stablecoin with its platforms, which have one of the largest user bases globally, with 2.4 billion monthly active users. If an estimated one-third of its users potentially used Libra, it would be twice the population of the United States. Facebook's initiative would instantly become a significant player in the global financial industry. Furthermore, Libra was a direct challenge to the sovereign currencies of the world, which are integral to the nation-state.

Libra encountered a united front of regulatory opposition. France and Germany jointly agreed to block Libra, stating that "no private entity can claim monetary power, which is inherent to the sovereignty of nations."[4] This was also at a time when Facebook was under scrutiny for privacy issues relating to Cambridge Analytica and alleged Russian interference in the 2016 US elections. Fed Chairman Jerome Powell also stated that "Libra raises many serious concerns regarding privacy, money laundering, consumer protection, and financial stability. These are concerns that should be thoroughly and publicly addressed."

In October 2019, the FSB published a report on regulatory issues of stablecoins in response to the G20's focus on "monitoring developments in crypto-assets," no doubt in response to Libra. It was followed by a subsequent report in April 2020 on the same topic.

Many aspects of Libra are interesting and could resurface in designs of other stablecoin projects. For further reading, see Regulating Libra by Zetzsche, Buckley, and Arner.[5]

6.3 Role of the Central Bank

Most individuals and businesses do not regularly interact with the central bank, which can make its operations appear mysterious and complex. However, the central bank plays a critical role in maintaining the monetary system that governs much of the modern world.

The primary responsibility of the central bank is to promote a stable and healthy economy, which includes managing inflation to stay within its target range and ensuring employment remains robust. In order to achieve these goals, the central bank regulates banks, maintains financial stability, and serves as a lender of last resort. During times of crisis, the central bank can also utilize various monetary policy tools such as quantitative easing and tightening.

In addition to these duties, the central bank is responsible for managing a country's foreign reserves. The relationship between the central bank and commercial banks also enables the creation of money through fractional reserve banking.

6.4 Structure of the Monetary System and a View Towards the Future

Figures 6.2 and 6.3 from the MAS illustrate the structure of the two-tier monetary system, and one possible future of the monetary system with the advent of FinTech platforms, stablecoins, crypto-assets, and CBDCs.

Figure 6.2 illustrates the structure of the two-tier monetary system, where commercial banks hold accounts at the central bank to settle payments with each other. The majority of the money supply is created by commercial banks through fractional reserve banking when they extend loans to households and businesses. Consumers and businesses do not directly interact with the central bank, except when using cash. The banking sector is regulated and supervised by the government, and consumer and business deposits in commercial banks are protected by deposit insurance schemes.

Figure 6.3 represents one potential future model of the monetary system, taking into account three types of disruptions. First, the declining relevance of cash as a medium of exchange is represented by the crosses. Second, the intermediation of FinTech apps between consumers and commercial banks is illustrated by the Technology platforms bar. Lastly, the introduction of digital asset alternatives from foreign central banks, stablecoins, and crypto-assets is represented by the dark square.

The digitization of money has led to the gradual displacement of cash by FinTech and digital banking apps. Professor Kenneth Rogoff's 2016 book, *The Curse of Cash*,[6] is a good reference for this trend. In the book, he argues that

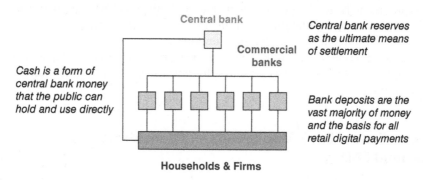

Figure 6.2 The two tier monetary system.

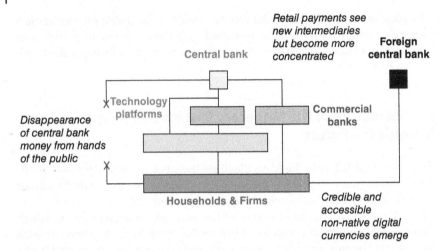

Figure 6.3 A possible future model of the monetary system and an envisioned future model.
Source: MAS. https://www.mas.gov.sg/publications/monographs-or-information-paper/2021/retail-cbdc-paper

large-denomination bills facilitate criminal activities and should be removed from circulation.

The emergence of FinTech platforms and features like Apple Pay has shifted the point of contact with consumers directly to the app, accelerating the decline of cash and creating potential concentration risks with these platforms. Moreover, these platforms utilize user data to make personalized recommendations and credit-score users.

Foreign central banks may soon enable citizens of other countries to access their CBDCs, leading to substitution effects for consumers and businesses who may prefer to hold foreign currency and pay for goods and services in a foreign currency. Similarly, consumers and businesses may opt to use stablecoins and crypto-assets issued by private companies and integrated with FinTech apps. This presents a potential threat to monetary sovereignty, as we previously discussed with Bitcoin and developing economies.

Libra represented the convergence of FinTech and alternative digital asset disruptions, which served as a catalyst for governments and central banks to take action.

6.5 Central Bank Motivations and Considerations around CBDCs

Central Bank Digital Currencies (CBDCs) could mitigate the risks as described in the three types of disruption taking place to the monetary system. CBDCs can function as an upgrade to money and FinTech infrastructure in service to the public good. As a claim on the central bank, CBDCs can reduce risks for consumers utilizing FinTech apps, while also safeguarding privacy and data as a public infrastructure. As a domestic form of digital currency that matches foreign CBDCs in functionality, it can protect monetary sovereignty and the effectiveness of monetary policy.

Central banks and governments may have different policy goals and objectives when it comes to CBDCs and their implementation strategy. This can result in different CBDC designs, as well as decisions about whether or not to implement a CBDC at all. Despite these differences, one of the key advantages of CBDCs is that they can function as a backup or alternative for payment systems within a country. For instance, in China, where Alipay and WeChat Pay hold a combined market share of over 90%, the e-CNY was developed as a redundancy system to provide an alternative payment option in the event of technical or financial failures on the part of these platforms.[7]

In addition to serving as an alternative payment system, CBDCs offer a range of potential benefits and risks that we will explore shortly. However, before delving into these aspects, it is important to distinguish between the two primary types of CBDCs, as they can differ significantly in their design and implementation.

6.6   Retail vs Wholesale CBDCs

There are two main types of CBDCs: wholesale and retail. These CBDCs serve different users and have distinct characteristics. Wholesale CBDCs (W-CBDCs) are networks that connect central banks and commercial banks. In contrast, retail CBDCs (R-CBDCs) are networks that connect central banks, commercial banks, and the general public, including consumers and businesses. R-CBDCs have the potential to have a much greater impact than W-CBDCs, as they introduce new features and capabilities to the financial system. This is because R-CBDCs can provide the general public with direct access to a digital version of central bank money, which can offer a range of benefits and opportunities that were not previously available through traditional payment systems.

6.7   Wholesale CBDCs

W-CBDCs can be seen as an improvement over the current settlement networks connecting central banks, commercial banks, and other financial institutions, such as Real-time Gross Settlement (RTGS) systems. One of the main benefits of W-CBDCs is their potential to facilitate faster and less expensive settlements between financial institutions, particularly in cross-border payments.

There has been a gradual expansion in the scope and vision of W-CBDCs, as evidenced by the three types of W-CBDC projects: domestic, bilateral, and multilateral models. Domestic projects deal with interbank settlements within a country, while bilateral projects pertain to payment corridors that are joint projects between two central banks. Multilateral CBDC arrangements are single systems that multiple countries operate on.

Corridor and multimodel projects are of greater interest due to their potential to address cross-border payment challenges. I should note that most of these projects are still in the pilot or experimental stage as of writing.

6.7.1   Domestic W-CBDCs

Since 2016, there have been several pilots with domestic W-CBDCs, including Project Jasper (Canada), Project Ubin (Singapore), Project Khokha (South Africa), Project Inthanon (Thailand), and Project Salt (Brazil).

The Cross-border Payments Problem

Cross-border payments remain a complex issue for both businesses and individuals looking to pay someone on the other side of the planet. According to a survey conducted by Oliver Wyman and JP Morgan, US$23.5 trillion, or 25% of global GDP, is moved annually, with transaction costs of US$120 billion, which works out to about 50 basis points. On average, *The Economist* estimates that a transaction costs about 7%, and Oliver Wyman estimates US$27. Settlement may take 2–3 days. Compared to many domestic real-time, near-zero cost transfers, this seems archaic. Let's break down why this is the case.

Currently, the model for cross-border payments relies on correspondent banks, which act as intermediaries in the destination country of a payment. For example, if a US citizen wants to pay someone in Zambia, it is very likely the payer's bank will need to use a correspondent bank because they do not have the local currency and do not have a banking license in the destination country. The costs of compliance and maintaining a presence in the destination country can be prohibitively high, so if the US bank has no domestic presence there, they must rely on the correspondent bank. The correspondent bank makes the payment for a fee that is usually passed on to the payer.

FinTech solutions like TransferWise, Mastercard, and Visa are global payment networks that facilitate cross-border, multicurrency transactions. However, it's important to note that they are for-profit companies, unlike public infrastructure designed for the public good. Additionally, while these solutions may work well for individual consumers, they may not be suitable for the high transaction volumes required by multinational corporations.

Banks have an advantage when it comes to facilitating cross-border payments due to their extensive financial resources and experience with regulations and compliance.

Cross-border payments are complex, involving different currencies, time zones, operating procedures, and legal jurisdictions. Some have compared them to connecting different systems of water pipes with varying flow rates and pressures. Intermediaries are required to bridge these systems of payment.

However, this issue is not improving. In fact, a survey conducted by the FSB found a decrease in correspondent banking relationships from 2011 to 2016, leading to longer payment chains and increasing reliance on a smaller number of correspondent banks. The survey identified high costs, low speed, limited access, and lack of transparency as four challenges to cross-border payments. The World Bank has also been addressing this issue through its work in supporting 120 national payment systems over many years.

While initiatives such as Europe's SEPA (Single Euro Payments Area) exist to integrate payment systems, it's unlikely that such initiatives will happen on a global scale due to the absence of a common currency and the lack of legal and regulatory harmonization.

6.7.2 Bilateral W-CBDCs

Bilateral W-CBDCs look to solve cross-border payments between two countries. Since 2019 many pilots have been conducted with payment corridors: joint projects undertaken by two central banks such as Project Jura (France / Switzerland), Project Jasper–Ubin (Canada / Singapore), Project Inthanon–LionRock (Hong Kong / Thailand), Project Stella (Japan / ECB) and Project Aber (Saudi Arabia / UAE).

Cross-border wholesale CBDCs can offer several benefits, such as improved efficiency, security, and liquidity of wholesale payment systems, reduced counterparty risk, enhanced delivery-versus-payment mechanisms, and new forms of conditionality for payments. Most of these systems also run 24/7.

6.7.3 Multilateral CBDCs (mCBDCs)

mCBDCs represent the full suite of capabilities that W-CBDCs have the potential for, including interoperability, smart contract functionality, and 24/7 operations. mCBDCs have the potential to transform the current correspondent banking model into a peer-to-peer model. Oliver Wyman and JP Morgan estimate that mCBDCs have the potential to reduce cross-border fees from US$120b to US$20b annually, an incredible 81%.[8]

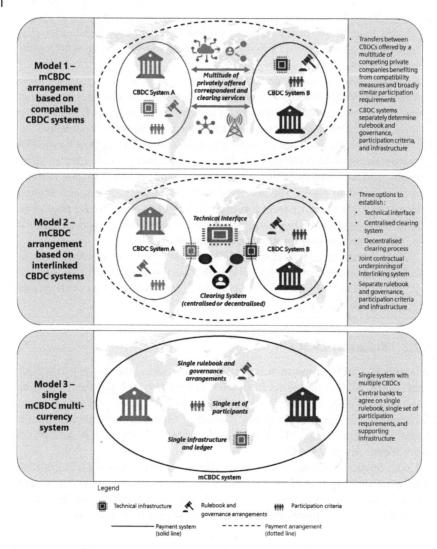

Figure 6.4 mCBDC models.
Source: BIS, https://www.bis.org/publ/othp38.htm

The BIS has conceptually described three types of mCBDC models: compatible arrangements, interlinked arrangements, and single systems – models 1, 2, and 3 respectively in Figure 6.4.

In Figure 6.4, the solid line refers to payment systems and the dotted line represents payment arrangements. The BIS makes a distinction between systems and arrangements. Systems have a single operator that maintains one rulebook and controls access to the system. Arrangements, on the other hand, is a broader term referring to a decentralized network of participants who collaborate to send and receive payments without a multilateral agreement.

Compatible mCBDC arrangements are those in which each country maintains separate CBDC systems. Transfers between systems are made possible by a multitude of private sector companies. This resembles current payment systems where a diversity of private sector companies such as FinTechs and banks compete.

Interlinked mCBDC arrangements have shared technical interfaces and clearing systems to bridge the systems. The FX exchange could be performed by the central banks or private sector companies. Examples of interlinked mCBDCs include Project Jasper–Ubin and Project Jura.

SWIFT has published results of experiments to connect mCBDC systems, solving for both models 1 and 2.

Single system mCBDCs are the deepest level of integration. Central banks adhere to a single rulebook and access criteria. The BIS postulates that the deeper integration allows for greater operational functionality and efficiency, but increased governance and control challenges. There would be a single message standard across the system that would eliminate mismatches. Compliance would also be equivalent across the system.

Examples of single mCBDC systems include the mBridge project from Hong Kong, Thailand, China, and UAE, and Project Dunbar from Australia, Malaysia, Singapore, and South Africa.

In a paper "Towards the holy grail of cross-border payments"[9] from two ECB researchers, Bindseil and Pantelopoulos postulated that "after more than thousand years of search, the holy grail of cross-border payments can be found within the next ten years" from the "interlinking of domestic instant payment systems and future CBDCs, both with a competitive FX conversion layer."

Could mCBDCs be part of this Holy Grail? Let's take a look at one of the most promising mCBDC projects.

6.8 Case Study: Project mBridge

Project mBridge is a joint project between the Bank for International Settlements Innovation Hub Hong Kong Centre (BISIH), the Bank of Thailand (BOT), the Digital Currency Institute of the People's Bank of China (PBCDCI), the Central Bank of the United Arab Emirates (CBUAE), and the Hong Kong Monetary Authority (HKMA) (Figure 6.5). Originally Project Inthanon–LionRock, a bilateral W-CBDC project between the HKMA and BOT, the project was renamed mBridge upon the joining of BISIH, PBCDCI, and CBUAE.

In March 2023, the Reserve Bank of India and CBUAE signed a Memorandum of Understanding on cross-border CBDC transactions for remittances and trade. This paves the way for India to join the mBridge system.

Figure 6.5 Participating commercial banks in the mBridge pilot project.

mBridge is the biggest pilot with W-CBDCs to date, with US$12m issued on the platform, facilitating over 160 payment and FX PvP transactions with over US$22m in value during the six week pilot. The four respective central banks and twenty of the region's largest commercial banks participated in the pilot. Four currencies, THB, HKD, AED, and CNY, were made possible to settle PvP.

The breakthrough here is enabling peer-to-peer transactions between commercial banks in these FX pairs. As briefly mentioned earlier in this chapter, the challenges with cross-border payments facilitated by correspondent banking are manifold. These include the requirement of a domestic presence and the availability of the domestic currency for the final leg of the transaction.

The CLS (Continuous Linked Settlement) system plays an important role in cross-border transactions in reducing counterparty risk, or Herstatt risk. Nonetheless, it only settles 18 major currencies.[10] Taking the mBridge pilot as an example, only HKD is a CLS-settled currency. AED, CNY, and THB are not. Enabling transactions to occur in native currencies without an intermediary currency can help mitigate risks associated with the monetary policies and other financial risks of the intermediary currency's country.

The other reason is China's involvement. All of the big four Chinese banks: ICBC, CCB, ABC, and BoC participated in the pilot. So far the news has been more about China's R-CBDC, the e-CNY, but not much has been said about their W-CBDC, which relates more to externally facing financial activity such as trade and remittances.

China looks to be a leader on CBDCs based on its economic strength. The mBridge project thus could well set mCBDC standards if it gets adopted by other countries. Their R-CBDC and W-CBDC systems will very likely be interoperable and have synergies which will increase transaction speeds, reduce risks, and lower costs.

mBridge thus is an early example of a global trade network outside the US-led financial system and an emerging sign of the multipolar world order.

In terms of technical specifications, while Inthanon–Lionrock Phase 1 used R3's Corda and Inthanon–Lionrock Phase 2 used Hyperledger Besu, the mBridge project uses "a new, fit-for-purpose" private permissioned blockchain that was developed "by central banks, for central banks" called the mBridge ledger. mBridge uses Solidity as its smart contract language and EVM as the blockchain virtual machine.

The pilot highlighted numerous fundamental issues pertaining to cross-border mCBDC systems, comprising policy, legal, and regulatory matters.

One of the most important issues is around monetary sovereignty – for the main reason that mCBDCs could allow foreign banks that are not domiciled or regulated by the domestic regulator / central bank to have access to domestic central bank money.

To mitigate this risk, foreign banks can hold and use domestic CBDCs but only domestic banks can issue and redeem CBDCs against reserve balances. There are also other limits on offshore CBDC circulation and holding restrictions.

The report for mBridge highlights a future roadmap for 2023 and 2024. Some key focus areas include:

- Automated interoperability with domestic payment systems;
- FX price discovery and matching, including additional jurisdictions and participants; and
- Exploring more services that the private sector can add to the platform.

6.9   Retail CBDCs

R-CBDCs represent a new type of M0 that is digitally native, functioning as digital cash issued by the central bank. From a consumer perspective, the experience of using R-CBDCs may not differ significantly from that of using existing digital banking and FinTech apps. In fact, the central bank probably looks to maintain the "singleness" of money – private and public money should all trade at par.

What is M0?

There are several measures of money supply, ranging from M0 to M4. They seek to measure the amounts of money circulating in the economy, ranging from the narrower definitions to the broader. Examples include notes and coins in circulation, bank deposits, and money-market funds. Different countries may have different definitions. The key difference between M0 and M1–4 is that M0 are the liabilities of central banks whereas M1–4 are liabilities of both central and commercial banks.

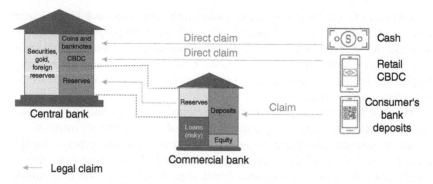

Figure 6.6 The legal claims of cash, R-CBDCs, and consumer bank deposits.
https://www.bis.org/publ/work976.pdf

The key difference is in the risk profile and the interoperability that R-CBDCs represent. R-CBDCs are a liability of the central bank, making the counterparty risk effectively zero. In the course of normal operations, this would not matter as much. But in times of crisis where the bankruptcy of a bank or a FinTech platform is in question, this would make a tremendous difference.

Figure 6.6 illustrates the legal claims of cash, R-CBDCs, and consumer bank deposits. In the case of cash and R-CBDCs, the claim is against the central bank. In the case of consumer bank deposits, the claim is against the commercial bank, which in turn has claims against the central bank on its reserves. As we have seen in the recent case of SVB's collapse, depositors are exposed to the balance sheet of commercial banks and their risk management practices.

Currently, central banks issue two types of M0: physical cash and central bank deposits. The former we are familiar with. Nonetheless, storing large amounts of cash is unfeasible and susceptible to theft. The latter is only available to commercial banks. R-CBDCs would result in the creation of a third type of M0, which would combine the benefits of physical cash with the advantages of digital currency, such as seamless and efficient payments and compatibility with FinTech applications.

The other difference is the interoperability of R-CBDCs and its nature as a public infrastructure. R-CBDCs would interoperate across private sector players and avoid "walled gardens" associated with private sector companies. This would enable R-CBDCs to be transferred seamlessly between different types of wallets.

There are many other possible implications of R-CBDCs such as programmability, enhanced monetary policy, tax, and data. Nonetheless many of these functions are experimental at this point and require careful deliberation as they have important societal implications. Central banks are more focused on payments than monetary policy in the context of CBDCs. In particular privacy and cybersecurity concerns have come to the fore.

R-CBDCs have significant implications for the two-tier monetary system, which involves the interplay between central banks and commercial banks in the money creation process, extending credit, and servicing households and firms.

While it is technically possible to disintermediate commercial banks with CBDCs, nearly all central banks seek to maintain the role of commercial banks in onboarding consumers, offering services, and extending loans. The private sector is better positioned to deliver these services, experiences, and technological integration, while the central bank's strength lies in conducting monetary and fiscal policy and managing the economy as a whole.

In short, although the technology allows for it, central banks don't look to disintermediate commercial banks with CBDCs. As we will discuss in further detail when exploring the various types of R-CBDCs, direct R-CBDC models that seek to disintermediate commercial banks are not widely adopted.

6.10 Benefits and Risks of R-CBDCs

These are some of the key benefits and risks of R-CBDCs:

Benefits

Continued access to central bank money

R-CBDCs provide public access to central bank money in view of the increasing decline of cash. As mentioned earlier this is one of the most important aspects of R-CBDCs in a digital economy that is increasingly being facilitated by the private sector. The availability of digital central bank money protects monetary sovereignty when households and firms may have the option of holding other foreign CBDCs and crypto-assets.

Resilience and redundancy

R-CBDCs can serve as a backup to private sector payments networks, which could fail for any number of reasons including operational, technical, or financial risks.

Payments diversity and interoperability

R-CBDCs can serve as a public payments infrastructure that serves as a counterbalance to closed-loop private sector payments systems. They can lower barriers to entry and increase competition, leading to increased innovation and greater diversity of payment service providers.

Financial inclusion

CBDCs can increase financial inclusion by providing access to digital payments for unbanked or underbanked populations. As a public-sector initiative, it would be less profit-driven and prioritize goals to onboard low-income groups to utilize digital services.

Privacy

Currently, consumers already grant access to their financial lives to commercial banks and FinTech platforms. It could be argued that the government and central banks are more accountable to the public and thus would be incentivized to provide a system that safeguards privacy whilst maintaining AML / CFT / sanctions compliance.

Direct fiscal transfers

Large scale fiscal transfer programs, such as those during the Covid-19 pandemic, could be made more efficient with R-CBDCs. The US pandemic stimulus check program involved complexity with paperwork and other operational frictions that hindered getting money into the hands of the most vulnerable.[11]

Better monitoring of corruption, money laundering, and tax evasion

R-CBDCs, through increased monitoring capabilities, could deter illicit and criminal use of the financial system. R-CBDCs could also assist in the automated collection of tax and reduce tax evasion.

Enhanced monetary policy tools

R-CBDCs could enhance the tools available to central bankers, allowing for a greater range of options and capabilities to manage the economy. These could include negative interest rates and direct fiscal stimulus based on certain preconditions such as income levels and set conditions on what the money can be spent on.

Data

CBDCs can improve the transparency and accountability of the financial system by providing more accurate and timely data on economic activity, money supply, and financial flows. They can also help combat money laundering, tax evasion, corruption, and illicit activities.

Risks

Big government

Having read most of this chapter, I imagine any proponent of limited government would be having a seizure by now. The high-level risk of R-CBDCs is clearly government overreach, control, and surveillance. R-CBDCs can give central banks excessive power and influence over the economy and society. They can also pose a threat to privacy and civil liberties by enabling excessive surveillance and censorship of transactions. This is a key reason why CBDC developments in the liberal democracies like the United States have trailed those of more centrally governed countries like China.

The libertarian Cato Institute performed sentiment analysis on the public comments solicited by the Federal Reserve on its CBDC discussion paper, and found that over 71% of the two thousand comments were opposed to a US CBDC, on the grounds of financial privacy, oppression, and risks of disintermediating commercial banks.[12]

The ECB had also run a public consultation on a digital euro.[13] Privacy emerged as the key requested feature by respondents, outranking security, low costs, and offline capabilities.

Privacy

A CBDC does not imply that the Government has a full and complete surveillance and control over one's financial life. My personal opinion is that this risk is overblown on social media and borders on scaremongering. Safeguards around privacy can be built in and this is most certainly something that nearly all central banks are aware of and look to address. In the first place, central banks are not in the business of monetizing user data, unlike many tech platforms.

Nonetheless, R-CBDC systems, specifically hybrid and direct systems, allow for transactions and balances to be viewed by the central bank. In my mind, the key questions around privacy are around how safeguards will be audited and be held accountable.

e-CNY's design is based on "controllable anonymity": anonymity for small transactions and traceability for large transactions.[14] Small transactions (5,000 CNY/day is about US$700/day) can be made with a mobile phone, but for larger transactions an upgrade is required by going through a KYC process.

As with DeFi, privacy in CBDCs can also be enabled with technologies such as Zero-Knowledge Proofs (ZKPs) and Trusted Execution Environments (TEEs).

Project Tourbillon, a project by the BIS Innovation Hub's Swiss Centre and cryptographer David Chaum, looks to improve cyber resiliency, scalability and privacy in a CBDC system.

Disintermediating banks

CBDCs can create competition between central banks and commercial banks for consumer deposits, interest, and lending. The option of holding digital central bank money is very attractive for households and firms, due to the lower counterparty risk. This can trigger bank runs and cause financial instability. If households and firms decide to hold more CBDC and less commercial bank money, this reduces the ability for commercial banks to extend credit and could lead to reduced economic growth.

Bank run risks

The ease of conversion and near-instant transfers between commercial bank money and CBDC could exacerbate financial instability in times of crisis.

Cybersecurity risks

The interface of the central banking system with the general public is a big undertaking and introduces a much larger attack surface and possibly the interest of state-level hackers. The infrastructure, operations and participants in a CBDC system will all need to be very resistant to cyberattacks.

Complexity

CBDCs can introduce new technical, legal, regulatory, operational, and governance challenges that need to be addressed before launching them. They can also create uncertainty and confusion among consumers, businesses, regulators, and policymakers about their design, functionality, adoption, and impact.

6.11 R-CBDC Design Choices

Auer and Böhme from the BIS introduced a CBDC pyramid as a framework to conceptualize CBDC design (Figure 6.7).[15] It maps consumer needs such as convenient real-time payments, privacy, and cross-border payments onto the design choices that central banks have to make in developing a CBDC system. Each design choice involves different trade-offs. The lower layers of the pyramid denote the fundamental design choices of the system that influence higher layers.

6.11.1 Nature of Claims and Role of the Central Bank

The first layer is the nature of the legal claim and the role of the central bank in the CBDC system. By definition, CBDCs are legal claims on the central bank and anything else would not be a CBDC. Nonetheless, indirect models are included in some CBDC research where the claim is on the intermediary. The other key design choice is the role of the central bank in maintaining the retail

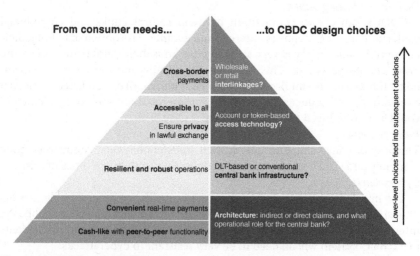

Figure 6.7 CBDC pyramid of consumer needs and design choices.
Source: BIS, Auer and Böhme (2020).

ledger and facilitating transactions. It can either perform this role or leave this to the commercial banks.

6.11.2 DLT or Conventional Centralized Ledger

The second layer is the choice to utilize DLT or a conventional centralized ledger for the database. Generally speaking, the main difference between DLT and conventional centralized ledgers is the way in which the ledger is updated with each transaction and how consensus among nodes is achieved. In a distributed ledger, the ledger has to be harmonized across all nodes of the system, often utilizing consensus algorithms. This involves messaging and broadcasting among nodes and requires time to achieve consensus.

In a centralized ledger, the authoritative entity (in the case of a CBDC, most likely the central bank) has the role of validating transactions. We can see this in RTGS systems where commercial banks settle transactions with each other on the central bank ledger, lowering settlement risk with finality.

Nonetheless, there are several benefits of using DLT including resilience and reliability, interoperability, and reduced need for intermediaries. To reiterate, DLTs are often used when there are a large number of parties that need to transact with one another, utilizing the network to maintain trust.

Risks of using DLT may include lower throughput and higher maintenance costs due to the overhead of the consensus mechanisms and maintaining a large number of nodes. Maintaining privacy in a DLT-based CBDC system also requires solving what is called the "backchain problem." This means that the receiver of funds needs to validate that the funds actually came from the central bank. However, by doing so, the receiver will need to trace the history of the token back to its origin, revealing its prior transaction history.

Central Banks' Preference for Permissioned DLTs

For most of this book, we have been discussing public blockchains and the ecosystems of applications that have been built on public blockchains. Now that we are discussing centralized systems, this distinction may not be so clear. So let me offer this clarification to address this important difference, and also address central banks' clear preference for permissioned DLT systems.

But before that, a clarification on the distinction between blockchain and DLT. Simply put, DLTs are a more generalized category of distributed ledgers which may include other types of DLTs. Some of these DLTs, such as directed acyclic graphs or hashgraphs, don't involve chains of transaction blocks. They may have different methods of ordering and batching transactions, achieving consensus, and synchronizing the ledger.

R3's Corda, for example, is one of the more popular permissioned DLT platforms for regulated financial markets and the banking industry. It has no blocks and no chains. To call it a blockchain would be misleading. Thus "permissioned DLT" is a more accurate term than "permissioned blockchain" in the context of CBDCs. Nonetheless I would say in more informal settings "DLT" and "blockchain" are interchangeable terms. To streamline semantically, I will just use the term DLT from here.

The difference between public and permissioned DLTs was covered briefly in Chapter 2. One of the key features of public DLTs such Bitcoin and Ethereum is trustlessness. This enables participants to join and leave the network, participate in validation and transact with other participants of the network freely. There is no central authority to screen participants based on their identities. The network enables trust between participants who may not trust one another to begin with.

However, banks have very strict requirements around compliance. Where anonymity is a feature in public DLTs, anonymity is a bug in permissioned DLTs. To quote directly from R3's Corda documentation:

> There is no place for anonymous actors in enterprise networks entrusted with sensitive information. Anonymous, and likely unaccountable, users pose a security threat to networks, either by compromising confidentiality or by interfering in the correct operation of the system. If such users have no business being there, then they should probably not be there. Further, regulated enterprises are subject to strict security requirements, so anonymous users must not be there.[16]

For DLT systems to be used in banking environments, node operators and participants must be known for a host of reasons including cybersecurity, data privacy, financial risk, and AML / CFT / sanctions compliance. Regulators have a requirement to know and understand financial transactions and the identities of actors according to their mandates for oversight.

Furthermore, enterprise-grade financial systems handle tremendous throughput which public DLTs may not be able to handle. To take an extreme example, Alipay handled 544,000 TPS (transactions per second) on "Single's Day 2019." Visa rates at about 1,700 TPS. Currently, although scaling solutions are in the works, Bitcoin can handle about 7 TPS and Ethereum about 30 TPS.

Settlement finality is also an issue with public DLTs. What PoW and PoS consensus mechanisms allow for is a probabilistic finality where the longer the chain of blocks is, the lower the probability of the transaction being reverted. Where centralized ledgers are concerned, barring cases where the central authority is compromised,[17] what the central authority decides is deemed final. Settlement finality is an explicitly stated principle in the CPMI-IOSCO PFMI (Principles for Financial Market Infrastructures).

To revisit the scalability trilemma, permissioned DLTs sacrifice decentralization in favor of throughput and security.

Permissioned DLTs also allow central banks to retain control over the governance of the network. They can decide which commercial banks and financial intermediaries participate in the CBDC network. The governance of the DLT can also be customized.

Finally, permissioned DLTs are designed to integrate with existing financial infrastructures. They are designed with legal norms in mind and are compatible with industry standards such as ISO 20022 and ISDA CDM.

For these reasons, central banks and commercial banks have a preference for permissioned DLTs.

In February 2023, Mr Agustín Carstens, General Manager of the BIS, gave a speech about "Innovation and the future of the monetary system." He made clear his position on public and permissioned blockchains, in the context of CBDCs. He stated that "programmability and composability do not require decentralized or permissionless platforms," and that "all the potential benefits I just outlined can be achieved in permissioned platforms with various degrees of centralisation."[18] He also outlined the idea of a "unified ledger" that would connect CBDCs, tokenized deposits, and tokenized assets, with the benefits of programmability, composability, and interoperability.

6.11.3 Token- or Account-based Access

The third design choice is around token- or account-based access. The difference here is around the specific method in which access to CBDC is granted.

In token-based CBDCs, knowledge of a private key is sufficient to honor claims. This is akin to bearer instruments such as cash where possession is sufficient to honor a claim. Advantages of token-based CBDCs include higher privacy and universal access. Disadvantages include AML / CFT risks and risk of losing funds if users mismanage their private keys.

Account-based CBDCs are akin to bank accounts where identity is used to grant access. Advantages of account-based CBDCs include easier recovery of funds, interoperability with other financial applications, and AML / CFT compliance. Disadvantages of account-based CBDCs include possible narrower adoption due to lack of identity and higher frictions required with verification.

6.11.4 Cross-border

The fourth design choice in the CBDC design pyramid surrounds whether it can be used in cross-border transactions.

Project Icebreaker is a joint project between the Bank of Israel, Norges Bank, Sveriges Riksbank, and the BIS Innovation Hub that tested the feasibility of

R-CBDCs in cross-border payments. It connected the three R-CBDC proto-types via FX providers that held CBDCs on both sides of the transaction. In this manner the domestic CBDC does not leave its own system. Notably all three of the CBDC prototypes used different DLTs: Quorum (Israel), Hyperledger Besu (Norway), and R3's Corda (Sweden), demonstrating that interoperability between systems is possible.

Given the infancy of R-CBDC projects, cross-border payments is perhaps more relevant for W-CBDC as we have earlier covered with mCBDCs.

As R-CBDCs evolve, they also could become more integrated with instant payment systems that are becoming more common such as Pix in Brazil and TIPS in Europe.

6.11.5 Holding and Transaction Limits

To limit the substitution effects of an R-CBDC on bank deposits, inhibit use for investment, and to limit the use of R-CBDCs to payments, most central banks considering R-CBDCs have mooted holding and transaction limits on CBDCs. Fabio Panetta, Member of the Executive Board of the ECB, has mentioned a possible holding limit of 3,000–4,000 digital euros per person.[19] A type 4 entry-level e-CNY wallet has a maximum holding limit of 10,000 CNY (~US$1,450).[20]

6.11.6 Interest Yielding

Another important design choice is whether or not the CBDC is interest yield-ing. Although unlikely, CBDCs can also be designed such that they yield nega-tive interest to promote spending. An interest yielding CBDC would naturally compete with bank deposits and be attractive to households and firms, boost-ing adoption.

6.12 Types of R-CBDCs

Auer, Cornelli, and Frost from the BIS classify four R-CBDC architectures according to the first layer of the design pyramid.

The two key dimensions of this categorization are:

1. Which ledgers the central bank maintains – just wholesale, or both whole-sale and retail; and
2. Who directly serves households and firms – onboarding, handling pay-ments, and other servicing.

These create more involvement by the central bank with the payments sys-tem and will increase technical, operational, and legal burdens on the central bank. It also changes more of the status quo with the two-tier banking system.

Table 6.1 Types of retail CBDC.

Name	Alternative names	Claim	Ledger recorded by Central Bank	Who handles retail payments?
Direct	Single-cell	Central Bank	Wholesale and retail	Central Bank
Hybrid	Platform, Two-tier	Central Bank	Wholesale and retail	Intermediaries
Intermediated	Two-tier	Central Bank	Wholesale	Intermediaries
Indirect	Synthetic, Two-tier, Narrow Bank	Intermediaries	Wholesale	Intermediaries

Source: BIS, The Book of Crypto, Henri Arslanian, author's summary

The direct, intermediated, hybrid, and indirect models are summarized in Table 6.1 and Figure 6.8.

6.12.1   Direct

The direct model is one where the central bank directly serves consumers and businesses, bypassing commercial banks. The central bank maintains both retail and wholesale ledgers.

It looks unlikely that this model will be implemented, for a few reasons. Central banks do not look to disintermediate commercial banks – this would simply be too much of a disruption to the existing system. Also, central banks don't have the technical capabilities to scale and handle the onboarding / KYC of users. Currently, commercial banks handle a significant amount of work, including credit scoring and a myriad of other services. It's better to allow the private sector to maintain its role and harness the innovative drive of the free market.

6.12.2   Two-tier Models: Hybrid and Intermediated

Two-tier models which are similar to the banking system today appear to be the most promising. In a survey done by Raphael Auer, Giulio Cornelli, and Jon Frost at the BIS (last updated January 2023), out of 39 R-CBDC projects that have specified a model, 74% of projects chose a hybrid / intermediated model. I should note for clarity that the majority of these projects are pilots and not live CBDCs (see Figure 6.9).

In hybrid and intermediate models, the private sector manages all customer-facing activity, similar to the current two-tier banking system today.

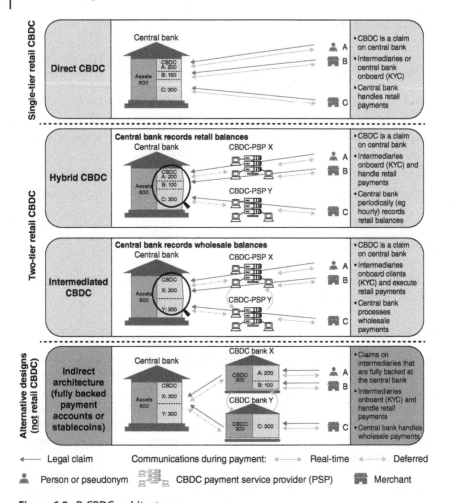

Figure 6.8 R-CBDC architectures.
Source: BIS, CBDC: The quest for minimally invasive technology, https://www.bis.org/publ/work948.pdf

The difference between hybrid and wholesale models is the ledger maintained by the central bank.

In the hybrid model the central bank maintains both wholesale and retail ledgers. The purpose of the central bank keeping a record of the retail ledger is more for backup than customer-facing. This allows for retail holdings to be transferred from one intermediary to another in the event of technical, operational, or financial failure.

In the intermediated model the central bank only records wholesale balances and transactions. This solves the privacy issue but might not enable the benefits of portability and enhanced monetary tools.

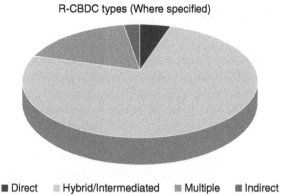

R-CBDC types (Where specified)

■ Direct   ▨ Hybrid/Intermediated   ▨ Multiple   ■ Indirect

Figure 6.9 R-CBDC types.
Source: Auer, R., Cornelli, G., and Frost, J. (2020). Rise of the central bank digital currencies: drivers, approaches and technologies. BIS working paper, No 880, August.

6.12.3 Indirect / Synthetic

CBDCs by definition are legal claims on the central bank. If they are claims on intermediaries they are not CBDCs.[21] Nonetheless I include indirect models for completeness as it is a model that has been considered before.

"Synthetic CBDC" was suggested by Tobias Adrian and Tommaso Mancini-Griffoli[22] from the IMF in 2019. The architecture suggested was intermediaries keeping client funds as central bank reserves on a 1:1 fully backed basis. In this manner clients would be protected from financial risks of other liabilities on the intermediary's balance sheet. This is a claim on the intermediary and more akin to "narrow banking" which is another topic of discussion.[23]

6.13 Examples of R-CBDCs

As of time of writing, there are four live R-CBDC projects:

- Bahamian Sand Dollar,
- Eastern Caribbean DCash,
- Nigerian eNaira, and
- Jamaican JAM-DEX.

Among these four, Nigeria has the largest population by far, of 230 million people. With 55% of the population unbanked,[24] it appears to be a good candidate to examine if CBDCs can address financial inclusion. Let's take a look at the eNaira project.

6.14   Case Study: Nigerian eNaira

Nigeria and the eNaira illustrate the complex web of monetary and economic issues that developing countries face in an era of crypto-assets and CBDCs.

The Central Bank of Nigeria (CBN) started research on CBDCs in 2017 and subsequently launched the eNaira in October 2021 as Africa's first retail CBDC. The CBN's motivations for the eNaira are financial inclusion, facilitating local and international trade, countering counterfeiting, and combating illicit financial activity.[25]

The Nigerian economy is largely informal and facilitated by cash. Since the naira's introduction in 1973, the currency has been devalued many times. From 1981 to 2021, the Naira has dropped in value by 99.8% against the US dollar.[26] The naira is also undergoing a redesign and an exchange of old for new banknotes is underway, amidst a shortage for new banknotes.

Cross-border payments are also a challenge in Nigeria due to blacklists, and inflation is currently at 22%.[27]

Not surprisingly, crypto-assets have been popular in Nigeria. A survey in 2020[28] found that 32% of Nigerians used crypto-assets, the highest proportion of any country in the world.

The CBN has acted to stem the use of crypto-assets. In February 2021, the CBN imposed a ban on individual and business users of crypto-assets from accessing the banking system. Nigerian banks have closed the bank accounts of crypto businesses.

The eNaira looks to be a solution to many of these issues. In March 2023, the Governor of the Central Bank of Nigeria (CBN), Mr. Godwin Emefiele, announced that 13 million eNaira Speed Wallets have been downloaded and N22 billion (~US$48m) has been transacted.[29]

How does the eNaira work? Initially developed[30] by Bitt, the same company that developed the Eastern Caribbean DCash, the eNaira is a hybrid architecture based on the Hyperledger Fabric DLT.

The Digital Currency Management System (DCMS) is the central administration for the CBN to issue and mint the eNaira. Financial institutions maintain an eNaira Treasury Wallet on the DCMS, and use the "FI Suite" application to manage holdings, requests, and redemptions with the CBN. Financial institutions can create sub-wallets for branches, funded by the Treasury Wallet.

At the retail level, the app has two versions: one for retail users, one for merchants. For individuals, wallets have tiered (0 to 3) transaction and balance limits according to KYC level using identity number and bank account. The wallet is linked with a phone number to begin with. Merchant accounts have no limits but require full KYC and compliance with AML / CFT rules.

The eNaira also works with non-smartphones using the USSD protocol for GSM cellular phones.

The eNaira does not yield interest.

As Africa's largest economy and population, Nigeria's eNaira project could pave the way for other CBDC projects in Africa. Ghana and South Africa are running pilots for retail and wholesale CBDC respectively.

In a similar vein, Africa has one of the world's largest adoption rates for mobile money,[31] pioneered by M-Pesa in Kenya by Vodafone and Safaricom in 2007. The M-Pesa project had been a revolution for financial inclusion, boosting access to financial services in Kenya from 27% of all households in 2006 to 84% in 2021.[32]

6.15 Case Study: United States

I would be remiss if I did not cover the leading reserve currency and the developments in a possible US CBDC. Here are some highlights.

In January 2022, the Federal Reserve published a report "Money and Payments: The U.S. Dollar in the Age of Digital Transformation" for the purposes of a public discussion between the Fed and stakeholders about CBDCs. The report identifies key characteristics of a possible US CBDC: privacy-protected, intermediated, widely transferable, and identity-verified. This is the hybrid / intermediated model we covered earlier. The Federal Reserve has no intention to allow direct access to central bank money for individuals, and would involve commercial banks and other financial institutions in its model:

> The Federal Reserve Act does not authorize direct Federal Reserve accounts for individuals, and such accounts would represent a significant expansion of the Federal Reserve's role in the financial system and the economy. Under an intermediated model, the private sector would offer accounts or digital wallets to facilitate the management of CBDC holdings and payments.

The Federal Reserve also makes clear that the issuance of a CBDC would require "clear support from the executive branch and from Congress, ideally in the form of a specific authorizing law."[33]

As mentioned in Chapter 5, US President Biden released an Executive Order (EO) on Ensuring Responsible Development of Digital Assets in March 2022. As part of the six objectives, it tasks the various agencies to research the potential design, deployment, and implications of a US CBDC, and the actions required to launch a US CBDC if it is determined to be in the national interest. As part of the EO, the Office of Science and Technology Policy (OSTP) has also released a report on key technical design choices for a US CBDC.[34]

Project Hamilton is a research project between the Federal Reserve Bank of Boston and the Massachusetts Institute of Technology's Digital Currency Initiative (MIT DCI). The goal of the project is to understand the technical challenges and potentials of CBDCs. The primary goal was to design a "core transaction processor" that meets speed, throughput, and fault tolerance requirements for a large retail payment system. The result of Project Hamilton Phase 1 was two architectures. The first achieved 170,000 TPS with settlement under 2 seconds, and the second achieved 1.7 million TPS with settlement under 1 second. The second does not create an ordered history for all transactions.[35]

Associated with Project Hamilton is OpenCBDC, an open source, collaborative technical research project on CBDCs also from MIT DCI. The GitHub repository includes work from Phase 1 of Project Hamilton. OpenCBDC also concludes that a DLT is not necessary for a CBDC, stating that "while CBDC is often associated with blockchain or distributed ledger technology, a CBDC does not require a blockchain if it is operating in one trust domain."[36]

Governors of the Fed's Board have made speeches on US CBDCs, highlighting their current position and discussing the pertinent issues related to a possible US CBDC.

Governor Michelle Bowman has raised doubts about a CBDC's efficacy in improving financial inclusion, citing that a majority of the remaining 4.5% unbanked in the United States simply do not want a bank account. She also raised concerns about a scenario in which CBDCs are used for fiscal stimulus, and that this could lead to the "politicization of the payments system."[37]

Similarly, Governor Christopher Waller has voiced his skepticism on a "compelling need for the Fed to create a digital currency."[38] He framed the discussion around the attractiveness of a CBDC to a non-US company engaging in international financial transactions. In his view, CBDC does not change the factors supporting the primacy of the dollar, as they are not technological. Rather, they stem from the "long-standing stability of the US economy and political system" and the liquid market for US Treasuries. CBDCs, in his view, are "unlikely to affect the openness of the US economy, reconfigure trust in US institutions, or deepen America's commitment to rule of law."

Finally, FedNow is an instant payments system at the wholesale level launched in July 2023. Designed as an upgrade to current payment systems such as ACH and Fedwire, the FedNow service is designed to operate 24 hours a day, 365 days a year, and reduce transaction costs. The Fed has denied rumors that it is a CBDC. Governor Bowman has mentioned that FedNow would address some of the needs that are discussed in a CBDC.[39]

In summary, many in the United States voice that the risks outweigh the benefits of a CBDC, including those within the Fed. Combined with the privacy concerns of the US population, a US CBDC appears to have significant challenges if it gets passed at all by Congress.

6.16   Case Study: eCNY 数字人民币

Last but not least, what is likely to be the most significant CBDC project of all – the eCNY by the People's Bank of China (PBOC).

China was the first civilization to utilize paper money as legal tender during the Tang dynasty in the seventh century CE. More recently, Chinese companies such as WeChat and Alipay have pioneered FinTech with QR code payments, savings apps, super-apps, and credit scoring with alternative data. Given China's enormous population of 1.4 billion and its status as the world's second largest economy, China looks set to forge new ground in FinTech once again with the eCNY, the country's new CBDC.

The use of cash in China is declining. In a survey conducted by the PBOC in 2019, the total value of payments was 59% mobile phone, 16% cash and 23% cards.[40]

Research started in 2014 when the PBOC set up a task force to study frameworks, technology, and global trends around CBDC. The Digital Currency Institute was set up by the PBOC in 2016 to develop a prototype of the eCNY. In 2020 internal tests of the eCNY were conducted in Shenzhen, Suzhou, Xiong'An, and Chengdu.

As of 31 December 2021, total downloads of the eCNY application totaled 261 million, with 87.565 billion yuan (US$13.78 billion) transacted.[41] WeChat Pay and Alipay have been integrated into the eCNY application as payment methods, showcasing the growing interoperability of eCNY. In April 2023 it was reported that civil servants in Changsu, a city in Jiangsu, would be paid in eCNY.[42]

The eCNY is a two-tier system based on the hybrid / intermediated model, and incorporates many innovations from DLTs and cryptography including private / public key pairs, account and token-based architectures, and smart contracts.[43] Notably, eCNY does not use DLT for its core processing due to limitations on throughput. Here is a quote from Mu Changchun, Director-General, Digital Currency Institute (DCI) on DLT vis eCNY:

> DLT is suitable for non-real time, low frequency and less sensitive business use cases such as registry or confirmation of property rights, or securities settlements. But there are some concerns and doubts about the capacity, scalability and finality for DLT in the payment system. For example, we don't

use DLT for the core system of the eCNY because the capacity and scalability cannot meet retail requirements. In China we have a big population and high concurrency requirements which DLT cannot meet. But for the reconciliation part of our system we do use DLT.[44]

Yao Qian, former Director-General of the DCI, had previously summarized the architecture of the eCNY as "One Money, Two Ledgers, Three Centers"[45] (一币, 两库, 三中心). The system is much more complex than this but it serves as a good high level overview. Let's examine.

"One Money" refers to the singleness of the CNY and the intent for the eCNY to complement cash. The eCNY is token-based and utilizes UTXO architecture.[46] Similar to crypto-assets, it uses public-key cryptography using decryption keys to use and verify tokens held in possession. Several fields of information are encrypted into each token, including issuer, ownership, "management attributes," "security properties," and "application properties."[47] The eCNY does not bear interest.

"Two Ledgers" refers to the two-tier model of the eCNY. One ledger (发行库) is kept by the PBOC. A separate ledger (商业银行库) is kept by the commercial bank. Issuance of eCNY starts at the PBOC ledger where CNY balance is debited from the commercial bank's reserves and eCNY is credited. When eCNY is requested by a bank's customer, the opposite happens on the commercial bank's ledger: the customer's balance is debited and eCNY is credited. eCNY held by commercial banks cannot be used as reserves for fractional reserve banking.

Currently, nine commercial banks are authorized to create / redeem eCNY as illustrated in Figure 6.10. They include the big four Chinese banks (ICBC, CCB, BoC, and ABC), WeBank (Tencent-owned), and MYbank (Ant Group-owned).

Figure 6.10 illustrates the architecture of the eCNY system, which consists of four layers: the central bank, the nine authorized commercial banks, other commercial banks, and licensed non-bank payment institutions, and users.

"Three Centers" refer to three components of the eCNY system that handles onboarding, KYC, validation and fraud prevention. They are the Authentication Center (认证中心), Registration Center (登记中心), and Big Data Analysis Center (大数据分析中心).

The Authentication Center is a centralized KYC database. It synchronizes various KYC information from the ID system for Chinese citizens and residents, mobile phone registration data from mobile phone providers, and KYC information from banks. This data is a key part of the "controllable anonymity" feature of the eCNY system which grants tiered transaction and balance limits according to KYC strength.

图 5：数字人民币发行流通体系架构

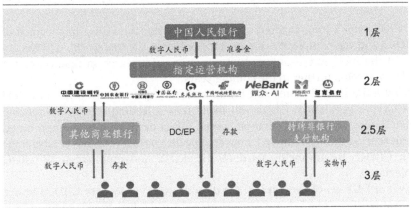

资料来源：《中国数字人民币的研发进展白皮书》，安信证券研究中心

Figure 6.10 eCNY Architecture.
Source: 安信证券 Essence Securities, 数字人民币:定位、特点和展望 eCNY: Positioning, Features, and Prospects, eCNY Whitepaper, PBOC

The Registration Center is a validation and registration engine. It has several functions, including registering tokens to accounts, managing eCNY creation and redemption, and validating transactions. It utilizes DLT as well as centralized database technologies.

The Big Data Analysis Center is a data processing engine for the purposes of fraud detection and AML / CFT compliance.

Offline CBDC wallets are a key feature in the eCNY system. This will allow for transactions between hardware wallets and PoS devices without an internet connection, making the eCNY as convenient as cash. The "loosely coupled account linkage"[48] allows for this functionality. It's not clear to me exactly how this works, but it could be a locking of funds until connectivity is achieved with the online system. Offline transfers are also likely to have low limits. The Postal Savings Bank of China has also trialed[49] a novel credit card sized hardware wallet with biometrics, showcasing things to come.

The other major area of discussion is the use of eCNY in international trade and its status relative to the US dollar. As covered earlier in this chapter, the PBOC is also participating in what looks to be also a landmark project in multilateral W-CBDCs with Project mBridge. The Guangdong-Hong Kong-Macau Greater Bay Area also seems a likely testing ground for the eCNY to play a role in trade, given Hong Kong and Macau's status as special administrative regions. Synergies between the domestic eCNY system and mBridge look very likely as they mature.

6.17   Chapter Summary

This has been a long chapter, but necessary given the future importance of CBDCs and the complexity of monetary policy in the real world. CBDCs are one of the most interesting and intense areas of research in finance, and it looks to develop further in the coming years.

Where the United States and European Union play outsized roles in DeFi and Crypto regulation, China will likely take a leading role in influencing CBDCs. Similar to how China pioneered QR code payments and app-based credit scoring through Alipay, China could gain a strong first-mover advantage with CBDCs by advancing its domestic eCNY and multilateral W-CBDC projects.

Even if DLT is not used in CBDCs directly, many aspects of CBDCs utilize innovations from blockchains, such as account and token-based models, smart contracts, consensus mechanisms, and cryptography.

At the inaugural DeFi conference of the BIS in April 2022, the question "Does safe DeFi require CBDCs?" framed many discussions. While the increased regulatory scrutiny following the FTX collapse has complicated integrating DeFi and CBDCs, there are promising areas where innovation is cross-pollinating. We will explore these in the next three chapters.

Notes

1. https://www.federalreserve.gov/publications/files/money-and-payments-20220120.pdf
2. https://www.bis.org/publ/othp33.pdf
3. https://www.atlanticcouncil.org/cbdctracker/
4. https://www.reuters.com/article/us-facebook-cryptocurrency-france-german-idUSKCN1VY1XU
5. Zetzsche, D.A., Buckley, R.P., and Arner, D.W. (2019). Regulating Libra. *Oxford Journal of Legal Studies*. https://papers.ssrn.com/sol3/papers.cfm?abstract_id=3414401
6. Rogoff, K.S. (2016). *The Curse of Cash*. Princeton, NJ: Princeton University Press.
7. https://www.bloomberg.com/news/articles/2021-03-25/china-digital-yuan-will-co-exist-with-alipay-wechat-pboc-says?sref=Fet8J5HC
8. https://www.oliverwyman.com/our-expertise/insights/2021/nov/unlocking-120-billion-value-in-cross-border-payments.html
9. Bindseil, U. and Pantelopoulos, G. (2022). Towards the holy grail of cross-border payments. ECB Working Paper Series No 2693. https://www.ecb.europa.eu/pub/pdf/scpwps/ecb.wp2693~8d4e580438.en.pdf

10. https://www.cls-group.com/products/settlement/clssettlement/currencies/
11. https://www.cnbc.com/2022/06/11/the-pandemic-stimulus-checks-were-a-big-experiment-did-it-work.html
12. https://www.cato.org/blog/update-two-thirds-commenters-concerned-about-cbdc
13. https://www.ecb.europa.eu/pub/pdf/other/Eurosystem_report_on_the_public_consultation_on_a_digital_euro~539fa8cd8d.en.pdf
14. http://www.pbc.gov.cn/en/3688110/3688172/4157443/4293696/2021071614584691871.pdf
15. Auer, R. and Böhme, R. (2020). The technology of retail central bank digital currency. *BIS Quarterly Review*, March. https://ssrn.com/abstract=3561198
16. https://training.corda.net/corda-fundamentals/introduction/
17. https://blog.ethereum.org/2016/05/09/on-settlement-finality
18. https://www.bis.org/speeches/sp230222.htm
19. https://www.ecb.europa.eu/press/key/date/2022/html/ecb.sp220615~0b859eb8bc.en.html
20. https://asia.nikkei.com/Spotlight/Caixin/China-launches-digital-yuan-app-in-pilot-cities-nationwide
21. https://www.bis.org/publ/othp33.pdf
22. https://www.imf.org/en/News/Articles/2019/05/13/sp051419-stablecoins-central-bank-digital-currencies-and-cross-border-payments
23. See Custodia Bank and The Narrow Bank
24. https://www.worldbank.org/en/publication/globalfindex/Report
25. https://www.enaira.gov.ng/
26. https://guardian.ng/business-services/osinbajos-prescription-and-painful-history-of-naira-devaluation/
27. https://tradingeconomics.com/nigeria/inflation-cpi
28. https://www.statista.com/chart/18345/crypto-currency-adoption/
29. https://www.thisdaylive.com/index.php/2023/03/22/emefiele-apologises-for-deluge-of-online-transactions-failure/
30. Nigeria is currently looking for more service providers to revamp the system. https://www.bloomberg.com/news/articles/2023-02-21/nigeria-seeks-new-tech-partners-to-revamp-enaira-central-bank-digital-currency?sref=Fet8J5HC
31. https://qz.com/africa/2161960/gsma-70-percent-of-the-worlds-1-trillion-mobile-money-market-is-in-africa
32. https://www.statista.com/statistics/1219362/access-to-financial-services-and-products-in-kenya/
33. https://www.federalreserve.gov/publications/files/money-and-payments-20220120.pdf
34. https://www.whitehouse.gov/ostp/news-updates/2022/09/16/technical-possibilities-for-a-u-s-central-bank-digital-currency/
35. https://www.bostonfed.org/publications/one-time-pubs/project-hamilton-phase-1-executive-summary.aspx

36. https://dci.mit.edu/opencbdc-faqs
37. https://www.federalreserve.gov/newsevents/speech/bowman20230418a.htm
38. https://www.federalreserve.gov/newsevents/speech/waller20221014a.htm
39. https://www.federalreserve.gov/newsevents/speech/bowman20220817a.htm
40. http://www.pbc.gov.cn/en/3688110/3688172/4157443/4293696/20210716145 84691871.pdf
41. https://www.chinainternetwatch.com/33050/cbdc-ecny/0
42. https://www.scmp.com/news/china/politics/article/3217996/chinese-city-changshu-plans-pay-employees-using-digital-yuan
43. Turrin, R. (2021). *Cashless; China's Digital Currency Revolution*. Gold River, CA: Authority Publishing. (p. 141).
44. 'The process of technological innovation at central banks', BIS, https://youtu .be/1QD-a8vYisI?t=920
45. https://www.yicai.com/news/100576775.html
46. Turrin, R. (2021). *Cashless; China's Digital Currency Revolution*. Gold River, CA: Authority Publishing.
47. 安信证券 Essence Securities, 数字人民币:定位、特点和展望 eCNY: Positioning, Features and Prospects
48. Progress of R&D of eCNY in China, PBOC, http://www.pbc.gov.cn/en/368811 0/3688172/4157443/4293696/2021071614584691871.pdf
49. https://en.pingwest.com/a/8347

7

Asset Tokenization

In Chapter 3, we briefly discussed the concept of tokenization of real-world assets and gave examples of startups that aim to connect on-chain capital markets with off-chain assets. However, in the next three chapters, we will delve deeper into the topic of asset tokenization, specifically focusing on asset tokenization in general, tokenized deposits, and tokenized securities.

You may be wondering, "Haven't we been discussing tokenization all along?" This is true, as crypto-assets are essentially tokens. However, most crypto-assets are on-chain assets and do not have a reference to a real-world, off-chain asset. When DLT is utilized in regulated, real-world environments, there are significant complexities that need to be addressed, such as asset servicing, lifecycle management, and legal and technical elements.

Therefore, in this chapter, we will narrow our focus to tokenized assets that usually reference an off-chain, regulated asset, which are often securities. We will explore how the tokenization of securities is a highly promising field with the potential to revolutionize the current way securities are issued, traded, and settled. Tokenized assets have significant potential benefits for both primary and secondary markets, and can increase efficiency in the securities market by enabling automation and disintermediation.

7.1   What Is Asset Tokenization?

The FSB defines tokenization as "the act of creating a digital representation of an off-chain asset and placing it on a distributed ledger."[1]

It is possible to tokenize virtually any asset. Since the early days of Ethereum, many entrepreneurs have attempted to tokenize various assets such as gold, real estate, art, commodities, and securities including equities and bonds (Figure 7.1).

Decentralizing Finance: How DeFi, Digital Assets, and Distributed Ledger Technology Are Transforming Finance, First Edition. Kenneth Bok.
© 2024 John Wiley & Sons Ltd. Published 2024 by John Wiley & Sons Ltd.

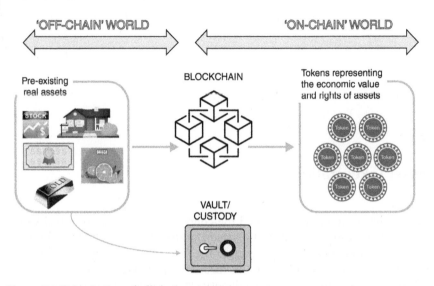

Figure 7.1 Tokenization of off-chain assets.
Source: OECD

Tokenization can be viewed as an extension of the dematerialization of securities that has been a trend since the introduction of computers in the 1960s. Dematerialization involves replacing paper stock certificates with digital book-entries on Central Securities Depositories (CSDs), where changes in ownership are recorded on the CSD's records.

Tokenized instruments may embed relevant information on the asset including asset type, ownership, legal framework, clearing, settlement, and custody requirements.

CSDs and CCPs

Providing a brief description of Central Securities Depositories (CSDs) and Central Counterparty Clearing Houses (CCPs) might be helpful, as these two components play a major role in the current securities infrastructure which could potentially change with the adoption of DLT.

Central Securities Depositories (CSDs) play an important role in the post-trade processing of financial transactions with securities. They serve as a register for securities accounts for banks, financial institutions, and individuals to hold and trade securities. Many of these financial institutions will hold securities on behalf of their clients. Securities may be in dematerialized, book-entry form, or in physical form that are held at the CSD.

CSDs facilitate the settlement of securities between buyers and sellers by maintaining the record of ownership. They may also provide asset servicing such as paying interest, paying dividends, administering corporate actions, and performing redemptions.

Most countries have one national CSD that is associated with the national stock exchange. An example is the Depository Trust Company (DTC) in the United States.

CSDs may also be international. They settle trades in international securities such as eurobonds (international bonds denominated in a currency not native to its issuing country). Examples include Clearstream and Euroclear.

Central Counterparty Clearing Houses (CCPs) serve a specific purpose of intermediating between buyers and sellers in order to reduce counterparty risk. By the process of novation, the CCP becomes the buyer to the seller and vice versa. This eliminates settlement uncertainty for market participants and protects against defaults.

In short, both CSDs and CCPs play an important role in post-trade processes such as clearing and settlement.

7.2 Benefits of Asset Tokenization

There are many potential benefits of asset tokenization that apply to all parts of an asset's lifecycle – including issuance, trading, asset servicing, clearing, and settlement. One way to get a sense of how tokenized assets would interact is in the DeFi world, where assets can be traded without a custodian and utilize innovations such as automated market makers, which run on smart contracts. The difference is that in the regulated world, participants would need to be identified and there would be more intermediaries involved due to the increased legal, regulatory, and operational requirements.

These are some of the benefits of asset tokenization via DLT:

- Efficiency gains due to automation and disintermediation,
- Enhanced resilience,
- Transparency,
- Fractional ownership, and
- International reach and direct access.

7.2.1 Efficiency Gains Due to Automation and Disintermediation

Global post-trade processing operations incur significant resources, with E&Y estimating costs ranging between US\$20 and 40 billion per annum.[2] In the United States, the settlement cycle has progressively shortened from T+5 (pre-1995) to T+3 (2004) and currently stands at T+2 (2017). The SEC has since announced requirements for T+1 in February 2023,[3] to be implemented by May 2024.

DLT has the potential to replace the centralized functions of CSDs and CCPs. DLT can reduce costs associated with settlement and clearing and shorten the settlement cycle to T+0 or near-instantaneous. Additionally, DLT can enable always-on, 24/365 operations for platforms, as is already common with public blockchains.

The reason for this is that tokenized assets are directly held on the DLT network. The transaction execution is linked with the settlement, making settlement immediate. If counterparties do not have the digital asset to trade, the transaction fails. This immediate settlement process eliminates the need for complicated netting and clearing processes, and allows for newly acquired tokenized assets to be immediately used.

Delivery versus payment (DvP) became a widespread industry practice after the October 1987 market crash, reducing settlement and systemic risks. However, DvP is not completely risk-free, as both legs of the transaction occur on separate systems. As we will examine, some central banks are conducting pilots that allow for both the asset and the payment to be settled *atomically* on the same DLT network, further reducing settlement risks and shortening the settlement cycle.

DLT can also reduce the cost of issuance and administration of securities. Smart contracts can facilitate corporate actions, dividend and interest payments, escrow arrangements, and collateral management.[4]

7.2.2 Enhanced Resilience

The distributed nature of DLT networks, where there is no single point of failure, combined with immutability and cryptographic proofs, can increase the resilience and reliability of securities platforms.

7.2.3 Transparency

DLT can reduce systemic risks related to counterparty risks and streamline operations involving multiple custodians with different due diligence and operational procedures by simplifying custody chains and increasing transparency. In a DLT network, all parties have access to the same information about the asset, including ownership, history, and associated metadata, which creates a single, verified, real-time source of truth.

DLT-based systems may also render the role of registrars and transfer agents redundant, as ownership records are maintained on the shared ledger and transactions are executed automatically via smart contracts.

Furthermore, DLT could increase the efficiency of regulatory compliance by programming regulatory restrictions and requirements into assets and informing regulators in real-time when relevant events occur. This could reduce the potential for errors and delays in compliance processes and increase visibility and transparency for regulators.

7.2.4   Fractional Ownership

Tokenization offers the possibility to divide assets into smaller claims, which could allow for more inclusive access for investors who prefer smaller minimum investment sizes. This could be particularly beneficial in markets such as private equity and real estate, where historically high barriers to entry have limited investor diversity. Tokenization could enable investors to diversify their portfolios with these asset classes.

Another advantage of DLT-based tokenization is the reduced cost of fundraising, which could make it easier for small and medium-sized enterprises (SMEs) to raise capital. By tokenizing their assets, SMEs can access a broader pool of potential investors, including those who may have previously been excluded due to the high cost of traditional fundraising methods.

Fractional ownership and tokenization have the potential to increase liquidity for an asset by allowing for a larger pool of investors and easier access to trading. If a market for the tokenized asset develops, investors can buy and sell fractions of the asset, which can increase the liquidity of the asset and potentially reduce its illiquidity premium.

7.2.5   International Reach and Direct Access

DLT-based securities platforms have the potential to enable a more global reach for investors and market participants, owing to the global nature of blockchains and interoperability. Tokenized assets could allow investors to participate directly in primary and secondary markets, subject to relevant KYC and AML laws and programs.

Tokenized assets could facilitate the issuance of securities globally, as they can be traded across borders without the need for complex and costly intermediaries. This could create new opportunities for issuers to raise capital from a broader and more diverse pool of investors and could increase the liquidity of the securities being offered.

Tokenization may also enable investors to participate directly in primary and secondary markets. Security Token Offerings (STOs) are a type of fundraising that uses DLT to issue tokens that represent ownership in an underlying asset, such as equity in a company or ownership in a real estate property. STOs may offer investors more transparency, increased liquidity, and more direct access to investment opportunities.

7.3 How is Tokenization Performed?

Several asset tokenization platforms, such as Polymath, Securitize, and Tokeny, have emerged in recent years. These platforms offer a suite of services that includes investor onboarding, KYC and AML compliance, token issuance, whitelisting, custody, distribution, and asset servicing.

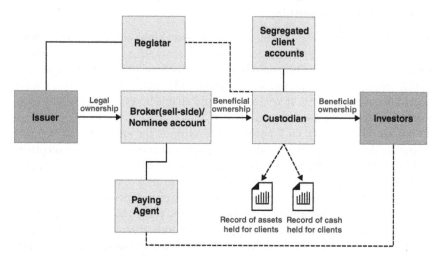

Figure 7.2 Current securities issuance.
Source: OECD, https://www.oecd.org/finance/The-Tokenisation-of-Assets-and-Potential-Implications-for-Financial-Markets.htm

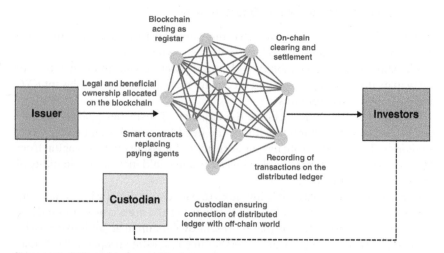

Figure 7.3 DLT-enabled securities issuance.
Source: OECD, https://www.oecd.org/finance/The-Tokenisation-of-Assets-and-Potential-Implications-for-Financial-Markets.htm

In addition to the asset tokenization platforms, there are also security token standards, such as ERC-1400 and ERC-3643, which have been developed to provide features tailored to security tokens.

These security token standards offer features such as identity and compliance, allowing issuers to ensure that only eligible investors can purchase the tokens. The standards also provide issuers and agents with the ability to control the tokens, ensuring that they are issued and traded in compliance with relevant regulations and laws. They also have features that manage documentation associated with the asset.

By providing a standardized framework for the issuance and management of security tokens, these standards can help promote interoperability across different tokenization platforms and increase the adoption of security tokens as a viable investment option.

Trusted third parties will still have a role to play in a tokenized platform. In particular, the role of the custodian could well be a key role,[5] as the centralized trusted authority that authenticates the connection between the off-chain asset and the on-chain token representation. The custodian will also ensure that the same asset is not being represented more than once on other platforms.

Figures 7.2 and 7.3 illustrate the parties and flow in the current architecture of securities issuance, and a securities issuance architecture enabled by DLT.

7.4 Considerations for Tokenization

Various reports and studies have suggested that certain characteristics make assets good candidates for tokenization. According to the Bank for International Settlements (BIS), good candidates for tokenization are systems with streamlined processes that involve little manual intervention, clear legal frameworks, and clear regulation.[6]

The BIS report suggests that tokenization is less attractive for systems that involve frequent manual workflow procedures and complex legal and regulatory frameworks. Such systems may require more frequent "transformations" in and out of the tokenization platforms, which could reduce the benefits of automation and disintermediation. While the potential gains could be significant, the challenges associated with such systems may also be more significant.

The OECD suggests a cost–benefit analysis that considers the potential benefits of tokenization, including corresponding efficiency gains, cost reductions, and increases in reliability, while also taking into account the technical challenges and operational risks. The OECD report suggests that benefits could be realized in markets where no current trading infrastructure exists, has a deficiency of trust, and has multiple layers of intermediation and limited liquidity. The OECD also suggests that the potential benefits could only be achieved if the network achieves sufficient scale.

7.5 DLT in Capital Markets

The Global Financial Markets Association (GFMA) has published a comprehensive report on the impact of DLT in capital markets (Figure 7.4). The report categorizes the capital markets into five distinct workflows or stages of a security's lifecycle and assesses the potential impact DLT could have on each stage:

1. Primary Markets
2. Secondary Trading
3. Clearing and Settlement
4. Custody
5. Asset Servicing

Let's look at each of these categories with some examples.

7.5.1 Primary Markets

The use of DLT in entrepreneurial finance has gained popularity since the advent of the first wave of initial coin offerings (ICOs) around 2017. The technology enables entrepreneurs to raise capital from a global pool of investors, which was seen as a lucrative opportunity. However, it also posed significant risks for investors due to the lack of accountability and other moral hazards.

Impact of DLT-based Securities on Workflow Efficiency, Financials and Value Creation, and Risk Mitigation Across the Securities Lifecycle

Implementation models Impact shown across both implementation models; detailed breakdown included in Chapter 2	Books and Records + Tokenized Securities				
	Primary Markets	Secondary Trading	Clearing and Settlement	Custody	Asset Servicing
Overall DLT Impact	Medium	Medium	High	High	High
Workflow Efficiency	Medium	Low	High	High	High
Financial Opportunity & Value Creation	High	High	High	High	High
Incremental Risk Mitigation	Low	Low	High	Medium	Medium

■ Low degree of positive impact　▨ Medium degree of positive impact　■ High degree of positive impact

Figure 7.4 Impact of DLT across the security's lifecycle.
Source: https://www.gfma.org/policies-resources/
gfma-publishes-report-on-impact-of-dlt-in-global-capital-markets/

It is important to note that while DLT changes the form factor and the underlying infrastructure of the asset, it does not alter the legal requirements for fundraising. Existing securities laws still apply.

DLT-based issuance of digital assets can streamline the various processes involved in primary market issuance, including origination and distribution. This technology offers a lower cost and faster alternative to traditional issuance routes.[7] In addition, it allows for bespoke instruments that have automated cash flows, asset servicing, and other lifecycle management functions that cater to the needs of both investors and issuers. DLT-based issuance also enables fractionalization, as discussed earlier.

The emergence of *security token offerings (STOs)* has provided entrepreneurs with yet another option for fundraising. It is important to distinguish between STOs, ICOs, and IPOs, as they differ in their characteristics.

The majority of STOs to date have been more similar to private placements than to public security offerings, as they have typically been sold only to accredited investors.[8]

STOs have been a significant topic since the advent of ICOs, as they represent a regulated version of the latter. STOs may offer a cheaper and more straightforward means of raising capital than an IPO, as DLT provides a more accessible method for implementing equity ownership and has a lower bar than a stock exchange with onerous listing requirements.

The largest STO to date has been by tZERO platform who raised US$134m at a valuation of US$1.5b in August 2018. tZERO is a digital securities issuance and trading platform that is licensed as an Alternative Trading System (ATS) in the United States.

Other STO platforms based in the United States include SharesPost and OpenFinance.

7.5.2   Secondary Markets

The GFMA assesses the impact of DLT on secondary market trading as medium, as trading is already highly efficient across asset classes and current centralized exchanges. However, DLT may help deepen liquidity in secondary markets for illiquid asset classes such as unlisted equities and unlisted investment funds, and broaden access to these assets to new investors.

DLT-based securities trading may also allow improved access and lower cost of market data, faster and more reliable settlement, improved order routing, and increased electronic trading.

One stock exchange that has undergone the full DLT transformation is the *SIX Digital Exchange (SDX)*. SDX is a regulated exchange for digital assets that is owned by the SIX Group, Switzerland's primary stock exchange. It offers a complete end-to-end solution for digital asset issuance, listing, trading, settlement, servicing, and custody, and also serves as a central securities depository (CSD) for digital assets. The SDX is particularly interested in serving the small and medium-sized enterprise (SME) sector, providing an opportunity for SMEs to raise capital in a market with lower requirements than the primary market.

Furthermore, SDX has also run two proof-of-concept projects in collaboration with the Swiss National Bank (SNB) and the BIS Innovation Hub Swiss Centre, Project Helvetia. The first phase of Project Helvetia involved W-CBDCs issued by the SNB and enabled for DvP settlements on the DLT-based platform utilizing W-CBDCs and the RTGS link respectively for the payment leg. The second phase added commercial banks into the experiment, integrated W-CBDC into the core banking systems of both the SNB and commercial banks, and ran transactions from end to end.

The SDX looks to be a prototype of the stock exchange of the future, fully integrating DLT in its operations, as well as other key partners in the securities and financial ecosystem.

While some DLT transformations have been successful, others have encountered significant challenges. The Australian Stock Exchange (ASX) announced a DLT-based replacement for its legacy clearing and settlement system, CHESS, in collaboration with US-based company Digital Asset in 2016. However, the project was eventually shelved in late 2022 after numerous delays, and the ASX wrote off AUD$250m of its investment in the project. An independent review by Accenture cited various technical and operational issues.

7.5.3 Clearing and Settlement

GFMA estimates that the impact of DLT on clearing and settlement in capital markets is high.

The current back-office operating costs globally are around US$20 billion per annum, of which around US$8 billion are on highly automated equity and fixed-income assets.[9] Capgemini estimates that cost savings from the use of DLT in clearing and settlement of cash securities, equities, repo, and leveraged loans could save US$12 billion a year.[10]

Faster settlement cycles unlock collateral held in margin and clearing arrangements, increasing capital efficiency. It has been estimated that total global outstanding collateral was around US$17 trillion[11] in 2022, with an opportunity cost of around US$500m[12] in foregone yield. Furthermore, margin requirements increase dramatically during volatile market conditions such as the UK LDI crisis in September 2022.

DLT looks to drive the evolution of CSDs and CCPs, as digital assets become more mainstream. DLT may not totally disintermediate CSDs and CCPs. CSDs and CCPs may integrate DLT and use it to supplement their existing operations and functions.

For example, one important role that CCPs provide is netting. The National Securities Clearing Corporation (NSCC) cleared an average of US$1.7 trillion daily and netted to a factor of 98%.[13] Netting is an important aspect of capital efficiency for financial institutions.

While DLT may reduce collateral requirements and unlock trapped liquidity due to accelerated and precise settlement, it may also increase collateral requirements due to pre-funding.

CCPs are taking notice. The European Association of CCP Clearing Houses (EACH) has published a paper on the potential impact of DLT on CCPs, with a focus on disintermediation.

Projects such as DTCC's Project Ion look to combine the benefits of DLT and CCPs. Based on R3's Corda, Project Ion supports up to T+0 netted settlement and interoperability with existing settlement platforms. Project Ion had gone live in a parallel production environment in August 2022.

DLT in clearing and settlement can be implemented in a number of ways. GFMA has outlined 4 models of DLT-based settlement[14]:

SS0: No DLT-based Securities or DLT-based Payment Instruments, DLT used as "Books and Records";

SS1: DLT-based Securities but no DLT-based Payment Instruments, payment settled in traditional accounts;

SS2: DLT-based Securities and DLT-based Payment Instruments, settle on different ledgers; and

SS3: DLT-based Securities and DLT-based Payment Instruments, settled on the same ledger.

DLT-based settlement may not drive a market-wide move towards shorter settlement cycles, but rather focus on specific asset classes where enhanced automation and precision can address existing pain points. Examples include repos (JP Morgan Onyx and Broadridge DLR) and OTC derivatives, the latter being prone to inefficiencies and high risks due to multiple intermediaries and duplicated information on legacy platforms.

DLT can enable more flexible settlement options where decisions on settlement speed can be made on a trade-by-trade basis, according to liquidity and cost requirements.

7.5.4 Custody

Custodian banks serve an important role in TradFi, and their role also looks to expand and evolve with the advent of digital assets. Custodian banks perform the safekeeping of assets for clients of brokerage firms and asset managers, with segregation to prevent commingling of assets with other clients or the agent's assets. Custodian banks also assist with settlement of transactions, record keeping, corporate actions, asset servicing, regulatory reporting, compliance, and proxy voting.

The custody business is highly consolidated. The four largest custodian banks in the world: BNY Mellon, State Street, JPMorgan Chase, and Citi collectively have US\$136.6 trillion[15] under custody and administration, about 50% of the total market share.

With digital assets, the role of custodians will become more technical, with the safeguarding, cybersecurity, and management of client's private keys. I covered some of the fundamentals of custody and types of wallets in Chapter 2 in case you need a refresher.

TradFi custodians such as BNY Mellon and State Street are responding proactively to digital assets, with both companies offering digital asset custody services. Approximately US\$16 trillion of digital assets under custody is projected by 2030.[16]

In a BNY Mellon / Celent survey[17] of 271 institutional investors, 65% had opted for a digital-native service provider, and 35% had opted for a TradFi service provider for their digital asset investment and custody needs. No one firm had more than 10% market share. Some of the leading companies included:

TradFi: State Street Digital, BNY Mellon / CIBC Mellon, JP Morgan, Fidelity Asset Management
Digital native: Coinbase Custody, PrimeTrust, Fireblocks

The survey also indicated that 72% of institutional investors indicated that they prefer an integrated provider for both TradFi assets and digital asset custody, as opposed to best of breed providers for individual needs, with 77% indicating they wanted access to enhanced DeFi yields through staking on crypto-assets.

GFMA suggests that the impact of DLT on custody is high, especially in systems where a full DLT transformation takes place on both the Books and Records layer as well as the asset layer.

7.6 Asset Servicing

Asset servicing relates to the administration of legal rights and obligations of asset owners post-trade. The three main work streams within asset servicing are corporate actions, tax withholding, and regulatory reporting. Asset servicing involves many parties including the issuer, custodian bank, administrator, asset manager, broker, paying agents, registrars, data providers, and the asset owners.

Many processes of asset servicing are still paper-based with physical mail and wet ink signatures. DLT can help streamline operations by enabling a single golden source of truth for data, and allow for smart contracts to automate legacy manual processes.

7.6.1 Corporate Actions

The total cost of corporate action errors has been estimated to be over US$1 billion a year,[18] with 57% of costs stemming from data errors and manual entry errors.[19] Mandatory corporate actions are dividends, bond coupons, and stock splits. Voluntary corporate actions include proxy voting, M&A, and rights issues.

DLT may enable increased voting participation from retail investors. The current system that involves a complex chain of intermediaries between the issuer and the asset owner results in many inefficiencies between meeting notifications and the voting process. In one survey, it was found that retail investors voted on 28% on shares held, as opposed to 92% for institutional investors.[20]

One example of the use of DLT in streamlining corporate actions is that with Digital Asset and IntellectEU with the Daml framework.[21]

7.6.2 Tax Withholding

The current system of taxation in many jurisdictions involves withholding at source with a subsequent reclaim. This applies to dividend and interest payments. Determining the correct withholding tax requires "synchronized data collection and reporting across a complex network of financial intermediaries and tax authorities."[22] Withholding tax can be reduced by tax treaties, provided the investor meets certain requirements and provides proof. Tax relief often takes time due to the manual processes in providing and verifying tax relief information. This incurs administrative costs and opportunity costs. The European Commission has estimated the overall cost to the European Union of withholding tax is to be €8.4b annually.[23]

The paper-based process and lack of transparency have also resulted in tax abuse and fraud. Starting in 2012, a €55 billion "cum-ex" tax fraud was uncovered in the European Union, resulting in calls for improvements in the tax system.[24] The fraud involved banks buying and reselling shares belonging to foreign investors on dividend pay-out days. Tax administrations were unable to identify real ownership and paid out fraudulent tax relief claims.

TaxGrid from EY is a global tax withholding solution that utilizes DLT to "automate, decentralize and securely share tax and financial information while maintaining data privacy between financial institutions and government agencies."[25] The project, started in 2020, involved Her Majesty's Revenue and Customs (HMRC), Netherlands Tax Authority, Norwegian Tax Administration, EY, BNP Paribas Securities Services, Citibank, JP Morgan Securities Services, and Northern Trust. The project aims to provide real-time data sharing between multiple parties while maintaining privacy through zero-knowledge proof technology.

7.6.3 Regulatory Reporting

Regulatory reporting is also another process which involves a significant amount of manual process. The current system is "spread over a patchwork of different databases"[26] and suffers from data quality issues that require manual reconciliation. The GFMA estimates the cost of compliance to be 3–9% of non-interest expense for banks.[27]

A DLT-based system could enable embedded supervision, in which the regulator can monitor compliance automatically by fetching information from the distributed ledger in real-time, instead of periodic requests from multiple parties. Such a system would also improve data quality and possibly be of lower cost to smaller banks.

7.7   Chapter Summary

This chapter has briefly outlined what asset tokenization is, why it is useful, and how it can be implemented. The implementation of DLT in capital markets globally is also a very promising field in which many challenges remain, but in which pilot projects have already proven promising results. In the next two chapters, we'll examine practical examples of asset tokenization in action through case studies of tokenized deposits and institutional DeFi.

Notes

1. Financial Stability Board (FSB) (2023): "The Financial Stability Risks of Decentralised Finance"
2. https://www.ey.com/en_cn/strategy/technology-driver-of-the-post-trade-operations
3. https://www.sec.gov/news/press-release/2023-29
4. https://www.oecd.org/finance/The-Tokenisation-of-Assets-and-Potential-Implications-for-Financial-Markets.htm
5. https://www.oecd.org/finance/The-Tokenisation-of-Assets-and-Potential-Implications-for-Financial-Markets.htm
6. https://www.bis.org/publ/bisbull72.htm
7. https://www.gfma.org/policies-resources/gfma-publishes-report-on-impact-of-dlt-in-global-capital-markets/

8. https://papers.ssrn.com/sol3/papers.cfm?abstract_id=3634626
9. https://www.broadridge.com/_assets/pdf/broadridge-charting-a-path-to-a-post-trade-utility-white-paper.pdf
10. https://www.capgemini.com/wp-content/uploads/2017/07/blockchain_securities_issuance_v6_web.pdf
11. https://www.gfma.org/policies-resources/gfma-publishes-report-on-impact-of-dlt-in-global-capital-markets/
12. Goldman Sachs, "Profiles in Innovation: Blockchain Putting Theory into Practice", 2016.
13. DTCC 2020 Annual Report
14. https://www.gfma.org/policies-resources/gfma-publishes-report-on-impact-of-dlt-in-global-capital-markets/
15. https://www.globalcustodian.com/custodians-assets-under-custody/
16. https://www.gfma.org/policies-resources/gfma-publishes-report-on-impact-of-dlt-in-global-capital-markets/
17. https://www.bnymellon.com/content/dam/bnymellon/documents/pdf/insights/migration-digital-assets-survey.pdf
18. https://www.gfma.org/policies-resources/gfma-publishes-report-on-impact-of-dlt-in-global-capital-markets/
19. https://www.broadridge.com/_assets/pdf/broadridge-asset-servicing-innovation-handbook-value-exchange-broadridge-nov-2021.pdf
20. https://www.cnbc.com/2021/10/12/few-individuals-participate-in-shareholder-voting-but-that-may-change.html
21. https://blog.digitalasset.com/developers/streamline-proxy-voting-and-regulatory-reporting-using-dlt
22. https://assets.ey.com/content/dam/ey-sites/ey-com/en_gl/topics/tax/tax-pdfs/ey-withholding-tax-distributed-ledger-report.pdf
23. https://ec.europa.eu/transparency/documents-register/detail?ref=COM(2017)147&lang=en
24. https://www.europarl.europa.eu/news/en/press-room/20181120IPR19552/cum-ex-tax-fraud-meps-call-for-inquiry-justice-and-stronger-tax-authorities
25. https://www.ey.com/en_sg/tax/taxgrid
26. https://www.gfma.org/policies-resources/gfma-publishes-report-on-impact-of-dlt-in-global-capital-markets/
27. https://www.gfma.org/policies-resources/gfma-publishes-report-on-impact-of-dlt-in-global-capital-markets/

8

Deposit Tokens

New ledger technology developed in the crypto world could allow tokenised bank deposits to circulate freely as 'tokenised deposit money', in what might be thought of as a digital banknote issued by a private bank. They would constitute claims on the issuing bank that could be held, for example in a wallet, without the holder having to have an account at the issuing bank.

—Sir Jon Cunliffe, Deputy Governor,
Financial Stability, Bank of England[1]

After discussing stablecoins, CBDCs, and tokenized assets, it's time to delve into deposit tokens, which could potentially revolutionize the banking industry by incorporating DLT technology into banking processes.

Deposit tokens are a way for commercial banks to implement DLT into their core business, offering the benefits of this technology.

8.1   What Are Deposit Tokens?

Deposit tokens are transferable tokens issued on a blockchain by a licensed depository institution, representing a deposit claim against the issuer.[2] At this point, deposit tokens are a very novel type of money that is currently being piloted by individual banks, consortia, and other private sector companies. Nonetheless, given the advantages of DLT and the importance of commercial banks in finance, this could well become a very significant trend.

But first, a point on terminology. The Global Financial Markets Association (GFMA) makes a distinction between the similar sounding "tokenized securities" and "security tokens." The former refers to a digital twin token that represents the underlying asset. The latter refers to an asset that is issued and custodized natively on a DLT exclusively with no underlying asset.[3] Even

Decentralizing Finance: How DeFi, Digital Assets, and Distributed Ledger Technology Are Transforming Finance, First Edition. Kenneth Bok.
© 2024 John Wiley & Sons Ltd. Published 2024 by John Wiley & Sons Ltd.

though "tokenized deposits" and "deposit tokens" appear to be used interchangeably in much of the literature I've seen, I will make this distinction between mirrored / twinned tokens and native tokens using this terminology. I should also note that deposit tokens appear to be more promising than tokenized deposits as they do not require an off-chain reconciliation process and can utilize the full functionality of DLT.[4]

To better understand deposit tokens, let's compare them to CBDCs and stablecoins. Bank deposits have unique characteristics that differentiate them from CBDCs and stablecoins. As we discuss the dimensions of digital fiat, the distinction for deposit tokens should become clearer. These dimensions are the issuer, regulatory status, participation in credit creation, and type of collateral.

Table 8.1 summarizes the four types of digital currencies.

Table 8.1 Types of digital currencies.

	Stablecoins	CBDCs	Deposit tokens	e-money
Issuer	Non-bank private companies	Central Banks	Commercial Banks	Non-bank private companies
Examples	USDC, USDT, BUSD	eNaira, eCNY	JPMCoin, RLN	PayPal, Square, Alipay, WeChat Pay
Regulatory oversight	Generally not well defined and still evolving	Central Bank and Governmental	Similar oversight as regulated bank deposits	Yes, most developed jurisdictions have e-money legislation
Collateral ratio	1:1	Backed by promise of central bank	Fractional reserve	1:1
Collateral type	Bank deposits, HQLA bonds, and other debt instruments	Domestic currency, Short- and long-term debt instruments, Foreign currency reserves, gold	Bank deposits, HQLA bonds, and other debt instruments	Fiat
Supports credit creation?	No	No	Yes	No
DLT-based?	Yes	Some	Yes	No

Source: Citi whitepaper, Author's elaboration

The primary distinction of the different types of digital fiat is the *issuer*. The issuer is the entity that bears the liability for the asset. CBDCs are liabilities of central banks, stablecoins are liabilities of private companies, and deposit tokens are liabilities of commercial banks. Each issuer has different counterparty risks, regulatory status, and collateral for the digital fiat.

Advocates of deposit tokens argue that by applying the existing regulations that govern traditional bank deposits to deposit tokens, they would be a safer alternative to stablecoins. This is particularly relevant as regulation around stablecoins is still evolving. Also, the main use case for stablecoins is currently crypto-trading, although this could change with more regulatory certainty.

While CBDCs would be the safest option in terms of counterparty risk, most CBDCs are not designed to compete with bank deposits. W-CBDCs can be seen as an upgrade to existing RTGS systems, while R-CBDCs are designed for payments rather than serving as a store of value or investment tool.

Another key issue is that of *credit creation*, and fundamentally that of how money is created in the current two-tier monetary system with fractional reserve banking. CBDCs and stablecoins are not designed to participate in the credit-creation process. As mentioned before in the CBDC chapter, nearly all central banks seek to maintain the status quo with the two-tier model. Central banks do not want to be in the business of extending credit or maintaining direct customer relationships with households and firms.

The ratio of commercial banking money to central banking money can be estimated by the M1/M0 ratio. In the United States, current M1 is US$18,943 billion and M0 is US$5,571 billion. This gives an M1/M0 ratio of around 3.4.[5] This means for every US$1 directly issued by the Fed, commercial banks have created US$3.40 of additional demand deposits in the United States.

The regulatory mandate of the issuer also dictates the amount and type of collateral that backs the digital fiat. In the case of stablecoins, they must be fully collateralized 1:1 for every stablecoin issued. These collateral are High Quality Liquid Assets (HQLA), usually in the form of cash and short-term Treasuries.

In contrast, commercial banks do not need to fully back bank deposits 1:1 due to fractional reserve banking. Banks must maintain certain liquidity ratios and requirements under Basel guidelines.

8.2 Benefits of Deposit Tokens

Why tokenize? As one might have guessed, the benefits of tokenizing bank deposits are in-line with the general benefits of asset tokenization. They include:

- Efficiency gains due to automation and disintermediation
- Enhanced resilience

- Transparency
- International reach and direct access

To that, we can add some additional benefits that are specific to deposit tokens. They include:

- Interoperability between banks
- Interoperability with CBDCs
- Atomic settlement, since they are the payment "P" leg of DvP and PvP transactions
- Reducing intermediaries and costs along the banking value chain
- Increasing liquidity of assets
- Enhance capital efficiency by eliminating "trapped liquidity" in escrow and margin arrangements
- Programmatic payments
- Enhancing AML and sanctions processes by automation, and other programmatic traceability
- Enabling DeFi innovations such as automated market makers which are built on smart contracts

Interoperability between banks could be one of the biggest benefits to deposit tokens. If adopted at scale, deposit tokens could greatly increase efficiencies in cross-border payments by reducing time to settlement. The move towards 24/365, always-on processing is already well underway in banking, and could be made a reality with deposit tokens.

Settlement risk in foreign exchange (FX) transactions is sometimes called Herstatt risk, after the German bank that collapsed. Counterparties that had sold Deutsche Marks to Herstatt in FX trades, expecting to receive US dollars in return, were left exposed when Herstatt's banking license was withdrawn by German regulators on 26 June 1974. The situation demonstrated the risk faced when one party in an FX trade settles their side of the transaction before receiving settlement from their counterparty, as was common practice at the time. After the Herstatt collapse, the FX market implemented payment-versus-payment (PvP) mechanisms to mitigate Herstatt risk by synchronizing the settlement of both sides of an FX trade. Atomic settlement by DLT takes this concept further.

8.3 Deposit Token Projects

There are several deposit token projects underway. Some of them are networks of multiple stakeholders, some are single stakeholders, and yet some of them are vendors offering solutions for deposit tokens.

8.3.1 Regulated Liability Network (RLN)

In June 2021, Citi published a report "The Regulated Internet of Value," authored by Tony McLaughlin, Head of Emerging Payments and Business Development at Citi's Treasury and Trade Solutions. The paper distinguished between *regulated liabilities*: CBDCs, deposit tokens, and e-money, and other unregulated digital assets such as Bitcoin.

Since then, the Regulated Liability Network (RLN) has published a Whitepaper and has collaborated with the New York Innovation Center (NYIC), which serves as the innovation hub of the Federal Reserve Bank of New York, on a proof-of-concept project. The team driving the initiative includes executives from Citi, OCBC, Goldman Sachs, BondeValue, Bank of America, Bank of New York, Payoneer, Paypal, Wells Fargo, SETL, and Linklaters.

The RLN proposes "a new shared ledger substrate for the sovereign currency system that is 'always on,' 'programmable,' and 'multi-asset.' The network would deliver 'on-chain' finality of settlement between the participating institutions in sovereign currencies and be compliant with all existing rules and regulations."[6]

The RLN is envisaged to be a regulated Financial Market Infrastructure (FMI) in accordance with the BIS's PFMI standards.

The shared ledger to be used has not been specified as yet, and may consist of one or several DLT systems and traditional database systems used in combination. SETL and AWS have published a paper to explore RLN's technical feasibility. R3 has also articulated what RLN would look like on Corda on their website.[7]

The RLN introduces the concept of legal and logical partitions, which can be compared to embassies. Similar to how an embassy of a foreign country is considered to be the home territory of the home country, decisions around access to a specific partition operated on the RLN are the exclusive right of the corresponding institution.

Partitions may be operated by central banks, commercial banks, e-money institutions, and possibly stablecoin institutions. Other deposit token consortia such as USDF and Tassat may also operate a partition on RLN.

8.3.2 Onyx by JP Morgan

The FSB maintains a list of Globally Systemically Important Banks (G-SIBs). These are banks that are considered critical to the global financial system due to their size, interconnectedness, cross-jurisdictional activity, substitutability, and complexity. Currently, there are 30 banks on the list. G-SIBs are subject to higher capital buffers and higher supervisory requirements. JP Morgan is the only bank to be in "Bucket 4" of the G-SIBs criteria, highlighting JP Morgan's importance in the global banking and payments system.

Onyx is JP Morgan's blockchain innovation unit, which launched its first product, JPM Coin, in 2020. JPM Coin is a permissioned system designed to function as a payment rail and deposit account ledger, enabling participating JP Morgan clients to transfer US Dollars held on deposit within the system. The platform is built on Quorum, a permissioned version of Ethereum that was initially created by JP Morgan in 2016 but later sold to ConsenSys. JPM Coin enables for 24/7 operations, atomic settlement, and programmable triggers.

Onyx's recent initiatives related to deposit tokens are intended to increase transferability to businesses and individuals outside the JP Morgan banking network. To enable this, Onyx is looking to utilize *verifiable credentials*, a new digital identity standard created by the World Wide Web Consortium (W3C). In a podcast, Naveen Mallela, Global Head of Coin Systems, explained that verifiable credentials perform a comparable function to KYC information used in correspondent banking, where the correspondent bank may accept KYC information if it is from a trusted source.[8]

Onyx's Digital Financing Application also allows for the fast and secure settlement of repo transactions within minutes. Repos, or repurchase agreements, are a common short-term borrowing mechanism utilized by banks, using government securities such as US Treasuries as collateral. The precise and more frequent intraday settlement cycles enable for the freeing of collateral that would otherwise be subject to longer T+2 settlement cycles. As of end 2022, US\$500 billion in transaction value has been settled on Onyx's platform.[9]

8.3.3 German Banking Industry Committee

The German Banking Industry Committee (GBIC) is the joint committee of the central associations of the German banking industry. In July 2021, the GBIC released a report titled "Europe Needs New Money – An Ecosystem of CBDC, Tokenised Commercial Bank Money, and Trigger Solutions," which proposed the development of a DLT-based monetary system with a potential digital euro CBDC. The GBIC refers to deposit tokens as "Commercial Bank Money Tokens" (CBMT) in the report. The proposal seems to be a collective response to the potential disintermediation of banks by retail CBDCs, but is also designed with integration with the digital euro in mind.

In March 2023, the GBIC released a follow-up working paper titled "Commercial Bank Money Token: Design and Considerations for a DLT-based Banking Network," which provides a detailed analysis of the potential design and considerations of a banking network built on DLT and deposit tokens. This paper is one of the most comprehensive reports on a deposit token network to date and explores various aspects such as settlement, legal considerations, fungibility, different operating models, and worst-case scenarios.

Considering the scope of this book, it is not feasible to provide an in-depth coverage of this topic. However, it's worth going a bit further into detail about fungibility considerations. How will deposit tokens maintain their "singleness" and fungibility across various banks that may use different DLTs?

The GBIC proposes three potential solutions for fungibility:

1. Fully collateralized stablecoin,
2. Special Purpose Vehicle (SPV), and
3. Commercial Bank Tokens.

In the fully collateralized stablecoin model, deposit tokens are the liabilities of the commercial bank, but are fully covered by central bank reserves. By maintaining full coverage by central bank reserves, counterparty risk is eliminated and all deposit tokens are fungible, regardless of the issuing bank. Reserves must be kept as collateral in an ECB trust account until the deposit token is destroyed. While this solution is relatively simple, it is capital intensive and requires close cooperation with the ECB / central bank.

In an SPV model, the deposit token is issued by a central SPV. This prevents a multi-issuer scenario and guarantees fungibility. The deposit token is a liability of the SPV and is issued to banks in exchange for collateral, in the form of securities. These could be HQLA such as government bonds and other short-term fixed income securities.

In the commercial bank token model, deposit tokens are liabilities of the bank, but are not collateralized in full by central bank reserves. This model maintains the credit creation by banks, but might lead to different exchange rates of deposit tokens owing to the differing counterparty risk of each bank. GBIC's proposal is that banks must grant each other credit lines and settle payments in central bank money.

A proof-of-concept is being conducted with DZ Bank, Commerzbank, Helaba and Unicredit, and selected corporates.[10]

8.3.4 Swiss Banker's Association (SBA)

The Swiss Bankers Association (SBA), the primary trade association representing Swiss Banks, has also weighed in on deposit tokens in a whitepaper published in March 2023. They suggested three models of deposit tokens, similar to the GBIC's proposals:

1. *Standardised Token*: Deposit tokens issued by respective banks that must comply with technical norms and fully backed by secure and highly liquid reserves;
2. *Joint Token*: SPV jointly owned by participating commercial banks, issuing a single deposit token that is fully or partially backed by secure and highly liquid reserves; and
3. *Coloured Token*: Deposit tokens are issued by respective banks but each bank is free to determine its own technology and collateral. All banks are regulated.

The SBA asserts that the Joint Token model is the most promising among the three, as it would enable "choice in terms of backing it with reserves without requiring excessive compromises," and would allow for "a certain degree of freedom with regards to money creation."[11]

8.3.5 Other projects

There are a number of other deposit token projects (and related projects) worth mentioning.

USDF is a consortium of US regional banks including New York Community Bank, NBH Bank, FirstBank, Webster Bank, Synovus Bank, and others. It uses a permissioned blockchain called Provenance, developed by Figure Technologies. It cites a number of use cases including automated mortgage payments, real-time international remittance, digital securities lending, and loan servicing.

Fnality, formerly USC (Utility Settlement Coin), was initially founded in 2015 by UBS and Clearmatics. It was based on a permissioned version of Ethereum. Fnality is a consortium with many financial institutions. Investors include Banco Santander, Bank of New York Mellon, Barclays, CIBC, Commerzbank, Credit Suisse, Euroclear, ING, KBC Group, Lloyds Banking Group, Mizuho, MUFG Group, Nasdaq, Nomura, SMBC, State Street, and UBS. It is planned to be multi-currency, including sterling, euro, US dollar, yen, and Canadian dollar. The Fnality system uses a central bank account for each currency to enable on-chain payments. Fnality's Sterling Fnality Payment System (FnPS) is due to launch in Q3 2023, and was recognized by HM Treasury as a payment system in August 2022.[12]

Tassat had powered the Signet network run by the now closed Signature Bank. Customers include Western Alliance Bank, Signature Bank, Customers Bank, Axos Bank, Byline Bank, and Cogent Bank.[13] In May 2023 it had announced a multi-currency functionality on its platform beginning in June 2023.

Partior, founded in 2021 as the commercial off-shoot of Project Ubin,[14] is backed by JP Morgan and other Singaporean entities Temasek and DBS Bank. Project Ubin is a MAS-led project to explore the use of DLT for clearing and settlement of payments and securities. The platform also intends to be a multi-currency network. Standard Chartered led the US$31m Series A funding round. Services include: multi-currency clearing and settlement, FX Payment vs Payment (PvP), FX Intraday Swaps, and Delivery vs Payment (DvP).

Project Orchid, from the Monetary Authority of Singapore (MAS), is an exploratory project on programmable digital currency. It is not strictly a deposit token project and the MAS does not plan to issue an R-CBDC at this point. Nonetheless Project Orchid is a forward-looking project that factors in all the various types of digital currency, including stablecoins, CBDCs, and deposit tokens, and explores real-world implementation of programmable money with examples.

The MAS's term for programmable digital currency is "Purpose Bound Money" (PBM). The MAS cites the "efficient disbursement of highly targeted or in-kind fiscal support (e.g., tourism vouchers)" and "machine-to-machine transactions" as possible use cases. The MAS distinguishes between "programmable payment" and "programmable money" in this way:

Programmable payment: "automatic execution of payments once a pre-defined set of conditions are met. For example, daily spending limits or recurring payments [...], similar to direct debits and standing orders."

Programmable money: "embedding rules within the medium of exchange itself that defines or constraints its usage. For example, [...] such that the medium of exchange could be denominated in fractional units of up to eighteen decimal places. [...] Unlike programmable payment, whereby the programming logic and the value itself are decoupled, programmable money is self-contained [...] When it has been transferred to another party, the logic and rules are moved as well."[15]

PBM looks to combine both programmable payment and programmable money. It works by wrapping the digital currency with the PBM smart contract. A wide variety of interaction patterns are suggested including payments between Governments, businesses, and individuals.

One use case that has been suggested, that Singaporeans are familiar with, are the "CDC voucher," vouchers issued by the Singapore Government designed to promote spending at small businesses. MAS proposes that PBM may assist in the redeemability, expiry, usability, and other conditions necessary in such a voucher scheme.

8.4 Chapter Summary

Deposit tokens are a novel type of digital currency that holds great potential for widespread application, particularly in light of the prevalence of commercial banks. The examples discussed in this chapter may have an advantage in terms of early experimentation, as they include some of the world's largest banks. However, there is still ample opportunity for innovation and growth in this field.

Notes

1. https://www.bankofengland.co.uk/speech/2023/april/jon-cunliffe-keynote-speech-at-the-innovate-finance-global-summit
2. https://www.jpmorgan.com/onyx/content-hub/deposit-tokens.htm
3 https://www.gfma.org/policies-resources/gfma-publishes-report-on-impact-of-dlt-in-global-capital-markets/

4. https://www.jpmorgan.com/onyx/content-hub/deposit-tokens.htm
5. https://tradingeconomics.com/united-states/money-supply-m0
6. https://regulatedliabilitynetwork.org/wp-content/uploads/2022/11/The-Regulated-Liability-Network-Whitepaper.pdf
7. https://r3.com/blog/the-regulated-liability-network-on-corda/
8. https://www.youtube.com/watch?v=_hZQ_jyCukI&ab_channel=DigFinVOX byAMTD
9. https://www.gfma.org/wp-content/uploads/2023/05/impact-of-dlt-on-global-capital-markets-full-report.pdf
10. https://www.ledgerinsights.com/deposit-tokens-german-banks-multi-currency/
11. https://www.swissbanking.ch/en/news-and-positions/news/the-deposit-token-sba-white-paper-on-a-digital-swiss-franc
12. https://www.ledgerinsights.com/fnality-dlt-payment-delay/
13. https://www.spglobal.com/marketintelligence/en/news-insights/latest-news-headlines/banks-blockchain-payment-networks-are-not-just-for-crypto currency-74222468
14. https://www.digfingroup.com/partior/
15. https://www.mas.gov.sg/publications/monographs-or-information-paper/2022/project-orchid-whitepaper

9

Institutional DeFi

In this chapter we'll synthesize the different components of what has been covered so far regarding DeFi innovations. This includes aspects such as AMMs, CBDCs, tokenized assets, tokenized deposits, and tokenized securities. By tying these threads together, we can gain insight into what the future institutional use of DeFi could look like.

Institutions have different requirements from individuals when adopting technology and working with counterparties. Licensed financial institutions are subject to stringent regulations such as KYC, AML, and technology risk compliance. This has made it challenging for them to participate in web3 and DeFi.

9.1 Considerations for Institutions to Participate in DeFi

Financial institutions interested in participating in DeFi or building a DeFi product will need to consider the following:

Regulatory compliance: Financial institutions will need to ensure that they are compliant with all applicable regulations. This includes ensuring that they have the appropriate KYC and AML procedures in place.

Counterparty risk: Financial institutions will need to assess the counterparty risk associated with DeFi protocols. This includes assessing the risk of hacks, smart contract vulnerabilities, and other security risks.

Technology risk management: Financial institutions will need to have a robust technology risk management framework in place to manage the risks associated with DeFi. This includes ensuring that they have the appropriate security controls in place and that they are able to monitor and respond to security incidents.

Decentralizing Finance: How DeFi, Digital Assets, and Distributed Ledger Technology Are Transforming Finance, First Edition. Kenneth Bok.
© 2024 John Wiley & Sons Ltd. Published 2024 by John Wiley & Sons Ltd.

Custody and key management: Financial institutions will need to ensure that they have a secure custody solution for their digital assets. This includes ensuring that they have the appropriate hardware and software security controls in place.

Auditing and reporting: Financial institutions will need to be able to audit and report on their DeFi activities. This includes ensuring that they have the appropriate internal controls in place and that they are able to produce audit reports that meet regulatory requirements.

Integration with TradFi rails: Financial institutions will need to integrate their DeFi activities with their traditional financial infrastructure. This includes ensuring that they are able to transfer assets between DeFi and TradFi systems.

On-off ramps: Financial institutions will need to provide on and off-ramps for their customers to access DeFi. This includes providing fiat currency gateways and other methods for customers to deposit and withdraw funds from DeFi protocols.

Cross-chain capabilities: Financial institutions might need to be able to operate across multiple blockchains. This is because DeFi protocols are not limited to a single blockchain.

Differentiating digital assets according to SCO60: Financial institutions will need to be able to differentiate between different types of digital assets. This is because different types of digital assets have different risk profiles and regulatory requirements under the Basel Framework.

Identifying and evaluating DeFi investment opportunities: Financial institutions will need to be able to identify and evaluate DeFi investment opportunities. This includes understanding the risks and rewards of different DeFi protocols.

Education and research for staff: Financial institutions will need to provide education and training to their staff on DeFi. This is because DeFi is a complex and rapidly evolving space.

9.2 Institutional DeFi Examples

"Permissioned DeFi" was first introduced in mid-2021 by crypto startups Aave and Compound to enable institutional participation in borrowing / lending liquidity pools. Custody company Fireblocks performed whitelisting. Aave's product was Aave Arc and Compound had Compound Treasury. These liquidity markets were designed to comply with AML and KYC/KYB regulations. As of writing, Compound Treasury is closed. I note that most institutions in these pools have been crypto-native, including OTC desks, market makers, and crypto funds.

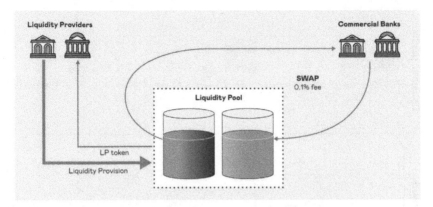

Figure 9.1 Liquidity provision in Singapore–France CBDC exchange trial.

One promising development in Institutional DeFi is the involvement of central banks, which have ventured into DeFi through the use of AMMs with CBDCs. We will explore some of these projects and the reasons behind this trend in more detail next.

In 2021, Onyx by JP Morgan, the MAS, and Banque de France conducted a pilot "*Liquidity management in a multi-currency corridor network.*" The project simulated cross-border transactions involving the Singapore dollar (SGD) and euro (EUR) CBDCs. Among the key objectives of the pilot, was the use of smart contracts in managing the exchange rate for the currency pair and providing automated liquidity pool and market-making services.

The pilot consisted of commercial banks being liquidity providers by staking their CBDCs from their wallets into the liquidity pool. Other commercial banks using the liquidity pool for trades were charged a 0.1% exchange fee debited from the liquidity taker's wallet (Figure 9.1).[1] The fees were retained by the liquidity pool and accrued to the liquidity providers, proportionally based on their staked assets to the pool.

The pilot used a fixed daily exchange rate for simplicity and did not use a constant product formula. Liquidity providers were required to stake EUR and SGD proportionally (1 EUR = 1.6 SGD) in exchange for 1 LP token. Liquidity providers were allowed to withdraw their staked CBDCs at any time

There are two other notable projects that involve the use of CBDCs and AMMs for liquidity provision in the FX market. The first is Project Mariana, which is a joint initiative of the Bank of France, the Monetary Authority of Singapore, and the Swiss National Bank, as well as their respective BIS Innovation Hub Centers.

Project Mariana extends the liquidity pool concept from two currencies to three, with CHF, EUR, and SGD W-CBDCs. The project had three objectives: (1) to examine a W-CBDC token design based on a uniform technical standard

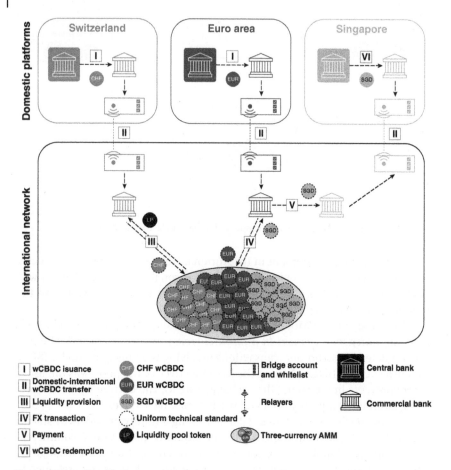

Figure 9.2 Project Mariana architecture.

and incorporate governance features that meet central bank requirements, (2) to design bridges for W-CBDC transfer between domestic platforms and an international network, and (3) to develop an FX interbank market using an AMM (Figure 9.2).[2]

Here are some key points from Project Mariana:

- Each central bank issues W-CBDCs on their respective domestic platforms, operates the bridge with the international network, and determines access.
- Central banks perform access control on commercial banks for W-CBDCs and transaction monitoring.
- Commercial banks request W-CBDC issuance and redemption on domestic platform.
- Commercial banks transfer W-CBDCs from domestic platform to international network.

- Commercial banks can provide and remove liquidity from the pool.
- Commercial banks may deposit one, two, or three currencies into the pool.
- Commercial banks can transfer W-CBDCs to other commercial banks in the international network.
- Commercial banks can exchange W-CBDCs via AMM in the international network.

The AMM is also intended to comply with the FX Global Code, a set of good practice principles for the FX market, such as transparency and market integrity. The system is Ethereum-based, with the W-CBDCs using the ERC-20 standard. A hybrid function market maker based on Curve V2 was used, which allows for slippage around frequently traded price ranges to be kept low.

The second is *Project Dunbar*, one of the two notable mCBDC projects, which involves collaboration between the BIS Innovation Hub, Reserve Bank of Australia, Central Bank of Malaysia, Monetary Authority of Singapore, and South African Reserve Bank.

One of the most significant projects with institutional DeFi and institutional grade digital asset networks is *Project Guardian*, led by the MAS. Project Guardian covers four key areas:

1. Open and interoperable networks,
2. Trust anchors,
3. Asset tokenization, and
4. Institutional grade DeFi protocols.

The Project Guardian report published in June 2023 defines various typologies of digital asset networks:

- *Platform types*: Public, private, and permissioned;
- *Asset types*: Native tokens, non-native tokens, account-based, fungible, non-fungible;
- *Access control*: Whitelisting, partitioning, verifiable credentials; and
- *Network structure*: Flat, layered, interlinked.

In the initial phase of Project Guardian, DBS and SBI Digital Asset Holdings collaborated on an AMM-based liquidity pool that held tokenized deposits and tokenized securities, including Singapore Government Securities Bonds, Japanese Government Bonds, and Japanese yen (JPY) and Singapore dollar (SGD) currencies. The project was conducted on a public blockchain, specifically Polygon, using an AMM (a modified version of Uniswap).

The pool consisted of three components: the tokenization system, verifiable credential issuance platform, and liquidity pool protocol (Figure 9.3).[3]

What is novel in the Project Guardian liquidity pool project is the access control system that uses Verifiable Credentials (VC) tokens, in line with W3C standards. VC tokens in accordance with ERC-721 token standards were issued with specific authorizations for liquidity providers and traders. In the project,

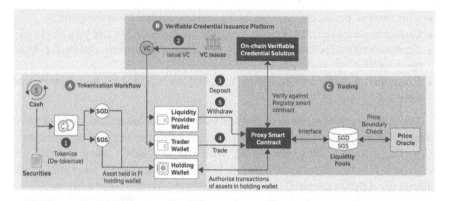

Figure 9.3 Project Guardian liquidity pool.
Source: Monetary Authority of Singapore, Project Guardian https://www.mas.gov.sg/publications/monographs-or-information-paper/2023/project-guardian-open-interoperable-networks (Pg. 26)

DBS and SBI served as trust anchors that performed screening and issued the VC tokens. The token contains various information such as participant identity, issuer identity, role, expiry, and digital signature.

The second project conducted with Project Guardian was a trade finance asset backed security token conducted by Standard Chartered, SGX Group (Singapore stock exchange), and Linklogis (Chinese supply chain FinTech). The project involved tokenizing trade finance receivables in the form of NFTs, and further tranching the assets into senior and junior tranches. The tranches were then tokenized to be made available for institutional investors.

I note that this design (specifically tranching and tokenizing by risk class) has also been done in the "real-world asset" / uncollateralized lending category in DeFi with platforms such as Credix and Goldfinch as covered in Chapter 3.

Project Guardian also elaborates on how the Principles for Financial Market Infrastructures (PFMI), an international standard for financial market infrastructures jointly developed by the BIS Committee for Payments and Market Infrastructures (CPMI) and the International Organization of Securities Commissions (IOSCO), applies to digital asset networks. It lists other relevant standards from IOSCO, BCBS, and FATF.

9.3 AMMs and FX

The previous examples illustrate the interest central banks have in using smart contracts and automated market makers with CBDCs and FX. This suggests a pathway in which CBDCs and tokenized deposits play more of a role with institutional DeFi. I note here as a counterpoint that crypto-native private sector players have also actively explored this topic, with the use of stablecoins.

While in theory, any asset class can be tokenized and research into how smart contracts can be implemented in traditional finance is ongoing, FX appears to be one of the more promising, being the largest market in the world (US7.5 trillion / day[4]) and their fundamental role in international and domestic finance.

Let's discuss more in detail how AMMs can play a role in the FX markets.

In a paper jointly published by Circle and Uniswap, "On-chain Foreign Exchange and cross-border payments," they explore the use of stablecoins and AMMs in the FX market. They suggest that on-chain FX can reduce the cost of remittance by up to 80%.[5]

In line with many other features of DeFi as mentioned several times in this book, FX markets based on stablecoins (or similarly, tokenized deposits and CBDCs) on AMMs can provide:

- 24/7 market,
- Near-instant settlement,
- Reduced settlement risks due to on-chain PvP,
- Data transparency, and
- Liquidity aggregation with smaller liquidity providers.

One of the key issues that AMMs solve in DeFi is liquidity provision for tokens with low liquidity. Coinmarketcap counts 26,114 cryptocurrencies as of time of writing, and many of them are tradable on AMM-based DEXs such as Uniswap. To utilize centralized market making facilities such as dedicated OTC market-making companies would be cost-prohibitive for these low liquidity tokens.

There is a similarity between this problem and illiquid currencies. There are currently 180 currencies recognized as legal tender by the UN. The vast majority of FX transactions are focused on a few major currencies such as USD, EUR, GBP, CHF, and JPY. The CLS system supports 18 major currencies. The trade of two illiquid currencies will frequently need to cross the spread twice with a major currency such as USD. The use of AMMs in FX could thus also be beneficial for developing and emerging economies for trade and market access.

Nonetheless, the market for non-USD stablecoins does not seem to have taken off, and appears to have significant headwinds, regulation being the primary challenge. The vast majority of stablecoin issuance is in USD, with USD representing 99.4% of all stablecoin issuance in USD value. EUR represents 0.54% and GBP represents 0.03% of total stablecoin issuance.[6] A report from Cumberland "The Growth Potential of Non-USD Stablecoins" examines this issue with regulations, use-cases, and technical considerations such as choice of blockchain.

A vibrant stablecoin-based FX ecosystem would necessitate a number of things:

- Consumers and businesses to have regulatory comfort and legal certainty over stablecoins.

- Stablecoin issuers that will likely be native to each country / currency, under a defined regulatory framework.
  - Or, banks issuing stablecoins, which is already happening in Japan,
  - For which stablecoins must be fully collateralized by cash or HQLA.
- There is an upper limit to stablecoins based on HQLA markets, and also bearing in mind that not all countries have liquid HQLA markets.

Japan has some of the most progressive legislation regarding stablecoins. In June 2022, Japan passed a law governing stablecoins, becoming the first G7 economy to establish a regulatory framework for them. In December 2022, Japan's Financial Services Agency, the country's financial regulator, lifted the ban on foreign-issued stablecoins.

Japanese bank trust companies, trust companies, and fund transfer operators are able to obtain authorization to issue stablecoins. Issuers must make fully backed security deposits, in monetary form or in HQLA such as government bond certificates.

A number of Japanese banks have already started developing stablecoin products.

Mitsubishi UFJ Trust and Banking, Japan's largest bank, is preparing to issue a stablecoin on their digital asset platform, Progmat.

Another group comprising Minna Bank, Tokyo Kiraboshi Financial Group, and Shikoku Bank are intending to issue stablecoins on Japan Open Chain, an Ethereum-based blockchain.

With stablecoins, Japanese consumers and businesses will have an option to make financial transactions without utilizing the national interbank clearing network, and is expected to cost less than wiring money through a bank.

9.4 Considerations for AMMs and Tokenized Assets

The use of AMMs in FX is very new, and there are a number of important issues that need to be addressed before it can be put into practice.

Liquidity providers to an AMM face a number of risks and opportunity costs. Staked assets in the pool are subject to loss due to technical risks. Staked assets also bear opportunity costs such as forgone interest and other uses for capital.

Perhaps the most problematic aspect of AMMs is the impermanent loss faced by liquidity providers. As discussed in Chapter 3, due to the programmatic nature of AMMs where price is a function of the balances in the pool, liquidity providers will always be at a disadvantage where price information is concerned. Impermanent loss is an effect of always having to take bad trades from arbitrageurs who have price information from other markets. One possible mitigation is to raise the exchange fee.

9.5 Unified Ledger

In a February 2023 speech on "Innovation and the future of the monetary system," Agustin Carstens, General Manager of the BIS, proposed the concept of a "unified programmable ledger." This public–private partnership would enable the interoperability of tokenized deposits and CBDCs through separate partitions on a unified ledger. This idea bears similarities to the RLN project, but also generalizes further to include tokenized assets.

This unified ledger aims to achieve two purposes[7]:

1. Combining all the components necessary to complete transactions on one platform.
2. Featuring money and assets as executable objects, so that transactions can occur without external authentication and verification.

The BIS takes into account the "large discrete changes entailed by new infrastructures"[8] and suggest incremental changes to the financial system by linking DLT-based systems with legacy systems by APIs. This would have lower upfront costs and require less coordination among stakeholders than creating a fully fledged unified ledger. Nonetheless, the BIS states that eventually these incremental fixes have limitations as they hold back the full benefits of DLT.

> [...] it is often the case that harnessing the benefits of technological advances necessitates a fundamental rethink of the financial infrastructure that supports new types of operation. Tokenisation presents another such opportunity, where the introduction of programmable platforms could bring long-term benefits that far outweigh the short-term costs arising from investment as well as the costs and coordination efforts in shifting to new standards and procedures.
>
> —BIS[9]

The BIS also discusses the key issue of privacy. Businesses will require assurances that confidential information can be protected. Safeguards and compliance with existing data privacy laws and standards, such as the EU's General Data Protection Regulation (GDPR), will need to be harmonized with a unified ledger.

The BIS envisions the unified ledger as having an execution environment and a data environment, which are subject to a common governance framework. Operating entities own and operate separate partitions in the data environment. Data encryption is also utilized in the execution environment. Cryptographic techniques such as homomorphic encryption allow for encrypted data to be used computationally. In this manner confidentiality and data control is achieved (Figure 9.4).[10]

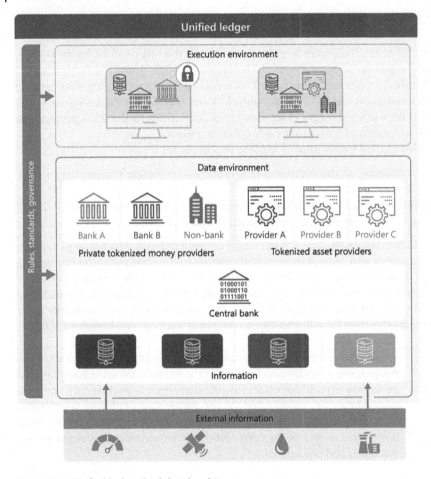

Figure 9.4 Unified ledger high level architecture.

Other privacy-preserving technologies that the BIS suggest could be used include

- Differential privacy,
- Secure multi-party computation, and
- Federated learning.

9.6 Chapter Summary

Institutional DeFi is an emerging and exciting field that is at the leading edge of DLT innovation and how it intersects with traditional finance. Significant work and time will be required for regulations, compliance standards, laws, and operational standards to evolve to allow smart contract-based innovations to be used in current financial operations. Nonetheless, the future is bright as the benefits of DLT are clear.

Notes

1. https://www.jpmorgan.com/content/dam/jpm/securities/documents/executive-summary.pdf
2. https://www.bis.org/about/bisih/topics/cbdc/mariana.htm
3. https://www.mas.gov.sg/publications/monographs-or-information-paper/2023/project-guardian-open-interoperable-networks
4. https://www.reuters.com/markets/us/global-fx-trading-hits-record-75-trln-day-bis-survey-2022-10-27/
5. https://uniswap.org/OnchainFX.pdf
6. https://www.theblock.co/data/decentralized-finance/stablecoins
7. https://www.bis.org/publ/arpdf/ar2023e3.htm
8. https://www.bis.org/publ/arpdf/ar2023e3.htm
9. https://www.bis.org/publ/arpdf/ar2023e3.htm
10. https://www.bis.org/publ/arpdf/ar2023e3.htm

10

Conclusion

I trust that you found this comprehensive guide to Digital Assets, DeFi, and DLT as enlightening to read as I found it fulfilling to write. Since I started writing in May 2022, the crypto landscape has changed dramatically. This period saw the downfall of Terra, followed by a similar fate for FTX in November of the same year.

The collapse of Terra and FTX serves as a stark reminder of the importance of adhering to established procedures in traditional finance. They highlight the potential risks involved with algorithmic stablecoins and the potential for mismanagement when assets are pooled without adequate oversight on cryptocurrency exchanges. While these incidents were not strictly related to DeFi, they undeniably had a significant impact on crypto and DeFi's future trajectory.

Although DeFi has experienced its share of security breaches, the core infrastructure has proven itself to be robust, maintaining reliability even amidst significant volatility. However, from a regulatory standpoint, these events have cast a shadow over the future of crypto-native DeFi.

Money has evolved tremendously over human history – from beads and shells to metal coins to paper bills and now digital currencies. The future of money promises more massive changes as technology continues disrupting how we store, use, and think about value.

Digital currencies like Bitcoin and Ethereum mark just the beginning of decentralized, global money powered by blockchain technology. As more assets become tokenized on blockchains, we may see a shift to programmable money with conditional logic and automated contracts built in. Money could become "smart," able to be customized, programmed, and regulated automatically via code rather than centralized control.

Regardless of the trajectory of cryptocurrency, the future of the broader digital-asset revolution is incontrovertible. The emergence of CBDCs,

Decentralizing Finance: How DeFi, Digital Assets, and Distributed Ledger Technology Are Transforming Finance, First Edition. Kenneth Bok.
© 2024 John Wiley & Sons Ltd. Published 2024 by John Wiley & Sons Ltd.

tokenized assets, and tokenized deposits seems inevitable. We are undoubtedly moving towards a future dominated by digital assets and currencies that promote innovation and new functionalities. From cash to credit cards, and from digital banking to FinTech applications, the future is evolving to one that is increasingly digital.

Decentralized networks, underpinning digital currencies, foster open ecosystems and fuel innovation. This ultimately leads to more secure, efficient, and cost-effective transaction methods.

Beyond blockchain, the growth of embedded payments through wearables, IoT devices, and biometrics may someday make physical cash and cards obsolete. Money could get integrated directly into identity and everyday objects through technology embedded in our bodies, clothes, cars, appliances, and environment. This would make money nearly invisible yet still enable transacting anytime and any where.

Of course, downsides abound, from deepening inequality if access is limited, to catastrophic failures if corrupted. Any major changes would need equitable oversight and regulatory guidance to align new monetary systems with human values. As money keeps evolving in the digital era, societies will need to balance promise and peril thoughtfully. But the possibilities for empowerment through access, automation, and advancing technology remain thrilling if we can steward change responsibly.

I'd like to conclude by articulating what I call the "Crypto-Fiat Innovation Dialectic" and some predictions around the future of DeFi and the future of digital money as a whole.

10.1 The Crypto–Fiat Innovation Dialectic

> Cryptocurrencies such as bitcoin, however, have spurred innovation in the banking system, both in technology and by challenging incumbents. Ultimately, this could be bitcoin's most valuable contribution to the public good.
>
> —(Kenneth Bok, "Harnessing decentralised finance innovation for the public good")[1]

The German philosopher Hegel suggested that history unfolds through a dialectical process involving three stages: thesis, antithesis, and synthesis. It appears that we are currently in the midst of such a dialectic between crypto and fiat.

Thesis: The dominant monetary system and fiat currencies (dollars, euros, etc.) promoted by traditional financial institutions and governments.

Antithesis: The invention of Bitcoin and decentralized cryptocurrencies built on blockchain, which challenge fiat currencies and traditional institutions.

Synthesis: The ongoing integration of blockchain into the mainstream financial world. Neither fiat nor crypto "win" outright but both evolve. Innovations from the crypto "Wild West" are adopted by regulated finance gradually.

The adoption of innovations, such as blockchain technology, automated market makers, and, in the near future, zero-knowledge proofs (ZKPs), will have a transformative impact on traditional finance. In conceptualizing a framework that includes both sides of the digital asset sphere, I believe it can be a useful guide for policymakers, technologists, and entrepreneurs in the ongoing transformation of digital money.

10.1.1 From Bitcoin to CBDCs

Before the advent of Bitcoin, digital fiat had never faced a challenger. Bitcoin aimed directly at the heart of central banking and its inherent flaws – specifically, the historical tendency of central banks to resort to printing money, particularly for the purpose of paying off national debt denominated in their own currencies. As Ray Dalio echoes:

> Of the roughly 750 currencies that have existed since 1700, only about 20 percent remain, and all of them have been devalued.
> —(Ray Dalio, *Principles for Dealing with the Changing World Order: Why Nations Succeed and Fail*)

The Austrian economist and Nobel laureate F. A. Hayek first articulated private money's benefits. Crypto catalyzes private sector digital money innovations. As Hayek wrote:

> As soon as one succeeds in freeing oneself of the universally but tacitly accepted creed that a country must be supplied by its government with its own distinctive and exclusive currency, all sorts of interesting questions arise which have never been examined.
> —(F. A. Hayek, *The Denationalisation of Money*)

Ethereum, following Bitcoin's lead, emerged as a platform for programmable money, allowing for the subsequent launch of stablecoins on smart contract platforms. Facebook, observing this, decided to launch Libra. As discussed in Chapter 6, the ambitious Libra project proved to be a significant catalyst, prompting notable responses from the G20. These developments were key drivers behind the creation of CBDCs (Figure 10.1).

There is a clear connection between crypto innovations and regulated finance's adoption of them, though this influence is often downplayed due to contrasting philosophies. Still, crypto innovations have impacted regulated finance's evolution significantly.

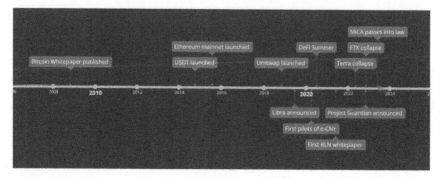

Figure 10.1 Digital asset evolutionary timeline.
Source: Author

Of course, if one looks further back, Bitcoin was also a synthesis of different technologies and innovations such as David Chaum's eCash and Proof-of-Work from Adam Back's Hashcash.

The public use of cryptography and strong encryption is a relatively recent phenomenon, closely following the advancements in personal computing and the increased availability of computational power, which made it feasible for daily use. The expansion of the internet, which necessitated secure communication and transactions, especially with the emergence of e-commerce, significantly contributed to the widespread adoption of strong encryption.

PGP (Pretty Good Privacy) encryption, for instance, was developed by Phil Zimmermann in 1991 and was one of the first widely available implementations of strong encryption for the public. Just a few decades prior in the 1970s, cryptography was classified as a munition in the United States, restricting its development and export. The public availability of strong encryption has been a boon to financial innovation as a whole.

10.1.2 Can DeFi Advance Financial Inclusion?

Central bankers and regulators often talk about financial inclusion as a key policy objective. I believe DeFi can assist in this noble mission. Amid a world seemingly paralyzed by bureaucratic impasses at the highest echelons, we somehow miss the fact that crypto enables anyone with an internet connection to create a bank account. Undoubtedly many aspects of DeFi need to be improved, such as consumer protections, key recovery, user experience (UX), and more. Nonetheless what DeFi has achieved to this point without government intervention is remarkable. Rather than constantly viewing crypto as the disreputable counterpart of traditional finance, regulators should focus on fostering and harmonizing DeFi, in line with their duty to encourage financial inclusion and innovation.

Several key projects, such as Kenya's M-Pesa, India's UPI, and Brazil's Pix, have significantly advanced financial inclusion. These projects, akin to roads and plumbing, are integral infrastructures of a country and are, therefore, public goods by necessity. However, the question arises: who will construct such a global public fintech infrastructure? There seems to be no regulatory body equipped for such an endeavor, possibly with the exception of the IMF. Given its early success, DeFi could step up to fulfill this role.

I once posed this question to a distinguished panel at an Official Monetary and Financial Institutions Forum (OMFIF) meeting, and was directed to the Bank for International Settlements' (BIS) Principles for Financial Market Infrastructures (PFMI). This document outlines the standards for financial market infrastructures in countries. If DeFi is to serve as a global fintech infrastructure, these principles seem to be an excellent starting point.

10.1.3 DeFi as Global FinTech Sandbox

Regulation and innovation often exist in a delicate balance, and the scales frequently tip against smaller entities. Crypto-native DeFi is one of the few areas where individuals can innovate freely without the need to engage vast teams of lawyers, lobbyists, and compliance personnel to appease regulators. Regulation often benefits established entities like large banks. Is this truly beneficial for consumers?

The innovative potential of this seemingly "Wild West" is an aspect often overlooked. Regulatory frameworks tend to favor incumbents and can hamper innovation. While it's true that cryptocurrency carries risks, it also empowers entrepreneurs and developers to share code via platforms like GitHub, engage in open-source innovation, and collaborate on a global scale. These opportunities are virtually non-existent in traditional finance, where banks maintain a tight grip on their source code, and developers operate within insulated silos.

Thus, a fitting analogy for understanding crypto and DeFi may be a "live" FinTech sandbox. By facilitating permissionless participation and innovation, crypto-native DeFi allows for experimentation without posing serious risks to the broader financial system. Ideally, participants in the crypto space should be fully aware of the associated risks and understand that government intervention or bailouts are not guaranteed. Disclosures and clear labeling from crypto companies should both be required and an industry standard.

What sets this sandbox apart is that real value is being transacted on this network. The stakes are genuine, attracting skilled talent as well as more nefarious elements such as hackers. However, it's worth noting that these real-world hackers are necessary to expose vulnerabilities in these complex systems.

10.1.4 Cybersecurity

Cybersecurity is of the utmost priority when it comes to CBDCs. The integrity of any CBDC system is only as strong as its weakest cybersecurity link, and a single major breach could significantly erode consumer and business trust in the central bank and the government it represents.

Interestingly, the cybersecurity challenges experienced in the DeFi space offer valuable lessons. For instance, Project Polaris undertaken by the BIS has closely studied these issues. When anticipating potential threats to CBDCs, BIS recommends utilizing established cybersecurity frameworks like the MITRE ATT&CK.

Inferences drawn from DeFi attacks and subsequent lessons are being utilized to identify potential tactics, techniques, and procedures that adversaries could deploy against CBDC systems. A direct excerpt from the Project Polaris report explains:

> since CBDCs are relatively new compared with other payment systems, there is very little historical data to predict threats specific to CBDCs. While DeFi is not a synonym for CBDCs, several of the current operational retail CBDC implementations are based on a similar technology stack or make use of one or more of DLT, smart contracts, tokens, digital identities and immutable data. This allows DeFi to serve as the starting point for this analysis of CBDC, although more tailored frameworks may need to be developed in future as the space matures.[2]

Therefore, the cybersecurity landscape within DLT should be viewed holistically, encompassing both realms of the digital-assets world. This perspective presents significant opportunities for strengthening security measures and enhancing the resilience of these emerging financial systems.

10.1.5 Moving Forward with Synthesis

The cryptocurrency community and central banking institutions should not perceive each other as adversaries. It's worth stating outright that the central banking community has a profound grasp of monetary matters, considering both historical and social dimensions, which significantly surpasses that of the cryptocurrency community.

If the goal of cryptocurrency is to genuinely serve the public interest through the facilitation of financial services, it should strive to operate within the guidelines and frameworks that history has painstakingly established. Delivering financial services at scale isn't merely a technological endeavor – it's an immense undertaking that necessitates the intricate coordination of legal considerations, geopolitical factors, policy, and regulation.

Thus, rather than positioning themselves in opposition, the cryptocurrency community and central banking institutions should seek productive dialogue and collaboration. This approach will be key to realizing the full potential of digital currencies and to ensuring their effective, safe, and equitable integration into the broader financial ecosystem.

10.2   Future Scenarios for DeFi: The Wild West, the Citadel, and the Bazaar

Looking ahead, it might be useful to draw some conclusions about the future of DeFi and the evolution of different paths of DLT and digital assets. What are its future prospects? What are the key developments that need to occur for it to go mainstream?

At this juncture it is fairly clear that the digital assets world is split into two fairly distinct paths:

1. *The Wild West*: A DeFi and crypto-native thread that stays true to the core tenets of decentralization, censorship resistance, community-governance, and pseudonymity. Public blockchains are the norm and tokens play an integral role in fundraising, utility, and governance.
2. *The Citadel*: A path within regulated finance that integrates DeFi innovations without actual linkage of crypto-native assets. Permissioned DLT is the norm and tokens are used in representing real-world assets.

To which we can also add a third possibility – the intersection of both:

3. *The Bazaar*: A path that combines both, with financial institutions incorporating crypto-assets into their operations, utilizing public blockchains, allowing for tokenized assets to trade with crypto-assets.

10.2.1   Path 1: Crypto-native DeFi / "Wild West"

10.2.1.1   Tailwinds

- Teams, especially top tier protocols, have very long runways and can build indefinitely
- Metcalfe's law and internet-native
- Open-source, permissionless innovation

10.2.1.2   Headwinds

- Regulatory risk
- Difficulty of serving real world consumers due to lack of integration with identity systems
- Tokens suffer from reputational issues whose utility is questionable

Just like the US Frontier in the 1850s, crypto-native DeFi can be a lawless, unpredictable place rife with risk. There is a lack of oversight and protections in this uncharted territory. At the same time, there is no shortage of opportunity in this wide open space for innovation and profit for the adventurous. Like the pioneers venturing west, those willing to brave the hazards of the frontier stand to gain handsome rewards.

Despite repeated proclamations of Bitcoin and crypto's downfall, they have consistently risen from the proverbial ashes. The crypto industry, mirroring broader economic trends, experiences its own cycles of boom and bust.

A prime example is the DeFi boom of 2020. In the 2017–2018 period, the crypto market witnessed an extraordinary surge from a market capitalization of less than US$20 billion to a peak of around US$800 billion. The market then crashed to US$100 billion by the end of 2018. However, this paled in comparison to the bull market of 2021–2022, which saw the market capitalization approach US$3 trillion.

Significantly, innovations within DeFi, such as Uniswap and Aave, were founded in 2017–2018 and *continued* building during the periods of stagnation when the sector was in the doldrums and largely ignored. These instances underscore the resilience and potential of the crypto and DeFi spaces, even amidst fluctuating conditions.

The public's fascination with extremes is a sentiment that the media is all too willing to capitalize on. Whether in seasons of boom or bust, the media's amplification often exacerbates the situation. However, beneath the surface tumult, tier 1 crypto teams and protocols maintain substantial treasuries that allow them to keep operations running. Regardless of the market's ups and downs, these teams persist in building their projects and ecosystems in line with their mandates and commitments.

Moreover, my focus thus far has been on crypto as it relates to finance. What falls outside the purview of this book is the expansive web3 industry, which incorporates other sectors such as Non-Fungible Tokens (NFTs), gaming, and various web3 infrastructure projects. Web3 could very well become a fundamental component of the future Metaverse, offering another dynamic arena for innovation.

Crypto-native DeFi is poised to experience a surge when these innovations are sufficiently developed and ready for the global consumer market. The intersection of these technological advancements promises to usher in a new era of digital interaction and transaction, further solidifying the role of DeFi in the evolving digital economy.

Crypto-native DeFi faces two primary challenges: regulation and identity, with the latter largely contingent on regulatory clarity. As of the time of writing, regulatory landscapes are varied. The European Union has passed MiCA (Markets in Crypto-assets), but the United States continues to scrutinize crypto practices, with little political will evident in either the Democrat or Republican camps to advance a pro-crypto agenda.

The absence of a well-defined identity mechanism poses a significant hurdle for DeFi in reaching mainstream consumers. Existing financial regulations and laws are fundamentally centered around Know Your Customer (KYC) and Anti-Money Laundering (AML) considerations. These regulations require payment providers to obtain and verify the identities of their customers, a mandate enforced by international bodies such as the Financial Action Task Force (FATF).

It remains to be seen whether initiatives like Decentralized Identity (DID) or projects like Worldcoin can successfully establish an internet-native identity layer compatible with DeFi. As these technologies evolve, their success or failure will play a pivotal role in determining the trajectory and potential for mainstream adoption of DeFi.

The other key difference between the Wild West and the Citadel is the role of tokens in products and in fund-raising. Tokens can be a double-edged sword. Tokens are fundamental to the running of projects in the crypto-native DeFi as utility tokens and governance tokens, and also as being a fund-raising mechanism.

Tokens can help with the fast adoption of products as they incentivize users to onboard early. Nonetheless, the use of tokens in DeFi products can be questionable. Many users may find that the mandatory use of tokens when utilizing products is not user-friendly, leaving the role of token in an uncertain state.

Teams may also find that having a liquid token subjects them to the pressures of appeasing vocal communities and anonymous token holders across social platforms like Telegram, Discord, and Reddit. Managing token-holder expectations becomes an ongoing challenge that can distract from the core focus of delivering a quality product that paying customers actually want.

Teams may be tempted to pursue short-term, inorganic actions such as paid partnerships or token financial engineering to pump the token price, instead of taking the harder, long-term path of building a good product. The liquidity of tokens creates complex community dynamics that teams must carefully navigate alongside building their core technology. A long-term, customer-focused mindset is required to build sustainable products versus chasing temporary token price spikes, or the latest shiny trend in Web3.

10.2.2 Path 2: DLT-enabled TradFi / "Citadel"

10.2.2.1 Tailwinds

- Compliance with existing regulations
- Interoperability with current norms and architectures of TradFi and traditional asset classes
- Implementation within the existing banking system and collaboration of central banks and commercial banks

10.2.2.2 Headwinds

- Innovation tends to be more incremental than revolutionary
- Limited talent base and developers

In historic terms, citadels are fortified structures designed for defense and stability, characterized by high walls and significant barriers to entry. Inside the citadel, a central authority governs through a hierarchy and formal regulations to maintain law and order. Essentially, citadels are constructed to repel invaders.

The existing banking system operates in a manner akin to a citadel, or a network of citadels. Information is stored in isolated environments, and software development is a closely guarded process. This high level of security serves to ensure the integrity and safety of clients and users.

Thus, the integration of DLT into the Citadel might result in more incremental advancements rather than a revolutionary shift. It's a cautious approach that maintains the existing structure while attempting to incorporate new technology, albeit at a slower and more methodical pace. This pathway emphasizes stability and regulatory compliance, albeit potentially at the cost of rapid innovation and transformative change.

Unlike the experimental and unregulated world of crypto-native DeFi, the measured development of CBDCs, tokenized bank deposits, and tokenized assets by central banks and commercial banks appears inevitable. The potential benefits of faster, cheaper settlements through peer-to-peer transactions are evident for these banking institutions. However, their adoption of these technologies will likely progress at a cautious pace, with a focus on stability, security, and consumer protections rather than rapid innovation. While the cryptocurrency ecosystem moves swiftly, the centralized banking system is taking a more methodical approach to leveraging blockchain-based payments and digitized assets. This contrasts the risk-embracing ethos of DeFi with the conservative nature of large regulatory bodies and financial institutions.

At its foundation, modern money represents a public–private partnership between central banks and commercial banks. While alternative monetary systems may emerge, the current one remains deeply rooted in history and the gradual evolution of finance. The intricate relationship between central banks, which regulate currency, and commercial banks, which manage customer deposits and lending, underpins today's monetary framework. This long-standing dynamic is unlikely to be abruptly upended solely by new technologies like cryptocurrency. Though innovations like blockchain may transform payment mechanisms, the essential role of centralized institutions in governing monetary policy will persist. The trajectory of money thus builds on existing systems, with technological change incorporated under regulatory oversight rather than displacing the fundamental public–private foundation altogether.

The BIS's preference for tokenized deposits over stablecoins demonstrates that central banks still prioritize collaboration with commercial banks. As previously discussed, innovation diffuses into the regulated sector by co-opting crypto concepts for traditional environments. Of the potential paths forward, DLT integration into mainstream finance holds promise given the vast resources of institutional backers. Adoption poses a challenge, but the support of major players like central banks makes this pathway hard to overlook. While crypto may pioneer disruptive ideas, traditional finance possesses the scale to integrate them in a regulated manner.

10.2.3   Path 3: Crossover DeFi / "Bazaar"

10.2.3.1   Tailwinds

- Combines the best of both worlds – open networks and regulated assets
- Allows for TradFi to tap into crypto liquidity and vice versa

10.2.3.2   Headwinds

- Regulatory uncertainty
- Interpretation of compliance may be difficult

Historically, bazaars facilitated exchange of goods between diverse cultures and currencies. They exemplify interfaces where monetary systems meet. Bazaars and marketplaces have also been key points of exchange of information and ideas, outside the boundaries of individual countries.

Similarly, the Bazaar path emerges when TradFi looks to tap into crypto liquidity, such as the SocGen – MakerDAO transaction,[3] and looks to invest in staking and other yield farming to earn DeFi yield. Other examples might include TradFi utilizing public blockchains, for issuing bonds and other institutional DeFi projects.

Tokenizing real-world assets on blockchains also blends these worlds, bringing regulated assets into decentralized environments. This direction seems promising, fusing the openness of DeFi with the stability of TradFi.

However, regulatory barriers persist. Financial institutions may be eager to engage with crypto but struggle to reconcile it with compliance frameworks. For example, the SEC has yet to approve a Bitcoin ETF despite industry interest.

While the Bazaar model offers opportunities, uncertainty around applicable regulation and jurisdiction prevents seamless integration. Until clear, technology-neutral policies develop, the overlap between decentralized and traditional finance remains constrained. Nonetheless, the allure of combining these spheres will likely compel regulatory evolution over time.

10.3 The Future of Money

To conclude, let's zoom all the way out and evaluate the future of money from the broadest perspective.

While I am an ardent supporter of DeFi, I am compelled to acknowledge that its impact on the global financial landscape – concerning the future of money – will likely be more indirect than direct. DeFi is poised to continue fostering innovation among central banks, commercial banks, and other FinTech companies. However, these innovative ideas will probably only be embraced within regulated financial frameworks once they have demonstrated their efficacy in the "live sandbox" of crypto, and have proven their ability to comply with existing financial laws and regulations.

Furthermore, DeFi and crypto are destined to persist in catering to the fringe areas that are beyond the reach of traditional banking systems and FinTech solutions. These situations often arise in extreme moments of institutional breakdowns when the internet becomes the only available lifeline. Consider the scenarios in Ukraine and Myanmar, for instance.

In the face of the Russia–Ukraine conflict, Ukrainians managed to preserve their life savings by converting their assets into Bitcoin before crossing the border. Cryptocurrency has also played a pivotal role in enabling Ukraine to mobilize funds for their resistance.[4]

Meanwhile, in Myanmar, following the military coup of 2021, the shadow government is striving to reclaim their banking system from the military junta, utilizing a digital bank underpinned by crypto.[5]

DeFi has filled a niche for an internet-native, digital-first money system that is independent of any government or institution, and will continue to grow and evolve in the coming years.

A diagram from the BIS (Figure 10.2) provides a depiction of the central banking vision for the future global monetary system. In this illustration, central banks act as the sturdy trunks of individual country's monetary "trees." Private sector payment service providers (PSPs), notably commercial banks, function as vital nodes within each tree, facilitating a variety of services like credit cards, electronic money, and autonomous wallets. The different trees are interconnected through fast payment systems (FPS) and CBDCs.

The envisioned future of the monetary ecosystem incorporates key features such as programmability, composability, and tokenization, elements arguably catalyzed by DeFi. Even prior to the rise of DeFi, open banking and APIs were already setting the stage for interoperability, data aggregation, data portability for consumers, and increased competition within the banking sector. The advent of DeFi has amplified the need for interoperability amidst the siloed nature of the banking ecosystem.

A strong canopy supports the global monetary (eco)system

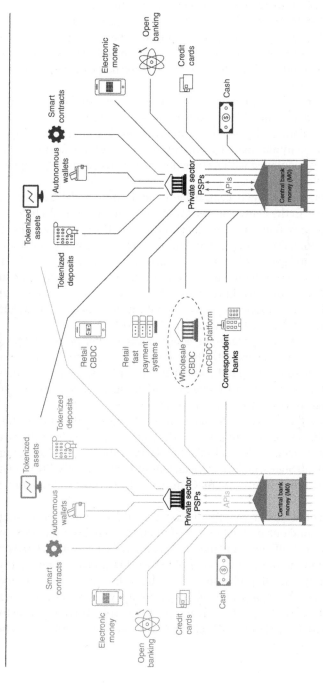

API = application programming interface; CBDC = central bank digital currency; PSP = payment service provider.

Figure 10.2 BIS vision of the global monetary ecosystem.
Source: BIS https://www.bis.org/publ/arpdf/ar2022e3.htm

The future of money looks to be shaped by a fusion of CBDCs, tokenized deposits, and stablecoins. DLT looks to be destined to be a part of these systems, if not the core technology underpinning them. All three mechanisms facilitate programmable, composable, and automated money flows, aligning with emergent trends such as Industry 4.0, the Internet of Things, and machine-to-machine payments.

AI appears poised to be integrated into nearly every kind of machine. What we once labeled as "smart" is set to become even smarter. For instance, self-driving cars fundamentally rely on AI and machine learning technologies. In a future dominated by automated payments, it would not be a far-fetched notion to envisage a car equipped with its own digital wallet, capable of independently paying for fuel and toll fees.

The relationship between central banks and commercial banks is deeply interconnected. In the United States, for instance, member banks hold stock in the Federal Reserve Bank and also elect members to the Federal Reserve Bank's board of directors. Fractional reserve banking, a key mechanism in credit issuance such as mortgages, hinges on commercial banks to evaluate potential borrowers. Commercial banks also play a significant role in maturity transformation and in providing banking services to a diverse range of consumers and businesses. This nexus appears poised to continue its evolution in tandem with DLT, ushering in tokenized versions of M0 and M1.

In this context, there appear to be considerable challenges for stablecoins in their current form, particularly their uncertain regulatory status and the requirement for stablecoins to be fully backed 1:1 by deposits. As banks start to issue stablecoins, a trend currently unfolding in Japan, the distinction between stablecoins and tokenized deposits may begin to blur.

mCBDCs may serve as key foundations of the future global monetary system. The shift towards a multipolar world seems increasingly likely, given the rise of countries such as China, India, Brazil, and other regional groupings like ASEAN, the Gulf States, and the African Union. Consequently, Project Dunbar, mBridge, and other future mCBDC initiatives are pivotal developments to monitor.

DLT's potential in our rapidly digitizing world is indeed promising. It is poised to redefine our understanding of finance, paving the way for a swifter, user-friendly, cost-efficient, and more secure financial ecosystem. Furthermore, it has the potential to integrate more of the world's unbanked population into the financial system. If you've found this book insightful and relished your journey through these pages, I would be grateful if you could leave a review on Amazon. Alternatively, you're welcome to share your thoughts directly with me at ken@blocks.sg. Your feedback is valuable, and I look forward to hearing from you.

Notes

1. https://www.omfif.org/2021/07/harnessing-decentralised-finance-innovation-for-the-public-good/
2. https://www.bis.org/about/bisih/topics/cbdc/polaris.htm
3. https://www.sgforge.com/refinancing-dai-stablecoin-defi-makerdao/
4. https://www.weforum.org/agenda/2023/03/the-role-cryptocurrency-crypto-huge-in-ukraine-war-russia/
5. https://www.coindesk.com/policy/2023/07/20/myanmar-shadow-govt-to-start-neobank-with-crypto-rails-to-fund-fight-against-military-junta/

Bibliography and Online Resources

Here are some books and online resources to continue your learning:

Crypto and DeFi

Antonopoulos, A. and Wood, G. (2018) *Mastering Ethereum. Building Smart Contracts and DApps*. The Ethereum Book LLC.

Arslanian, H. (2018) *The Book of Crypto. The Complete Guide to Understanding Bitcoin, Cryptocurrencies and Digital Assets*. Springer.

Buterin, V. (2022) *Proof of Stake: The Making of Ethereum and the Philosophy of Blockchains*. Seven Stories Press.

Dalio, R (2021) *Principles for Dealing with the Changing World Order: Why Nations Succeed and Fail*. Avid Reader Press.

Harvey, C. R., Ramachandran, A., and Santoro, J. (2021) *DeFi and the Future of Finance*. John Wiley & Sons.

Lewis, A. (2018) *The Basics of Bitcoins and Blockchains*. Mango Publishing.

McDonald, O. (2021) *Cryptocurrencies: Money, Trust and Regulation*. Agenda Publishing.

Narayanan, A., Bonneau, J., Felten, E., Miller, A., and Goldfeder, S. (2016) *Bitcoin and Cryptocurrency Technologies: A Comprehensive Introduction*. Princeton University Press.

Russo, C. (2020) *The Infinite Machine: How an Army of Crypto-hackers is Building the Next Internet with Ethereum*. Harper Business.

Werbach, K. (2018) *The Blockchain and the New Architecture of Trust*. MIT Press.

Decentralizing Finance: How DeFi, Digital Assets, and Distributed Ledger Technology Are Transforming Finance, First Edition. Kenneth Bok.
© 2024 John Wiley & Sons Ltd. Published 2024 by John Wiley & Sons Ltd.

CBDCs

Prasad, E. S. (2021) *The Future of Money: How the Digital Revolution is transforming Currencies and Finance*. Belknap Press.
Turrin, R. (2021) *Cashless: China's Digital Currency Revolution*. Authority Publishing.

Payments and FinTech

Laboure, M. and Deffrennes, N. (2022) *Democratizing Finance: The Radical Promise of Fintech*. Harvard University Press.
Leibbrandt, G., and De Terán, N. (2021) *The Pay Off: How Changing the Way We Pay Changes Everything*. Elliott and Thompson Ltd.
Rogoff, K. S. (2016) *The Curse of Cash: How Large-denomination Bills Aid Crime and Tax Evasion and Constrain Monetary Policy*. Princeton University Press

Monetary History

Ferguson, N. (2008) *The Ascent of Money: A Financial History of the World*. Penguin.
Graeber, D. (2011) *Debt: The First 5,000 Years*. Melville House Publishing.
Hayek, F. A. (1976) *The Denationalisation of Money: An Analysis of the Theory and Practice of Concurrent Currencies*. The Institute of Economic Affairs.

Online Resources

Bankless: https://www.bankless.com/
CoinDesk: https://www.coindesk.com/
John Kiff's newsletter: https://kiffmeister.com/
The Block: https://www.theblock.co/
Vitalik Buterin's blog: https://vitalik.ca/

Index

*Decentralizing Finance: How DeFi, Digital Assets, and Distributed Ledger Technology Are
Transforming Finance,* First Edition. Kenneth Bok.
© 2024 John Wiley & Sons Ltd. Published 2024 by John Wiley & Sons Ltd.